BARNSTORMING AMERICA

Stories from the Pioneers of Women's Basketball

JOHN A. MOLINA

With Charles A. Francis *Foreword by Donna Orender*

Acclaim Press
MORLEY, MISSOURI

Acclaim Press
— Your Next Great Book —

P.O. Box 238
Morley, MO 63767
(573) 472-9800
www.acclaimpress.com

Editor: Charles A. Francis
Book & Cover Design: M. Frene Melton

ISBN-13: 978-1-942613-56-5 / 1-942613-56-3
Library of Congress Control Number: 2016917197

Second Printing: 2018
Printed in the United States of America
10 9 8 7 6 5 4 3 2

This publication was produced using available information.
The publisher regrets it cannot assume responsibility for errors or omissions.

1968 All American Red Heads promotional picture

Contents

Foreword

By Donna Orender

Basketball has been a part of my life for as long as I can remember. The rhythmic bouncing of the ball became a clarion call for me. To this day, when I hear the "rubber hit the road," it will cause me to stop what I am doing and see where the music is being played. As a six-sport athlete in high school, basketball ultimately proved to be my passionate pursuit. We played just six games on my high school team. So, when I couldn't practice with the boys or pick up a game in the park as the guys asked me, "really, *you* got next?" or play AAU, I would be on my driveway, making music, pounding the dribble, and working on the beautiful rotation that would make the ball gently tickle the net. Swoosh. Sweet!

I would sometimes sneak my dad's car out of the driveway and travel to the Mecca of basketball, Harlem. I played in the Rucker League when it was the true gathering point for basketball greatness and where schoolyard ball was the show. So many greats played up there, and I remember playing with Nancy Lieberman and other New York City greats as we followed the path where we could play. There was not much in the way of scholarships in those years, and I sorely felt the gap in opportunities that my male friends were afforded as opposed to me and mine. I never let that impede my desire to play, and it was while watching Queens College play Immaculata for the national championship when I was still in high school that I knew what I wanted to do. I wanted to play with the best and be coached by the best. Coach Lucille Kyvallos was a legend, and I wanted to learn from her. So, even with an athletic scholarship to the University of New Mexico and an academic scholarship to the University of Chicago, off I went, just 10 miles from home, to play for one of the great pioneering teams in the game, Queens College. It was a decision that shaped me as a person and the path that my life would ultimately take.

It took me on a path that wrote history, that introduced me to history makers and to the importance that history has in creating a world that was better off if it deployed all of the talent that was offered in our global community. I had the privilege of playing professional basketball in the first women's league—the WBL—so I felt when it came to being an elite athlete, I had scaled the mountain. But when the call came from Adam Silver and David Stern regarding the WNBA, I knew it was time to pay it forward. I had a successful career in sports television and the business of sports at ABC Sports, Sports Channel, and the PGA Tour, and it was time to be a part of elevating the business of women's sports, clearly where I learned how to compete and win.

I arrived at the WNBA during a pivotal stretch in our young league's history. A year into my tenure, we began making preparations for our 10th anniversary. Our game was still growing, and our superstars were finally making inroads in the increasingly important front of popular culture. We had arrived. We had secured a tenuous foothold on the collective conscience of sports-minded Americans. I saw the proof in every new fan we reached, in every new corporate partnership we forged, and in every skeptical mind we changed. I knew our history. I knew the struggle because I had lived it. Still there were gaps in my knowledge, and soon I realized what a big uphill climb it was. The cultural and social gap was a yawning one, and it was as if the game was just invented. What a rich history the game had, and the lack of awareness of the women's game prior to 1972 seemed swept under some rug, long since forgotten.

John Molina's wonderful book has lifted that rug as he celebrates charismatic, committed, and talented athletes whose stories you will find compelling and endearing. The stories that unfold in the following pages offer a rare glimpse into the lives of a band of basketball sisters. You will begin to understand the sacrifices these women made, the challenges they faced, and the victories they won for us all. These are personal accounts, so you should not expect to piece together the entire history of women's basketball. But you will find wonderful tales that will remind us all that truth really is stranger than fiction. In most cases, the thought of blazing a new path or breaking through the proverbial glass ceiling rarely, if ever, crossed the minds of these young athletes. There was always another game to play, a new skill to master, or some other absurd obstacle to overcome. But make no mistake. These women shattered stereotypes and broke down barriers that had existed since the dawn of time.

To say that the women featured in *Barnstorming America* were ahead of their time says so much but, in my experience, really says too little. For these women were movers and shakers, and they had to be. For them to take up the game with such fierce determination at a time when a game where you sweated, used your elbows, and dove across the floor was not deemed very feminine, you had to be willing to defy social convention. On the court, these pioneers played the way the game was originally intended. They ran the give-and-go, the pick-and-roll, the motion offense, and the "man-to-man" defense. They pushed their bodies to the limit, even as the issue of "women and muscles" were an ongoing whisper of concern. When the game ended and the final horn sounded, sneakers were packed away, and the transition to the real world was immediately resumed. Basketball became a balancing act, where the dictates of the time were that you had to choose between being a woman or an athlete.

What was also readily apparent in this basketball romance is just how much these women sacrificed. The game represented opportunity, but for most, pursuing a life of basketball meant making choices most people never have to face. Leaving home. Putting education in the rearview. Postponing marriage. Giving up motherhood. Missing holidays, graduations, and life's little moments with family and friends. That these women embraced this reality with grace and a smile stands as testimony to their love of the game.

It is said that we stand on the shoulders of those who came before us. There is no doubt that today's generation of players owes a debt of gratitude to the women who came before us. These wonderful women and their stories that John has lovingly brought to the fore will help all of us — basketball players, athletes, and all women who look to blaze trails and cut our own path in the world of today — be inspired by their strength and commitment. From the small-town girl who wanted to see the world from the backseat of a stretch limousine to the farmer's daughter who left the cotton fields and everything she knew to chase a dream. There is a college freshman who just wanted the opportunity to play. That's all I ever wanted and still desire—opportunity, born from an equal playing field. In the big book of women who have made a difference in this world, these are all of our stories. For those of us in particular who love the game or any pursuit of passion for that matter, these stories are the kind that fill your heart with gratitude, remind us that challenges are to be overcome, and inspire us to reach forward to help lift our next generations. Thank you, John, for your embrace and your special ability to share the stories of those who will help us write new ones.

Donna Orender has been CEO of Orender Unlimited, a consulting and advisory company. She was an All-Star in the first professional women's basketball league—the WBL—and has been a sports and broadcasting executive, including service as the president of the Women's National Basketball Association (WNBA) from 2005–2010. Today, she is a sought-after speaker on issues such as teamwork, motivation, gender/diversity, and leadership.

Introduction

I grew up in the little farming community of South Glastonbury, Connecticut, where it seemed everyone's yard shared a boundary with one of the numerous cornfields, sprinkled in with some of the best broadleaf tobacco fields grown this side of Havana.

As a little kid, I spent much time at my grandparents' house. I was probably like any other little kid growing up in the 1960s. My curiosity meant I had to investigate everywhere I went. Their house was no exception.

I would often go upstairs into their unfinished attic. When I opened the door, it was like walking into the past. Old furniture and mementos from world wars past told stories that were passed along through the family, though hidden out of sight. Yet above an old mahogany bookcase hung a single picture on an unfinished wall with only some insulation between the studs. It was a picture of a women's basketball team. Not just any women's basketball team but my grandmother's basketball team. My grandmother was one of 17 children born to Polish immigrants who would farm the local lands alongside Connecticut River in the early 1900s. Here she was, standing in the second row, tallest of them all, on the J.B. Williams Soap Factory team during the Great Depression. It was pretty cool.

Then, like any other kid, my mind would wander, and I would go on and find something else to investigate and explore.

Over the next 20 years, I would go through high school and a bit of college, as did many others that I grew up with. My days of being young and inquisitive gave way to first relationships, dances, and cars. Yet, I always had a special bond with my grandmother. Even when I went to a local college, I would go down and have lunch with her virtually every day, and she would serve me raisin bread toast and Pepperidge Farm Milano cookies.

By the early '90s, I had fallen in love and married my wife, Roxanne. We had three children. My life was on fast forward, as many of us can relate to. It was during this time my grandmother became very sick with bone cancer. She passed away just as the lilacs bloomed in her yard on May 1, 1994. She was the first person who I was so very close to who would die. It struck me hard in my soul. A bit of the innocence of my childhood died that day, as well.

The only thing I really had to remind me of her was that picture hanging on that attic wall from her house.

Later in that fall of 1994, my family and I started watching University of Connecticut women's basketball games at the suggestion of a friend. I had pretty much given up on sports because it had become too much about the individual and not the team and the egos were as inflated as housing prices. But this was different. This game was about *team*, not the individual. My family became hooked overnight. In the spring of 1995, that UConn team, led by Rebecca Lobo and coached by Geno Auriemma, won the national championship and went undefeated with a record of 35–0.

I thought back to my grandmother and to that black-and-white picture of all those women in their bloomers playing basketball after work during the Depression.

How did we get from my grandmother to Rebecca Lobo?

I realized that I had never asked my grandmother about her playing days. I had missed out on that opportunity, and it was gone forever.

But a desire was born, a desire that could only be filled one way—to search for stories of other women who played basketball and to preserve those stories and share them with others so that what happened to me would not happen to them.

So, what follows in these pages springs from my desire—though unfulfilled—to hear all the stories of my grandmother. I wanted to learn what it was like when *she* played basketball.

I did it by learning a little about the early days of basketball.

Dr. James Naismith invented the game in 1891 for his men's physical education class. It was soon brought to Smith College, though the rules were changed to make it a bit less competitive and rough, so women could play it, as well.

You see, there were major concerns about women playing basketball back then. Those concerns were even mentioned in the 1901 Spalding rulebook for women's "basket-ball," as it was called. Among the concerns were that women were not as team-oriented as men and could not play a team sport like men because women were more selfish than men. The rulebook even mentioned that playing basket-ball could affect a woman when it came to having children.

But when watching the UConn women win the national championship, I saw the exact opposite. I saw cooperation. I saw unselfish play. In short, I saw a *team*.

The photo that sparked author John Molina's interest in the history of women's basketball — the J.B. Williams Soap Factory team, 1930s. Bernice Gondek Molina is standing, third from left.

But before women's basketball came into the mainstream in our sports culture, it was a curious novelty in the middle of the 20th century. Barnstorming teams of women, such as the All American Red Heads, Arkansas Lassies, Ozark Hill Billies, and more, traversed the country, performing in local high school gymnasiums, playing against teams of local All-Stars—always men—in a seemingly endless series of one-night stands. These barnstorming teams brought women's' basketball to the masses. Though crowds may have shown up at these performances as a matter of curiosity, many came away convinced that women *can* play this game—just as I was convinced by watching the UConn women's team in the '90s.

This book contains the stories of women who played on these barnstorming teams, as told by the athletes themselves or by their families. I would take programs that I came across and attempt to locate these players, either online during the earlier days of the Internet or even the old-fashioned way, writing a letter to a name and address I thought might be one of these players. Most never replied. For those who did, I was usually able to network them into other contacts, and this is what you will read in these pages.

These women have graciously opened up the windows to their past and shared some of their memories and photographs from a very special time in their lives and in the history of women's basketball. Some of these stories may have a bit of familiarity with another, as some of these players were on the court at the same time, even the same team, and thus shared many of the same experiences. Read a few of them, set it down, and come back and enjoy again.

Please find your special little place where there is no noise — a special chair by a window or a lawn chair in the backyard with a cup of tea. Let your mind leave the worries and cares of life for a few hours and join me as we go back in time. Jump in one of the special wagons these women traveled in on their barnstorming tours and sit alongside them.

Let's go together on a little trip—*Barnstorming America*.

Acknowledgments

They say it's not the destination, rather the journey, that's important.

Well, the destination is certainly a fun place to arrive. Yes, this has been an incredible 20-year journey.

I want to thank my grandmother Bernice (Gondek) Molina for having played basketball during the Great Depression for the J.B. Williams Soap Factory in Glastonbury. It was a picture hanging in her attic that served as my initial inspiration for all of this work.

To all of the players I have met over the years, including All American Red Heads as well as other teams and leagues dating back to the 1920s, and to every one of you who has ever stepped out on the court to play the game before it was a socially-accepted thing to do — thank you.

To all of those women who took the time and were gracious in opening up and sharing a piece of their own lives with others — my sincere gratitude to lend each and every one of you.

To four special people who assisted virtually every single day, morning, noon, and night, to help with anything that needed to be done on this project—Jolene Ammons, Sandy Mann, Dianne Warren, and "Spanky" Losier. I tip my hat to you and my coffee mug is raised high.

To Donna Orender — My thanks for taking the time out of a schedule that would rival a barnstorming season on the road to write the "Foreword" and your own story. You have been an inspiration on and off the court for five decades, and we need more women like you.

To Doug Sikes and Charlie Francis of Acclaim Press — Thank you for all of your support and vision to help give this book an even even wider audience appeal. To Keith Ellebrecht from Acclaim Press — On every team, there is usually a 'sixth player' award. From e-mails, to phone calls and texts (many times seven days a week) you made me feel this was more than just another project for you and believed in this book as much as I do. You are an asset to Acclaim and an ambassador for this book.

To Orwell Moore, a man I simply call "Coach" — While your own story is not in here, the effect you had on so many is evident, even between these pages. A mentor in my life and a man I love very much and miss daily. Coach, thank you for trusting me with your knowledge. We had something special as we trusted each other and the integrity of our word and never betrayed each other — something rare in today's world.

To my mother Lee Nielson — No matter what I've ever wanted to do in life, you always supported me. Just prior to this book going to print, my mother unexpectedly passed away. No words can describe my feeling of her not being able to sit in her chair and read this. To my dad, Ron Molina, and others who are no longer with us — I wish you could have seen this. Then again, if you were here, I would simply like to talk with you all and tell you how much we love and miss you.

To my children Sandra, C.J., and Rebecca-Lee — You all watched Dad start off with a hobby in the cellar. The first exhibit was held in our house, and you've all been a part of this. You have all supported me and helped me along the way. It never would have been as enjoyable without each of you being a part of it. My love to you forever.

To my wife Roxanne — When we got married, something like this was never in the cards. It's been a lot of fun, but it's also been a lot of work and even a lot of sacrifice. No one knows how much all of this has taken, except for you. The 11 p.m. phone calls, the 3 a.m. research. I thank you from my heart for putting up with me in the tough times and sharing the good times.

Yet one thing all of this has taught me over the years is that no matter what kind of passion a person may have for something, there is nothing comparable to the love that a person can have for another. People talk about "bucket lists." The only item on my list is to have you by my side through all of the ups and downs of this journey we call life. *You* are my bucket list.

John Molina, 2016

Barnstorming America

Stories from the Pioneers of Women's Basketball

All American Red Heads, circa 1937-38. Front, L-R: (Olympic Gold Medal winner) Helen Stephens and Ruth Osborn: Standing: Lila Blue, Gladys Lommler, Kay Kirkpatrick and Peggy Lawson.

CHAPTER ONE

The Birth of Basketball and Barnstorming

"Barnstorming"

"The term 'barnstorming,' which first appeared in the early 19th century, applied to theatrical troupes that toured in rural areas, often mounting their shows in, you guessed it, rented barns.

"The 'storm' in barnstorming is a bit more difficult to untangle. This figurative use led to the military sense of 'to storm' meaning ... to capture or take over.

"The use of 'storm' in 'barnstorm' is apparently a playful, slightly sardonic use of the term, referring to the need of the troupe to 'conquer' one barn full of bumpkins after another in the course of their tour."

– from Word-Detective.com

"Basket ball," as it was commonly known, had just been invented by Dr. James Naismith for his students at the YMCA training school in Springfield, Massachusetts, in the winter of 1891. A few miles up the Connecticut River was the home of Smith College for girls in North Hampton. In 1892, the school had just hired their first director of physical education, Senda Berenson.

Miss Berenson had read in *YMCA Magazine* about the new sport being played by the men in Springfield. She inquired of Dr. Naismith about the game and if women could play it. The game was very physical at the time, somewhat resembling lacrosse, one of Naismith's favorite sports.

Senda brought basket ball back to Smith to use it in her classes. The purpose of the game was for physical fitness for her ladies. During her era, it was frowned upon for women to participate in competitive, physical sports. Senda would have to change some of Naismith's rules to stress teamwork and cooperation rather than competition. She would break the court into three zones. Due to the large size of the court, nine players would compete on each team, with three players in each zone. No player could leave her zone.

A player could only hold the ball for three seconds and dribble the ball three times before passing, making it difficult for a single player to become a star. The effort and cooperation of all nine players was required. No snatching of the ball was allowed, either. Even though they were playing a sport, they remained ladies at all times, even when playing defense.

Whitewater Normal School girls enjoy a game of "basket ball."

On March 21, 1893, the first collegiate game was played at Smith. The freshman class played the sophomore class. No one knew what to expect. Berenson thought only a few would show up to watch the contest between the classes of 1895 and 1896, but she was surprised to find the gymnasium filled with students and banners with class colors hanging everywhere. Even though the girls' uniforms covered every bit of them but the face and hands, the doors to the gym were locked, and no men were allowed in to watch as it was not considered socially acceptable.

When Senda threw up the first ball, it hit the hand of the freshman center, dislocating her shoulder. Injuries such as this would only continue a decades-long argument that women shouldn't play competitive sports.

In the first game, each basket was worth one point. The Class of 1896 would go on to defeat the Class of 1895 5–4, and history was born. Women's basket ball would spread very quickly across the country.

By 1896, it was established at several colleges, and in April of that year, the first intercollegiate game was played. Seven hundred women would witness the event at the Page Street Armory between Stanford and Berkeley. This was a game of nine versus nine. The male sex would again be barred from the event.

Differences between the two teams on the court were hard to miss. The Stanford girls were slender and small, while the girls at Berkeley were more like the Gibson girls. They were bigger and stronger, but not as fast.

Stanford won the toss up. In this game, no player was allowed to run more than five feet before passing it on. Like the game at Smith, the ball couldn't be held for more than five seconds.

In the first half, most of the play remained on Stanford's side. As big as the Berkeley girls were, the ladies of the cardinal red were great jumpers, constantly keeping the ball on their side of the court. There were no zone defenses employed in this game, as each player had to guard a single player on the opposite team. The first goal was scored by Stanford, accounting for one point and prompting trumpet playing that created a deafening noise.

An aspiring young girl practices her basketball skills.

Not only were the rules of basket ball different in 1896, but so was the basket itself. The goal was not the legendary peach basket utilized by Naismith when he invented the sport but a rim with a net sewn into it. There was no opening in the net for the ball to pass through. When a basket was made, the umpire would pull a string attached to the inside of the net, pulling out the net and popping out the ball.

Five minutes after Stanford scored its first goal, Berkeley scored to tie the game. Stanford went on to win the game 2–1.

It was in these early days of basketball that concerns arose about women playing the sport, even appearing in the 1901 Spalding *Women's Basket Ball* rule book. Women were considered to be more selfish than men, so it was believed that they couldn't play a team-orientated game the way men could. It was even felt that the ability to bear children later in life could be adversely affected.

During this time, the outfits varied from school to school. While some wore bloomers, others wore skirts that went down to their ankle.

In 1920, women finally earned the right to vote, yet little progress had happened on the basketball court. The Amateur Athletic Union wouldn't even recognize women's basketball until they sponsored the first national championship in 1926.

On the other hand, during the 1920s, men's basketball was beginning to flourish. Barnstorming was becoming the way of the land, especially in the Midwest. Teams were being organized, taking to the open road in station wagons, buses, or other means of transportation that could accommodate eight people, playing game after game, night after night, as they worked their way across the back roads of small-town America.

In 1929, the stock market crashed, and the country went into the Great Depression. Millions were out of work; people lost their homes, farms, and just about everything they owned. With little to smile about in small-town and rural America, barnstorming sports teams helped lift the spirits of the common folks. A barnstorming men's team pulling up to the local gym brought a much-needed distraction from the misery that was the Depression.

While the Dust Bowl of the 1930s altered the landscape of the Midwest farms, the decade also resulted in a season of change in women's basketball. The women's game had just gone from a three-zone court game to a half court game in 1934. Now, a mere 16 years after women got

Early women's basketball team, 1905

the right to vote, women were about to hit the road of America and beyond, successfully barnstorming through these towns, just as the more dominant male teams had done. But these women would have nothing to do with three-zone or half court rules — they would not only play by men's rules, but play *against* men's teams, a drastic change from the three-zone game that had only ended a couple of years before the most successful women's traveling team would hit the road in 1936. They would be showcasing how women could play a game like a man and even beat him at his own game.

They didn't know it at the time, but these barnstorming women were pioneers, much like the pioneers of the 1800s who blazed the trails of westward expansion. While their 19th century counterparts traveled in covered wagons, the barnstorming women traveled in station wagons (although some of the more successful teams could afford vans and buses). The pioneers of westward expansion faced challenges, such as weather, rugged terrain and Indians, on their trek westward; the barnstorming women faced attitudes and perceptions about their gender that were just as daunting — that a woman's place was at home, that women couldn't play a man's sport, and that women could never hold their own with men on a level court. When these teams set out on the road, they weren't just playing basketball. They were pioneers in helping break down all of these stereotypes, affecting attitudes not only about women and sports but also about women in society. But the barnstorming women were oblivious to the impact that their efforts would have on gender. They were just women who had a great passion to play basketball and were thrilled to be able to get paid for doing what they loved!

Had they not been able to play basketball, what would have happened to these women? Some may have worked on the farms and factories in and around the small towns where they lived. Some may have become secretaries or clerical workers in the business world, although the corporate boardroom was still a man's world in the mid-20th century. Some may have become teachers, and still others might have been stay-at-home moms.

But getting paid to play basketball and travel the country at the same time? That was as far-fetched as the idea that a woman could be her party's nominee for President of the United States.

This book will introduce you to many of the women who were pioneers that helped change attitudes about women in sports and society. But first, a bit about the barnstorming teams they played on:

All American Red Heads (1936–86)

C.M. "Ole" Olson had a men's barnstorming team called the Terrible Swedes. They had been traversing the country since the 1920s out of Cassville, Missouri. He was so successful he would spin off and create other teams, like the Giants. The region also happened to be a hotbed for women's basketball with many of the nation's top AAU teams in the states surrounding Missouri.

His wife, Doyle, owned several beauty salons in the Missouri and Arkansas areas. Ole came up with the idea of creating a women's barnstorming team that would have a special gimmick — all of the players have red hair. It would be an instant eye catcher and serve as a 24/7 promotion wherever they went.

The Red Heads would be the first barnstorming team to be successful at traversing the country year after year.

They were an instant success, filling gyms to standing-room-only crowds. Ironically, it was primarily men that packed the gyms to see the Red Heads play. While many may have been initially intrigued by women playing against men in a male-dominated sport, those in attendance quickly witnessed that women could not only play the game of basketball by men's rules, but they could also beat men at their own game.

Across small-town America, gyms would overflow with fans hoping to catch a glimpse of some of the greatest players in the world on the same team. Crowds of over 1,000 were not uncommon.

In 1948, Olson offered a coaching job to an English teacher and high school coach, Orwell "Red" Moore. Moore was married to Lorene "Butch" Moore, one of his students. Butch loved the Red Heads. Orwell accepted the job on one condition — his wife would play on the team. The decision to hire Orwell Moore to coach the Red Heads was probably the most important decision Olson ever made.

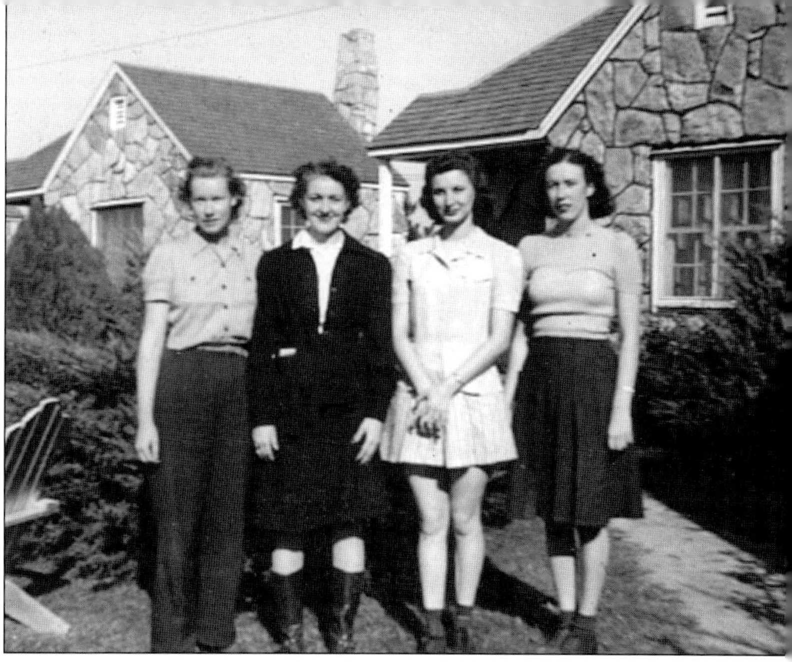

Darlene "Tex" Nabors, unidentified, Nota Lee McCain and Evelyn "Toby" McGee of the Red Heads in owner and founder C.M. "Ole" Olson's hometown of Cassville, Missouri

In 1955, Olson would sell the Red Heads to the Moores and retire to a farm and a life of fishing and one of his favorite pastimes, golf.

It was during these halftimes that the Red Heads started putting on an extra show, while the team of local men's all-stars that opposed them was catching their breath for the second half.

The Red Heads delighted the crowds with fancy ball handling, trick shots, and other displays of skill and entertainment. Coach Moore realized the importance of not only putting a competitive team on the court but also entertaining the crowd.

In 1969, the Moores bought an old boys' camp in Mississippi. They created "Camp Courage," a girls' camp designed with heavy emphasis on basketball.

In the early '70s, Moore had three teams on the road at the same time. The Red Heads machine was fully-oiled and running on all cylinders. Each team played more than 200 basketball games a year, with some of the teams winning nearly 90 percent of their games.

By the mid-1970s, the Red Heads were back down to one team. Title IX, while one of the most important laws to ever pass to help bring gender equality to education and sports in public schools, was beginning to have a negative effect on traveling teams.

Kay Kirkpatrick (second to the right of driver Wilbur Surface) joins her All American Red Heads in their station wagon as they travel in the Southwest desert, 1937.

Red Heads visit basketball Hall of Fame, 1973-74. Standing, L-R: Paula Haverstick, Cheryl Clark, Lynnea Sjoquist, Lynnette Sjoquist, Karen Logan, Donna "Spanky" Losier. Kneeling, L-R: Paula Allbritten and Jolene "Jo Jo" Ammons. In 2012, the Red Heads would themselves be inducted into the Naismith Memorial Basketball Hall of Fame.

Women had many more opportunities to play basketball at the college level. Even local school systems now had to have a girls' team if it had a boys' team, and equal time had to be given to the girls for court time in the gym. Professional women's leagues were only a few years away. With the source of players drying up, the Red Heads played their last game in 1986.

In 2012, the All American Red Heads became the first women's basketball team ever inducted into the Naismith Memorial Basketball Hall of Fame.

Helen Stephens Olympic Co-Eds (1938–43)

Olympic gold medalist Helen Stephens, known as the "Fulton Flash," would create her own barnstorming team a year after she played a single season with the All American Red Heads. Helen was able to keep her team on the road during the first two years of World War II. This was a feat in itself as gas rationing and other restrictions took many sports teams off the road during this time. Abe Saperstein, owner and founder of the world-famous Harlem Globetrotters, would handle the booking of Helen's games.

Grover Cleveland Alexander Stars of the World (late 1930s)

Grover Cleveland Alexander pitched in the major leagues from 1911 to 1930 and was best known for his heroics in the 1926 World Series as the St. Louis Cardinals won their first Series, beating the New York Yankees. He was elected to the National Baseball Hall of Fame in 1938.

He stepped off the pitcher's mound of the major leagues and turned to some barnstorming in the 1930s, playing baseball for the famous "House of David" until 1940. His women's traveling basketball team played during the late 1930s, with Abe Saperstein booking the team's schedule, as he did for Helen Stephens' Olympic Co-Eds.

Alexander battled alcoholism, drinking heavily in response to lung and hearing issues related to his service during World War I. He died in a hotel room in Nebraska in 1950, reportedly penniless, at the age of 63.

Ozark Hill Billies (1938–43)

The Ozark Hill Billies was the second women's team created by All American Red Heads' owner C.M. Olson. The Red Heads had a gimmick — their henna-colored hair. The Hill Billies would be no different. They showed up for pre-game warmups in hillbilly attire, then removed them to reveal their game uniforms.

During the first season, they also featured one man on the team, as well. Some considered the team to be the baby sister of the Red Heads, but they could hold their own on the court with their "big sister," as they showed on one occasion when they played the Red Heads and lost only by two points in double overtime.

Around 1941, former Red Head Ruth Osborn became the owner of the team and continued the team for a couple of more seasons.

Hill Billies Vinia Hobbs, Eleanor Laich and Lucy Peters in front of their cabin in Chelan, Washington

Arkansas Travelers (1948–67)

Anyone that knew women's basketball from the '30s to the '60s knew of Hazel Walker. One of the most dominant to ever step on the court in her day, Hazel was on some of the greatest amateur teams in the '30s and '40s, including the Tulsa Stenos, El Dorado Lions, and the Norwood Flyers, for which she became a national champion three times and a runner up once.

Hazel traded her amateur status in to become a professional basketball player, joining the All American Red Heads after World War II. She spent two seasons with Olson's teams before deciding to take it to the next level and start her own team.

Based out of Little Rock, Arkansas, the Travelers would become one of the most dominant and sought-after barnstorming teams of the time.

The Arkansas Travelers at the DeSoto dealership with their new station wagon, 1949-50. L-R: Carolyn Daniel, Peggy Dean, Wilma Bogan, Hazel Walker, Allegra "Stubby" Winters, Mary Alice "Peachie" Hatcher, George "Moon" Mullins and Phyllis White.

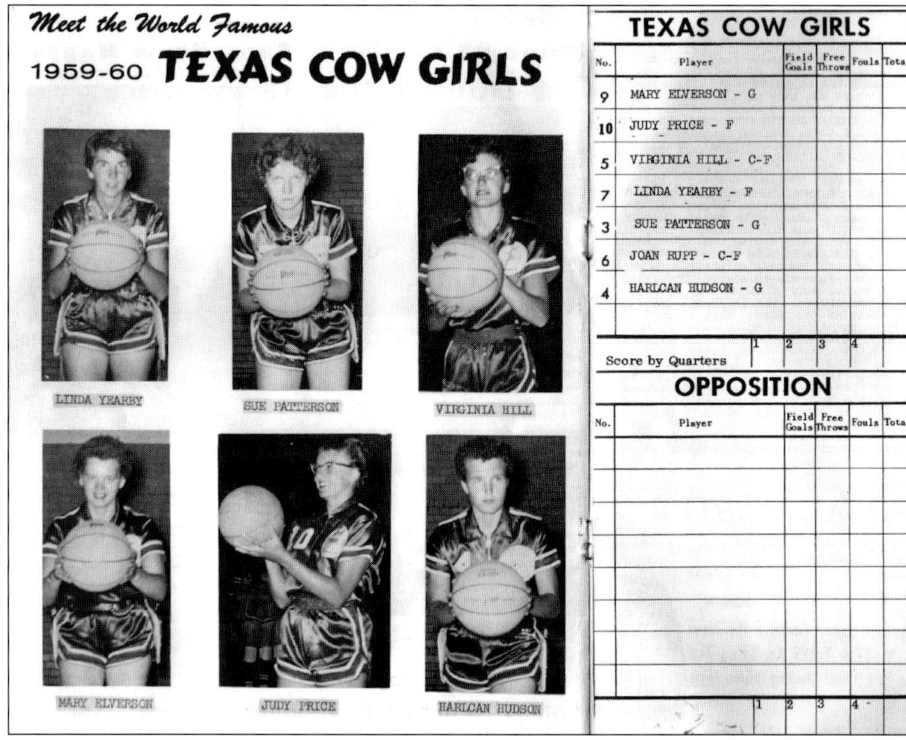

10th anniversary Texas Cowgirls program with Linda Yearby, Ginny Hill and Harlean Hudson, 1959-60

Linda Yearby of the Texas Cowgirls, between Philadelphia 76'ers Red Kerr and Connie Dierking, 1963-64

Texas Cowgirls (1949–77)

With the second-longest existence of any women's barnstorming team to ever take the court, the official name of the team was "Dempsey Hovland's World Famous Texas Cowgirls." Despite their name, the team started in Chicago.

Similar to other barnstorming teams, the Cowgirls played against men yet had the distinction of being the opening bill for the world-famous Harlem Globetrotters, as well as the Los Angeles Lakers.

The Cowgirls traveled and played in Morocco, as well as Mexico and Canada.

Shooting Stars/Arkansas Lassies (1962–76)

Elvera "Peps" Neuman and Linda Yearby were stars for the famous Texas Cowgirls from Chicago. They would leave and form a partnership in 1962 to start their own team. The result would be the Shooting Stars. Eventually, they would change their name to the Arkansas Lassies to help book more games.

Yearby ended up with the "Lassies" name and continue to travel. She had a vision for the future, and along with barnstorming her own team, she became involved with potential professional leagues twice. Despite the famous "Arkansas" label, the team was actually based out of Ionia, Michigan.

Poster promoting Shooting Stars game, 1965. The Shooting Stars later became the Arkansas Lassies.

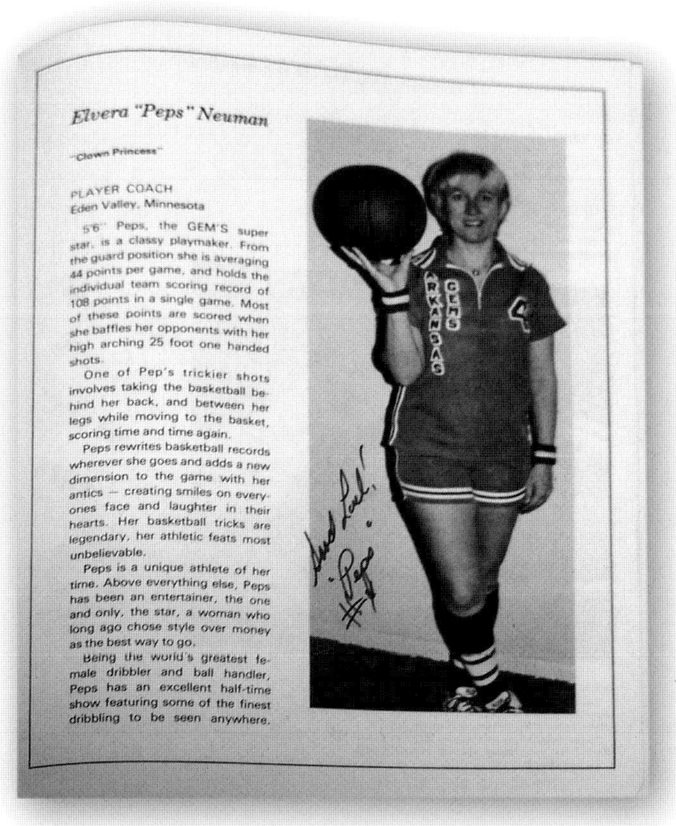

Elvera "Peps" Neuman signed this Arkansas Gems picture in souvenir program, mid-1970s.

The Lassies defeated the Indianapolis Pink Panthers in what was believed to be the first women's professional basketball game that featured two professional women's basketball teams. The league idea didn't make it off the ground, but some who were involved tried again the following year with Orwell Moore as president of the league and Linda as vice president. This ill-fated league never got off the ground.

In 1975, Linda became co-owner with former All American Red Head Jolene Ammons in an attempt to keep the team on the road. As the days of barnstorming days were waning, Yearby and Ammons parted in 1976, and the team disbanded.

Royal Maids (1971–72)

Two businessmen out of Kansas City saw the opportunity of barnstorming and dollar signs. The All American Red Heads had three teams on the road, and the Southern Belles had wrapped up another season.

With the Kansas City Royals baseball team as a strong foundation for sports in the city, this was an area ripe for a team and some money to be made. They convinced a coach from the All American Red Heads, as well as some of their players, to head west.

However, Title IX had become law, and the window of opportunity for starting a barnstorming team was closing rapidly. They lasted one year.

Arkansas Gems (1973–88)

Peps and Linda parted ways in 1973, and Peps would go on to form the Arkansas Gems. Despite the Arkansas moniker, the Gems were based in Clearwater, Minnesota, and put on upwards of 75,000 miles a season barnstorming.

This team ended up being the last survivor of the well-known barnstorming teams when it finally came off the road in 1988.

Southern Belles (L-R) Kathy Gaither, Linda Shanks, Lucille "Lucy" Thomason, Lenna Carey and Madeline Hoing in a display of sisterhood, 1969

Southern Belles (1967–71)

Ben Overman was a coach for the All American Red Heads for several years. He left the Red Heads and started his own team, the Southern Belles, in the fall of 1967.

His wife, Pat, who played for the Red Heads, joined her husband during that first season, as did some of the other Red Heads.

The Belles played by the same rules as the Red Heads and put on a similar show. They even had Caraway, Arkansas, as their home base, like the Red Heads.

The Belles' last season would be 1970–71, and Ben would return to the Red Heads.

The Pink Panthers (1974–75)

The Pink Panthers were a team that Lee Bakunin "wanted to take what had been done with barnstorming teams over the previous 40+ years and move it to the next level with an actual league. No more playing men." That was the vision of Panthers owner and founder Lee Bakunin. Lee was a Yale graduate and had a law practice in Phoenix, Arizona, in 1974.

"I read about the All American Red Heads in *Sports Illustrated* and thought, 'Hey, I could do that,'" Bakunin said. A vision of becoming an owner of a team in a women's pro basketball league, which had not done before, was born.

Lee had previously met up with Eddie "The King" Feigner, who was known for his fast-pitch softball barnstorming as "The King and his Court." Eddie traveled the country with his team of only four players — a catcher, a first baseman, a shortstop, and himself as pitcher. He recorded over 140,000 strikeouts, including many Major League baseball players like Willie Mays, Roberto Clemente, and Brooks Robinson. Bakunin became friends with Feigner, who invited him on the road to learn about the methodology of traveling and booking games. Lee took him up on the offer and drove around with him for a couple of days on the East Coast as the King and His Court were playing at Fort Dix, New Jersey, in 1974.

Lee sat on the bench with the players and learned about the business of barnstorming. He learned about merchandising and about connecting with the fans.

Lee Bakunin's plan was simple. "I wanted to take what the All American Red Heads were doing to the next level. I called Jolene Ammons of the Red Heads and told her about my idea." She had the same idea as Lee and saw what

Pink Panther Jolene Ammons and owner Lee Bakunin, 1974

the future was going to bring and wanted to be a part of it. Lee also spoke with Jolene's teammate, Karen Logan.

"I then sat down and developed a marketing plan, with the focus on displaying the athleticism of the women. I envisioned a league of teams like the Pink Panthers." Despite a tight budget, with the help of Jolene Ammons, a team was formed, and all of the players came to Phoenix in the fall of 1974. Lee was a member of the Jewish Community Center and arranged for free use of the center as a practice facility — the same place the NBA Phoenix Suns held their practices.

The first game was held at the Jewish Community Center, playing for just half the gate. "I saw a woman named Gwen Bachman who was almost seven feet tall," recalled Lee, who talked her into joining the team. He wanted to put together a team that had some real height. The forwards were 6-foot-3 and 6-foot-4.

The halftime show at a Panther game normally featured Karen Logan playing one-on-one against a player from the opposing men's team. This was nothing new for Logan, who frequently took on members of the Suns, who shared the practice facility.

At one point, the Suns' owner, Jerry Colangelo, asked if maybe they could use the Panthers in a preliminary game during the season. It was a wonderful idea that could help promote the Panthers and the upcoming league, but the team failed to draw enough crowds in Phoenix to be profitable. Lee had a friend who could get the team a lot of bookings in Indiana, so the team moved from Phoenix to Indianapolis. Lee remained in Phoenix, where he practiced law, and his friend Conrad "Connie" Stephens managed the Panthers.

In Indianapolis, they were making a little bit more money than in Phoenix, but like Lee, Connie wasn't taking any of the money for his work but continued because they all believed in the vision.

Connie had come up with an idea. He knew that there had never been a basketball game featuring two women's teams. He contacted the Arkansas Lassies, and they agreed to play. The historic game was held in January 1975. The game was well promoted and there was even a basketball signed by both teams. It was a very close game throughout, and the Arkansas Lassies beat the Panthers 65–63. It even scored an article in the *New York Times*, but that was about it.

Unable to gain any traction in marketing and publicity, the Indianapolis Pink Panthers folded soon. Afterwards, Connie contacted the owners of the Lassies (Linda Yearby) and the Red Heads (Orwell Moore) and some other barnstorming teams and got them all to get together in Indianapolis to discuss the formation of another league, with hopes of beginning play that fall. Orwell Moore would become the president of that league and Linda Yearby of the Lassies the vice president. That league never got off the ground, but it wouldn't be long before it would be attempted again.

WBL — Women's Professional Basketball League

Started in 1978 by Commissioner Bill Byrne, the first player ever signed in the Women's Professional Basketball League was Molly "Machine Gun" Bolin by the Iowa Cornets. The league featured some of the world's best players of the day, including Ann Meyers, Nancy Lieberman, Rosie Walker, and Carol Blazejowski.

The WBL was the first women's pro league to make it even a season, lasting three seasons before folding. The WBL also had an All-Star game each year. The first season, the East would beat the West at Madison Square Garden with Althea Gwyn leading the way for the East with 19 points and 16 rebounds.

Game tickets, Iowa Cornets vs. Milwaukee Does, 1979. The Cornets and Does played in the Women's Professional Basketball League (WBL), which played three seasons beginning in 1978.

CHAPTER TWO

Hoop Dreams Can Come True

As America scratched and crawled its way out of the Great Depression in the late 1930s, employment opportunities were becoming more common. FDR's "New Deal" offered families some financial relief early in the decade, with programs such as the Works Progress Administration putting men to work. Women, by the societal norms of the day, supported their families primarily by staying home and doing what homemakers do. Women who were able to work outside the home were usually single, widowed, or had husbands who were absent or disabled.

When the government began making New Deal jobs available to women late in the decade, they still involved jobs that would traditionally come under the umbrella of "women's work."

The stereotypes of women's role in the workplace continued as the recovery progressed. Jobs became more plentiful, but for women, the options were normally limited. If a woman wanted to earn a living in a factory making garments or shoes, great. Teaching? Good. A secretary? Fine. A nurse? Have at it.

But if a woman wanted to support herself as an athlete? Until the late '30s, that wasn't an option. Professional sports were almost exclusively the domain of men. At one point, the most popular baseball player, Babe Ruth, earned more money than the president.

Ironically, it was another "Babe" that helped to open the doors for women to earn a living in sports. Mildred "Babe" Didrickson had played on an Amateur Athletic Union champion basketball team in 1931 as a member of the Golden Cyclones, a team sponsored by a Dallas insurance company where she was employed. But she became a national celebrity by winning two gold medals in track and field in the 1932 Olympics.

Red Heads Peggy Lawson when she was with the Des Moines American Institute of Business AAU team, circa 1934

In 1938, Didrickson made headlines by becoming the first woman to compete in a men's Professional Golfers Association tournament, entering the Los Angeles Open. She missed the cut after the first two rounds but met her future husband, pro wrestler George Zaharias, at the event.

While Babe Didrickson helped break the barrier of women and professional sports, she was an anomaly. But it was basketball that proved to be the vehicle that put more women on the road to earning a living in sports.

One of those women was **Peggy Lawson**, who, according to daughter Mary Kay Pfeiffer, was to the 1930s what Sue Bird is to the 21st century. "If there was a basketball game of national importance being played," Pfeiffer said, "Peggy was probably on one of the teams." She played with the Walkers, an AAU team based in Wetumka, Oklahoma, and the Tulsa Stenos, playing for national AAU titles several times. Based on her play with the Walkers, she was recruited to join the American Institute of Business AAU team for a five-game series in Canada against what was billed as "the best team in the world," the Edmonton Grads.

Left: Red Head Peggy Lawson (fourth from left, back row) played with the three-time National AAU Champion Tulsa Stenos in 1935.

About this time, C.M. "Ole" Olson, who owned men's professional basketball teams, began organizing a women's pro team based in Cassville, Missouri. He sent a letter to a pair of twins — Vera and Lera Dunford — to play on the team that he called the All American Red Heads, whose players were required to dye their hair red to help plug the Olson hair salon business. Vera decided not to join the Red Heads as she was engaged to get married, but Lera did, and this was the first time the twins would ever be separated. Peggy Lawson and friend Vicki Cone engaged in a bit of subterfuge that changed her life forever.

"Vicki and I began corresponding with Olson in Vera's name and completed the deal," said Lawson. "He knew nothing about it until we were all in Cassville and playing."

Lawson played four seasons with the Red Heads, which became perhaps the most well-known of many barnstorming women's pro teams that emerged over the next four decades. The Red Heads played by men's rules against teams of men.

Another player who honed her skills in the AAU system who joined the Red Heads was **Kay Kirkpatrick**. Kirkpatrick and her two brothers all attended Baylor University in Waco, Texas, where the brothers were both on the basketball team. Kay practiced right along with her brothers, shooting 500 shots a day. A local sporting goods store in Waco sponsored a women's AAU team, and Kay became good enough to not only earn a spot on the team but also to get the attention of Ole Olson and the Red Heads.

Daughter Kathleen Ethington says that Kay was hesitant to join the Red Heads at first.

"Her parents wanted her to finish school before she made any decisions about playing women's basketball," says Ethington. "But Mr. Olson informed his associates that he wanted the girl from Texas on his team, so they contacted her a second time, and Mother decided to go ahead and play." And so Kay Kirkpatrick became a member of the first professional women's basketball team in December 1936.

Apart from intramural programs, there were no collegiate programs for women in those days. But many high schools had girls' basketball teams playing a version of the sport that was designed to be less demanding on the weaker sex. Teams played six per side, with three guards on the defensive end and three forwards on the offensive end. Players weren't allow to cross the half court line into the other zone. An Oklahoma woman became a legend coaching six-on-six girls' basketball.

Bertha Teague coached at Byng High School in Ada, Oklahoma. Byng won 98 straight games between 1936 and 1939 and compiled a 1,157-115 record over a career that spanned four decades. Her Byng teams were undefeated in league play for 27 consecutive seasons.

With no collegiate programs available to her exceptionally talented players, Teague often recommended players to Ole Olson, who not only owned the All American Red Heads but also the Ozark Hill Billies as well. Among the players she coached that went on to pro careers were **Vinia Hobbs, Nora Muncrief,** and **Lorene "Danny" Daniels**.

Hobbs was one of the players on the Byng High School team that won 98 straight games. After scoring 518 points during her senior season — an astounding total during the two-zone era when low-scoring games were the rule — Hobbs became a member of the Hill Billies in the fall of 1938.

Muncrief, who graduated from Byng in 1939 and was also part of the 98-game winning streak, played two seasons with the Hill Billies after Teague wrote a letter to Olson saying that Nora had the skills he was looking for. Nora wasn't the only athlete in the Muncrief family to turn pro. Brother Bob pitched in the Major Leagues and appeared in the World Series with both the St. Louis Browns and Cleveland Indians.

While Ole Olson often decided whether or not to sign a player based on a recommendation or seeing them play in person, he had an instinct for the intangible traits that went into a good player. That was the case with Lorene Daniels.

Red Heads poster advertising 1939 game vs. Rochester Royals

"One day in 1938, Ole Olson came out to the farmhouse," relates daughter Cindy Wilkes Thoren. After Olson asked where he could find Lorene, who had been recommended by Bertha Teague, the family pointed out to the back forty and said he would find her there. "She was planting peanuts — walking the planter behind the horse. When Mr. Olson saw her, he said, 'I have to have her on my team. That girl can work!'" Lorene joined the Hillbillies and was a member until 1950.

Georgia Washington, who played five seasons with the Red Heads under new owner and coach Orwell Moore, said her reputation as a high school player led to her pro career from 1961–1966. Moore had asked a girl in a nearby town, "Who was the roughest girl you have every played basketball against?" Her answer: "Georgia Washington." Moore tracked down Washington and asked if she would be interested in playing professional basketball. "The next thing I knew," said Georgia, "I was an All American Red Head."

Like Ole Olson, Orwell Moore looked for intangibles when recruiting players. "I always thought you would simply go out and look for the five best players you could find," said Washington. "That is not how he worked. He had a vision in his head, and he would assemble it that way. It could be that sometimes he looked for a scorer, at other times for a person he felt would get the crowd into the game. On occasion, he would look for a rough and tough player. I was simply in the right place when he was looking for that player."

While Olson often took the initiative in recruiting talent for his team, sometimes talented players reached out to him, as did **Gene "Careless" Love.**

Love played high school basketball at Standard High School in Olla, Louisiana. In college, she and a roommate saw ads for an appearance by the All American Red Heads. While they didn't have the money to go to the game, they had the money for a stamp and wrote to C.M. Olson and asked for an opportunity to try out.

The girls were surprised when Olson showed up one day to see what the girls could do. He liked what he saw in 6-foot-4 Gene enough to accompany her back to Olla and ask for her father's permission to join the Red Heads.

While most families of the girls who turned pro at that time supported their decision, others did not. **Helen Onson**, an outstanding Minnesota High School player, was in the stands in 1937 when Grover Cleveland Alexander's Stars of the World played in Rhinelander. When one of their players was injured, Helen was asked to join the team on its barnstorming tour. But her family didn't like the idea of Helen leaving home to join a traveling basketball team and even refused to lend her money for train fare or a meal for the 100-mile journey to the team's next stop in Chippewa Falls, Wisconsin. She borrowed the money for the train fare from a friend's mother, then found a quarter under a bench at the train station — her first meal money. Onson went on to play with the Olympic Co-Eds as a teammate of double gold medalist Helen Stephens, and later with the Ozark Hill Billies before ending her brief pro career.

The father of **Marvalee Jo Darrow** also was against her playing pro basketball. She was a junior college student in Oklahoma when the Ozark Hill Billies came calling. But Daddy was afraid that she would never finish her education. "Just let me go. I promise I will finish school," she pleaded. When her father still hadn't relented after a few days, Marvalee's mother interceded and gave her permission to go and join the Hill Billies. After a stint with the Hill Billies, Darrow finished her pro career with the All American Red Heads before keeping her promise to her father and entering college.

For prospects like **Brenda "Brooksie" O'Bryan**, getting permission to sign a pro contract wasn't an issue.

O'Bryan met former Red Head Pauline Barbo while playing softball in Louisiana. When Barbo found out that basketball was O'Bryan's favorite sport, she got her in contact with Orwell Moore, who arranged a tryout at the Red Heads Mississippi training facility, Camp Courage. After a two-day tryout, Moore offered O'Bryan a contract but with one stipulation. Since married players tended not to stay with the team very long, he told her if she had to call and check with her husband, don't bother signing. O'Bryan's answer? "Give me the pen!" O'Bryan stuck with the Red Heads for three seasons, long enough to score over 10,000 points.

Elvera "Peps" Neuman didn't let a negative comment from a local school administrator dissuade her from pursuing a career in basketball. Having already been contacted before graduating from Eden Valley High School in Minnesota by the Texas Cowgirls, she stated in her yearbook that her plans for after school were "playing women's professional basketball." The superintendent of schools took note and was heard saying, "Can you imagine? That Neuman girl wants to play professional basketball!" Elvera made the Cowgirls team and played with three other barnstorming teams during a 26-year career.

The decision to sign a player or not often hinged on their performance during a tryout or an informal private workout. **Jolene "Jo Jo" Ammons** remembers her tryout for the Arkansas Travelers in 1960 in Pearson, Georgia.

"I was so I nervous. After changing into shorts and getting on the court, I looked back at the dressing room door and there was the entire [Travelers] team watching, including the world famous Hazel Walker. Hazel said to shoot a few free throws to loosen up. My first shot didn't come close to the rim. I missed the whole thing. She came over to me and told me to settle my nerves. So, I did what I loved most, taking the ball and spinning it, doing some ball handling. She seemed to like what she saw. After that my confidence was restored."

Although the Travelers offered Jolene a contract, she didn't sign, but she did sign with the Red Heads two years later. She went on to enjoy a 14-year career in pro basketball as a player, coach, and owner.

There were times when a recruit's tryout was a bit unconventional, as was **Janet Cox**'s audition for the Red Heads in 1968. Cox had written to owner Orwell Moore, asking for a tryout, and Moore replied that the team had a vacancy and asked her to join them for a tryout in Gainesville, Georgia.

"My tryout was to put on a uniform and play in the game that night," remembers Cox. "It was a dismal performance and very humiliating. I did not have red hair, was quickly out of breath, and knew none of the twenty-something plays that were used every night." Moore, in need of a player and seeing her potential during her "tryout under fire," signed Cox to a contract. The natural blonde became a redhead and a Red Head.

Playing pro basketball was the culmination of a long-term dream for players like **Sandy Mann.** As a seventh-grader in Desha, Arkansas, she saw the All American Red Heads play and was smitten.

"I went home from that game and said to my parents, 'If you will put a basketball goal up in the backyard and get me a basketball, I'm going to play with the Red Heads.' They did, and I did." She played for eight seasons as a member of the Red Heads and the Southern Belles.

While the roads that led women to join barnstorming pro basketball teams were varied, the girls shared many of the same personality traits — desire, pride, discipline, perseverance, and a love of the game. Once they joined their teams and started their new lives, they all shared a common experience necessary to be successful — work.

Southern Belles in a sister huddle. Clockwise from bottom: Lenna Carey (with pigtails), Sandy Mann, Madeline Hoing, Linda Shanks, Dianne Kirkland, Kathy Gaither, Lucille Thomason.

CHAPTER THREE

Welcome to Pro Basketball, Ladies

Mickey Hendricks left Gate City, Virginia, in 1962, headed on a bus to Paragould, Arkansas, to begin training camp with the All American Red Heads. At the bus depot at West Memphis, Arkansas, she saw a girl who was quite tall who was traveling alone. Hendricks went over to the stranger and said, "You're a Red Head." Her educated guess was a good one, even though the girl didn't have red hair. The girl was Jolene Ammons, another Red Heads rookie. The two boarded the bus for the short ride to Paragrould and became good friends and roommates.

Ammons recalls her first meeting with Hendricks at West Memphis: "In my mind, I was thinking, 'This is really great. I don't have red hair, and someone recognizes me!'"

The status of Ammons and Hendricks as non-Red Heads didn't last long after they got to camp. Coach Orwell Moore met the bus, and Ammons remembers the welcome they got. "His greeting wasn't 'Hello' or 'Welcome to the team,'— it was 'The hair has to go.'"

As members of the Red Heads, new players had to dye their hair red, a requirement that began with original Red Heads owner C.M. "Ole" Olson, who owned five beauty salons in Missouri and Arkansas with his wife, Doyle. A shrewd entrepreneur, Olson knew that the red hair would not only be a good promotional gimmick for the basketball team but also a way to plug the salon business. In the early days of the team, for players like **Toby McGee** (real name **Evelyn Turner**) becoming redheads was a professional job at the hands of Doyle Olson herself when they reported to Cassville, Missouri for training. But for most Red Heads, changing hair color was either a "do-it-yourself" or "do-it-to-a-teammate" task. Cindy Thoren recalls her mother, **Lorene Daniels** — a Red Head from 1938–1950 — telling her about the hair-dyeing process.

"Like teens at a slumber party, they would dye each other's hair with henna and sit in front of the gas stove to dry it and set the color. The heat made the red color brighter."

L-R: Vinia Hobbs, Coach Bernard Cowden, Lorene "Danny" Daniels and Lucy Peters of the Ozark Hill Billies ready for practice near owner Ole Olson's home in Cassville, MO.

Most new Red Head players submitted to the change of hair color cheerfully, but sometimes their hair wasn't as cooperative. For players with jet black hair, becoming a redhead was something that required several bottles of dye initially and retreatment several times during the season. "The first thing we did was get acquainted with Miss Clairol!" said **Debbie Smith**, who played with the Red Heads during the 1967–68 season. "I had long, thick, black hair. It took several bottles to get to the auburn color. After that, we just had to touch up every few weeks. After I finished playing, it took many trips to the salon to get the red out. At one point, I had spotted hair."

Debra "Shak" Parashak, who played for the Red Heads from 1975–77, remembers that for owner/coach Orwell Moore, it wasn't enough to have just red hair "but as bright as you can get it. And to Coach and Mrs. Moore, it was never red enough, so back again for another bottle!"

Carolyn Grantham played only one season with the Red Heads, 1966–67 but said, "It took two years to get that red color out of my hair after I stopped playing."

Once the hair coloring was taken care of, rookies were treated to a healthy regimen of conditioning — not hair, but physical.

"I was nowhere near ready for that first training camp my rookie year," said **Brenda Moon** of her first training camp in 1965, a camp that featured two intense weeks of training. The training got the team in shape, "real shape that would allow a body to play six or seven games a week, every week. There were three-a-days and two-a-days and an occasional scrimmage against some local Caraway, Arkansas, men that I think got a kick out of testing out the skills of the new crop of Red Heads every fall. I was so sore and used so much Absorbine Jr. that it ate holes in my undergarments." Moon played three seasons with the Red Heads.

Judith Coghlan had not only played basketball but also ran track before joining the Red Heads for a season in 1968. "Even though I was a track athlete, running up and down stairs and other drills in training camp made me realize I needed more work on my endurance."

To understand why conditioning was so important to the pioneers of women's basketball, consider the schedule of today's NBA or WNBA player compared to that of a barnstormer.

An NBA team plays an 82-game schedule; a WNBA team plays 34 games during a shortened summer season. Barnstorming women's teams typically played 150 games or more.

NBA/WNBA teams normally play about three games a week — occasionally four and occasionally on back-to-back dates. Barnstorming teams usually played seven days a week, with doubleheaders in separate towns routinely scheduled on weekends. Off days were rare.

NBA/WNBA teams travel on chartered airline flights. Barnstorming teams traveled in station wagons, vans, or limos, often having to drive all night to make it to their next game. Players became accustomed to sleeping on the road.

NBA/WNBA teams have active rosters of 12 players to share playing time in a game. Barnstorming teams normally traveled with only seven players. At times, injuries required they play with only five players.

NBA/WNBA teams go to their locker rooms at halftime to rest. Most barnstorming teams used halftime to entertain fans with demonstrations of ball handling and trick shots. (Their opponents, however, got to rest.)

NBA/WNBA teams travel with a staff of professional trainers and have access to a team physician to help them deal with minor injuries and get their bodies ready to play. Barnstorming players had each other.

NBA/WNBA teams played against players of their own gender. Barnstorming women played against physically-stronger men.

Little wonder why the pioneers of women's basketball had to be in super physical condition to endure the brutal schedule that faced them.

"We practiced three times a day and ran lots and lots of laps, as well as going up and down stairs," recalls **Debbie Smith** about Red Heads camp in 1967. "I hated that, but after we started the games, I understood why!"

Dianne "Kirk" Kirkland, who spent two seasons with the Southern Belles starting in 1969, remembered how tough the long season they played was on her and her teammates.

"The grueling pace was tough at times, but playing with a group of girls in tip-top condition who loved the sport made it seem easier."

Aaronette Eiffling, remembers training camp during her first and only season as a Red Head. "I reported to training camp on October 1, 1965, in Caraway, Arkansas. And my, my — after two days, I realized I had never been in shape — I just thought I had," Eiffling said. "Sore was not a strong-enough word to describe the pain. Every muscle in my body hurt. Even smiling was painful."

While the rookies and teammates hoped that their hard work in camp would lead to "the thrill of victory" once competition started, players like Janet Cox had to deal with "the agony of the feet."

"My worst physical complaint, that I remember, was the blood blisters on the soles of my feet," recalled Cox, who played a season with the Red Heads in '68–'69. "We wore Converse tennis shoes with minimal cushioning. … I wore two pairs of socks and would need to soak my feet in a bathtub in order to remove them." Cox said teammates had to hold her feet in buckets of ice water to condition her feet. To strengthen her arches, she rolled soda bottles on the floor under her feet.

A common ailment during training camp came as a result of the pounding the feet and legs took from all the running. "As a rookie with the Cowgirls, we had training camp in a gym with a tile floor," said Elvera "Peps" Neuman. "I'd run over 100 laps around the gym, with each step pounding on that hard floor. I eventually got shin splints."

"I can still feel the pain from the workouts and sprints," says **Becky Harp**, who played four seasons with the Red Heads from 1965–69. "I remember one girl who had to go home for a while to get over shin splints." Other players, like Debbie Smith, battled through the pain. "Back then, we didn't have fancy weights to work out by," Smith said. "Our leg weights were bags filled with sand and tied together by a rope. I had shin splints and didn't have time to rest my legs, so I played in leg pain most of the time. We just played through it."

Brenda Ragan, with the Red Heads during 1968–69 season, said all the work on conditioning and endurance gave them an advantage over their male counterparts when the season started.

"We had to be in shape to play 100% at a matinee, then travel 50 miles or so and play that night, again at 100%," Ragan said. "We played hard every game to please the crowd that paid to see us, and they loved it. I think the men sometimes were quite embarrassed that we could run circles around them."

Of course, training camp wasn't all just about conditioning. To compete with the men on the scoreboard, the women had to not only run with the men, but they also had to outshoot them.

"We couldn't outmuscle the men, and we couldn't out jump them. But we could outshoot them," said **Frances "Goose" Garroutte,** who played 16 seasons with the Arkansas Travelers from 1951–67. "I practiced shooting for hours at a time, sometimes 500 shots a day."

All aspects of a team's play had to be perfected during training camp, including the ones that had to do with the entertainment side of the business, which was part of the attraction for most of the barnstorming teams.

"Training was intense. We only had two weeks before the first training game," recalled **Ruth Simmons**, a member of the Red Heads from 1979–82. "We ate, slept, lived, and breathed Red Head basketball. We worked on conditioning, learning plays, perfecting routines, and orchestrating the signature All American Red Head halftime show. There was nowhere else I'd rather be."

For new players, learning the tricks that were part of a halftime show didn't happen overnight.

"When I arrived in Arkansas at training, the coach gave me three basketballs and said, 'Lucy learn how to juggle,'" recalls **Lucy Thomason,** who spent a season with the Southern Belles in 1970–71. "It took practice, practice, practice. For the Southern Belles halftime show of entertainment, I juggled; I shot a "behind-the-back" shot; and from the foul line, with my back to the goal, I would step backwards toward the goal and bounce the ball over my head and into the goal. All of this took hours and hours to perfect and be consistent."

Sue Branham remembers how hard it was to get up to speed on the Red Heads offense and the tricks that each team member had to be able to perform.

"Learning to do all the tricks and plays in just two weeks of training camp was the biggest challenge I had faced to that point in my young life," Branham said. "I was trying to remember everything, and it was overwhelming. I was worried I wouldn't be able to get it. But the veterans pulled me aside and worked with me until I figured it out. These women were my heroes, and now they were teaching me one-on-one."

Not all the work to be done during training camps was physical in nature but necessary nonetheless. **Carolyn "California Girl" Wooldridge**, a member of the Red Heads during the 1975–76 season, remembers sewing buttons on uniforms that had fallen off during the previous season.

And then there was selling to do — selling themselves.

"We had to head up to Arkansas to take pictures for programs, billboards, and even Christmas cards," Wooldridge said. "Coach [Orwell] Moore would promote us every way he could dream about."

Since the Red Heads' limousine was a virtual traveling billboard, Moore believed in keeping it looking great. During Wooldridge's training camp with the Red Heads in '75, Moore decided that the limo needed a paint job. The team had another task to add to its to-do list that year.

"First, we had to sand it down, and it was so huge (close to 30 feet long), it took us two full days," Wooldridge said. "Yet as we built up some muscles from all that hand sanding, we were also building up a sense of team and weren't totally aware of it at the time."

While training camp featured more than its share of work, campers found time in the evenings to play a little.

"While [the Red Heads] trained in Caraway (Arkansas), we stayed at the Jami-Bee Motel in Jonesboro, Arkansas," relates Sandy Mann. "The Jami-Bee had a little coffee shop. These were the years when you put a nickel in the jukebox and played and danced to some of the greatest songs of the day — the same songs we heard on Dick Clark's 'American Bandstand.'"

The rigors of training camp served to prepare the barnstormers for the endurance test that lay ahead of them for the next six months on the road, where they would face opponents such as mental fatigue, burnout, sleep deprivation, and exhaustion. It also put them in a better position to compete successfully against their opponents *on* the court — men.

During training camp of 1975, Red Head players got a workout sanding and painting the team limos, "Big Red" and "Whitey."

CHAPTER FOUR

Battles of the Sexes

By the time barnstorming women's basketball teams hit the road in the late 1930s, several men's barnstorming troupes were already operating. The Harlem Globetrotters had been on the road since the mid-1920s and were the most well-known of the teams of the day, but they weren't the first professional men's team. The Original Celtics and the New York Renaissance Five were among teams that competed in loosely organized leagues that came and went almost as often as the players did. The instability ultimately forced teams to turn to barnstorming to make ends meet.

C.M. "Ole" Olson owned and played on a men's team based in Cassville, Missouri, that he called "The Terrible Swedes" as early as 1920. The Swedes blended competitive basketball with a splash of showmanship, such as Olson's own innovative backhand passing. The competition they played against was often organized college and pro teams, although they did at times play against teams of local amateurs who took their best shot at taking down the Swedes in front of the home crowd. As Olson set out to bring women's professional basketball to the public with the All American Red Heads in 1936 and two years later with the Ozark Hill Billies, the question was "whom would the women play?"

College basketball for women didn't exist in those days. For the most part, the only organized basketball open to women after high school (in the few high schools that offered it) was through clubs that competed in the Amateur Athletic Union programs. Putting together teams of women on a local level who could play a competitive game against Olson's pros was difficult and, in most cases, out of the question. So, Olson's teams would have to play against men. But where would the opponents come from? Olson relied on the strategy that had been so successful with the Terrible Swedes — scheduling games against local teams of men. This "killed two birds with one rock" — the Red Heads and Hill Billies had competition, and the local competition helped put more fans in the seats.

While the Red Heads and Hill Billies integrated comedy and tricks into their games, the competition was real. The men's teams they played against weren't going to be satisfied to show up and make like the Washington Generals — perennial patsies of the Harlem Globetrotters — who were on owner-promoter Abe Saperstein's payroll and whose job was to make the Globetrotters look good. The locals showed up to play and, hopefully, to win.

"Playing night after night after night, you encountered a variety of teams with different skill levels," said **Willa Faye "Red" Mason**, who traveled with the Red Heads from 1948–56. "You might play an AAU team that had a regular schedule that it was playing, or you might run into a team of just a bunch of local coaches getting together for a pickup game to see if they could beat a bunch of girls."

Many of the men's teams who thought that playing against women would be a cakewalk had a rude awakening once the games started.

"We had to prove ourselves many times," remembered Becky Harp. "You could tell a men's team would not know what to expect at the beginning of a game, but it wouldn't take long before they realized they were up against some very talented and very

Poster promoting game between Olson's Terrible Swedes and the Middletown Aviation Five, 1928

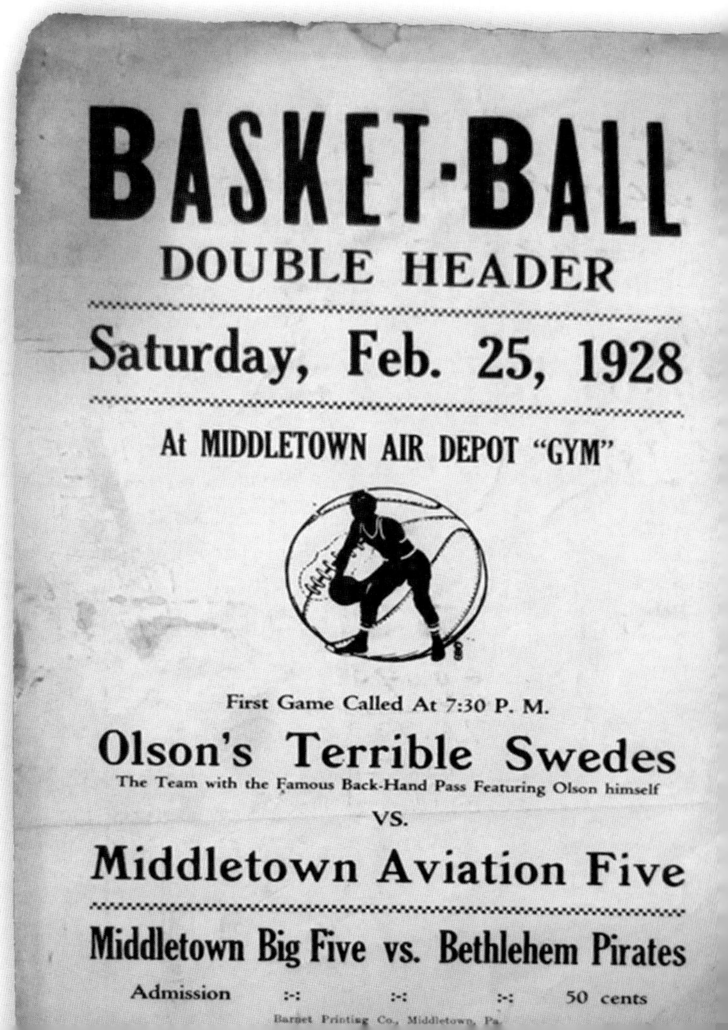

One of the earliest games featuring women versus men basketball. Red Heads Gladys Lommler at foul line and Kay Kirkpatrick ready to defend under basket, circa 1937-38.

competitive ballplayers. Before long they would realize they were going to have to put out some effort to stay in the game. We won their respect many, many times."

Sue Petzold, who traveled with the Southern Belles during the 1969–70 season, recalls a game in Missouri that both teams wanted desperately to win. On this occasion, the competitor wasn't a team thrown together for one night but an organized club that hadn't lost in three years.

"That was definitely our goal — to bring them down," said Petzold. "It was a tough, hard-fought game, with the men treating us just like any other men's team they played. We were up for the challenge."

After regulation time expired, the game was tied at 80–80 and went into "sudden death" —not the normal overtime period, but the first point scored wins. "I'm not sure how long it was without anyone scoring — it seemed like another whole quarter — but we persevered," Petzold continued. "It was tough and rough under the goal and out at the circle. Each player was holding his or her ground on both teams. Finally, there was a shooting foul against the men that was so obvious it had to be called. We needed to make only one of the two free throws to win the game, but we sealed the deal with the first shot and won 81–80. That game had to be my favorite. To win was great, and to do it against that particular team was like icing on the cake."

The competition between the barnstorming women and their male opponents was very real, and there were often battle scars to prove it — on both sides.

"During the first half of the game, the men would typically be having fun, acting nonchalant and not taking us seriously," according to Red Head Janet Cox. "The majority of the time, the Red Heads would be leading at halftime. ... During the second half, the men were more solemn, serious, and aggressive in their physical play. The pats and pinches on the derrières were replaced with swinging elbows and body shoving. During my tenure (one season), I received a broken nose from an elbow and a broken index finger."

Frances "Goose" Garroutte, who saw it all during a 16-year barnstorming career with the Arkansas Travelers, recalled a game when the physical play got out of hand and the perpetrators were ones you'd expect to be promoters of sportsmanship.

"Once I had a fist thrown at me that hit me — and that was from the principal of a high school," Garroutte said. She also remembers other educators that sometimes played "dirty" when tempers flared. "Sometimes our opponent was a team made up of all the coaches of the surrounding area, which was a great drawing card. ... But the coaches' teams were by far the worst, since they did not want to get beat in front of their kids by a bunch of women. Most of them were nice, but some of them did get nasty."

"Red" Mason agreed that the coaches were very motivated not to lose. "The coaches were in front of their peers, as well as the players they coached," Mason said. "They couldn't afford to look like fools. After all, we got to leave town 30 minutes after the game, but they had to coach the next day and explain to their players why they lost to a bunch of girls."

Embarrassing the local men folk by beating them on the basketball court was not without repercussions, remembered Helen Onson, an early barnstormer who played with Helen Stephens Olympic Co-Eds and the Ozark Hill Billies prior to World War II. After one victory by the barnstormers, "a restaurant owner in Colorado threw [us] out of his establishment, saying he 'didn't want any trouble.'"

Kay Kirkpatrick, one of the original All American Red Heads that hit the road in 1936, related to her daughter a story about an occasion when the Red Heads gave the local males a beating.

Red Head Ruth Osborn (back to camera) watches as Kay Kirkpatrick gets a hand on the ball, circa 37-38.

"Mother recalled one time in particular in the Detroit area where local police officers formed a line for the women as they exited the arena to get into their bus and leave after the men's team suffered a humiliating defeat at the hands of the Red Heads," said Kathleen Ethington. "Usually the local police would escort them to the outskirts of whatever city they were in. This occurred more in the larger cities than the smaller venues, but it occurred frequently in the beginning."

When the play got too rough, the barnstormers sometimes had to take matters into their own hands — or, to be more precise, their knees. Bernie Hudgens King related a story told by her mother **Nellie Marlow,** a Red Head of 1955–57.

"Mom told us about a situation during one game where one of the men they were playing against got very rough. He had been pushing her around and elbowing her all night. Lo and behold, my mother went up for a rebound with him and got outjumped. As he came down with the ball, he elbowed her in the mouth and knocked two of her teeth out. My mother was *not* going to come out of the game for good. As the night went on, the coach let her come back in after she had begged him. She got the perfect opportunity to remind this player not to play dirty and that what a man can do, a woman can do better. She got a rebound, and when he came down, she popped her knee up, and he fell to the floor. As he lay on the floor with a bruised ego (among other things), she told him, 'Don't *ever* elbow another lady in the mouth.'"

Teammates of **Lorene "Butch" Moore**, a Red Heads player and coach from 1947–58, recalls the time she defended center Emogene Shelton.

"Butch was the general on the court," said Jolene Ammons, who played 14 seasons with the Red Heads herself. "Once, when one of the guys was doing something to Emo, she told Emo to step aside when she was ready to do a backhand pass, which she could throw very hard. You can imagine where it went. Emo had no more problems that night."

While you might say that such retaliation wasn't very ladylike, keep in mind that the pioneers of women's basketball were playing against men, playing by men's rules. It follows that they would have to resort to men's tactics from time to time. **Hazel Walker**, who played briefly for the Red Heads before owning and coaching the Arkansas Travelers, had these simple expectations for decorum for the players she coached: "My players should look like women, act like women, and play basketball like men."

Once, when a game against a college team in Colorado was getting out of hand, Coach Orwell Moore of the Red Heads told his team to let the opponents win, hoping to avoid injuries. But the women would have none of that.

"The [opposing] team was young and undefeated, and they were not going to allow a 'bunch of girls' to beat them," remembers **Gwen Reed**, who played a season with the Red Heads and later played with the New York Stars of the WBL, the first pro women's league to make it through a season. "I was determined that they were not going to win, so we went out and had another huddle on the court. All I said was, 'I want this game!' It was like a miracle. The girls couldn't miss. We ended up winning the game and came out of it with just a few scrapes and bruises. I was so proud of each member of our team."

The games that got out of hand were the exception rather than the rule. Aaronette Eiffling remembers one game in which one of the locals playing against her Red Heads happened to be a celebrity — and a gentleman.

Red Heads Jolene "Jo Jo" Ammons with Cheryl Clark (back to camera) taking on the men during a 1973 game in Memphis, Tennessee.

"I remember playing — I think it was Indianapolis — and one of the men playing was a former NBA player, Clyde Lovellette. It was an honor playing against a professional. He was the first player to ever be on a team that won the NCAA Championship, NBA Championship, an Olympic gold medal, and then be inducted into the Basketball Hall of Fame. (He was a) big, big guy, but so nice!"

"Peps" Neuman recalls the welcome her Arkansas Gems got in 1982 in New York from opponents that you might not associate with gentlemanly manners — Lawrence Taylor and the New York Giants of the National Football League.

"We all had our hair done for the big game. After introductions, each of us received a beautiful bouquet of roses from a different Giant player."

That gesture was typical of the warm welcome the Lassies received in their travels, Neuman said.

"When we pulled into town, people would tell each other that we had arrived and showed us great respect. On the basketball floor, we had mutual respect for the men's teams we played, for the referees who were donating their time, and for the people in the audience who were part of our stunts."

Competing against males, the pioneers of women's basketball proved not only that women could play the game, but also play it at a high level. Records are incomplete, but for seasons where win-loss records were tracked, the barnstormers typically won between 80–90 percent of their games. Even more impressive is the fact that they enjoyed that success despite the fact that they never had a home court advantage.

The opposing teams were not the only foes the pioneers had to overcome during the season. What may have been their toughest foe dogged them 24/7 for the duration of their six-month schedule — the road.

Red Heads pose with their male opponents during the 1970-71 season. Red Heads are (L-R) Kathy McCall, Emma Bartmess, Cheryl Clark, Pat "Watusie" Deroche, Charlotte "Sweetie" Adams, Carolyn Reeves and Lois "Sugar Bear"Glover.

CHAPTER FIVE

Queens of the Road

Depending on the year and the team, the barnstorming pioneers of women's basketball traveled somewhere between 36,000 and 70,000 miles per season, based on recollections of the players interviewed for this book. The points on the scoreboard weren't the only ones these teams had to be concerned about during their marathon seasons. Sometimes, the biggest challenge proved to be getting from "point A" to "point B."

Arkansas Travelers' Frances "Goose" Garroutte, prior to packing bus for another game in 1955

While there were a few times when the itineraries of the barnstormers required air or boat travel, the mode of transportation for teams almost always included a vehicle with four wheels that traveled on concrete, asphalt, gravel, or dirt.

While on the court, Frances "Goose" Garroutte drove down the free throw lane toward the basket. Her duties with the Arkansas Travelers included sharing driving time with Hazel Walker. In the days before cruise control, GPS navigation, and wide highways, driving the lanes of America was hard work.

"Hazel and I were the only ones that ever drove," remembers Goose. "We just looked at the map at night, then took off the next day. There were no superhighways — just a bunch of little 'pig trails' through the little towns. I think I traveled every pig trail in America!"

While the more successful barnstorming teams in later years were able to travel in the relative comfort of stretch limousines, the early pioneers traveled in more modest vehicles, such as station wagons.

Sandy Mann recalled her first season with the All American Red Heads in 1963.

"In later years, we would travel in four-door stretch limos. However, let me tell you, that first year, there was no such thing. We traveled in a "funeral family car" … It was one of those old gray Cadillacs that had the front seat and backseat, which was way back there. Out of the back of the front seat, you pulled two little jump seats out, and that's what two of us had to sit on. It was so cold in that thing that ice would freeze on the INSIDE of the back windows. We would stuff Kleenex all around those windows, trying to stay warm. Yessirree, that was barnstorming in 1963!"

Even more primitive travel was the plight of the Royal Maids, a team that played only one season, 1971–72. "We traveled in a converted Checker Cab," said Teresa Bergeron. "It was forever breaking down."

Before they upgraded their mode of travel to limos, the Red Heads traveled in a three-row station wagon, according to **Jessie Banks**, who played from 1954–59. The seating arrangement was "three riding in the front seat, three in the middle, and two in the back. Luggage was on top, carefully loaded in order to get bags for eight people to fit, and covered with a large, heavy green tarp. Our uniform bags went behind the back seat."

Since luggage was carried on top of the wagon, loading it was an ordeal in itself.

"We traveled by station wagon, learning the routine of arranging the luggage on top of the vehicle, covered by a specially-made tarp," said legend-

Station wagon loaded, Jessie Banks is ready to hit the road with her All American Red Heads teammates, 1959. The vehicle had three rows, and the players luggage and was loaded on top, protected by a tarp.

ary Red Head Jolene Ammons. "On freezing cold, snowy mornings, *yuck*!" Since the job of loading the luggage was a big one, the players took turns. "When it was my turn, it was really rough on the hands on those cold mornings," said Red Head Shirley Beckman.

Ozark Hill Billies Nota Lee McCain and Phyllis White in front of their bus in St. John, Kansas.

Teams that were fortunate enough to travel by limousine in later years didn't have to worry about loading the luggage on top of the vehicle — it was stowed in the back. This provided an advantage for the shorter players on those occasions that required the team to travel overnight and the women to sleep on the road.

"Being the smallest player on our team, I did a lot of sleeping on top of the luggage in the back on occasion and would use a sweater or a jacket for a pillow," said **Lynn Holst**, a Red Head from 1971–73. "Most of the sleep was short naps, and the taller players could get a bit jealous at times, but sleeping in the back did come with its own issues. Coach (and driver) Ben (Overman) happened to be colorblind and didn't always see stop light changes. The brakes would get a hard and quick stomp of the foot and everything would come to a quick stop — except for me."

Being the shortest girl on the team sometimes meant taking on tasks that were more suited to a woman who was "vertically challenged."

Red Head Bessie Shelton takes her turn at the morning ritual of loading the car for the drive to the next town, circa 1963.

"Because I was the shortest, I was also relied on to help with tasks that others could not do easily," said Holst. "We were traveling to a town called Happy Camp, California, way up on a mountain. On our way up, the muffler fell down. I had to crawl under and wire it up with a coat hanger, but we made it."

Mechanical problems were a frequent issue for vehicles that often took on 40,000 miles in six months.

"One time when we were traveling to a game, we had a mishap with our car," said Pat "Watusie" Deroche. "We were traveling on the road, and all a sudden, we heard a big thunderous noise. It had us all jumping in our seats, wondering what happened. Coach was trying to steer the car on to the shoulder, so we wouldn't get in a wreck and get hurt. As we were pulling over to the side of the road, we looked out our window, and what do we see but a tire passing our limo and continuing up on the road. It was initially a bit amusing, until we realized the tire we saw going by was our own. We had lost the back tire. Needless to say, we had to stay out on the side of the road until a wrecker came, and we were able to make the game that night."

One Red Head team had trouble so frequently that they carried their own spare parts. "We carried a spare axle, true story, with packed bearings, as we seemed to have an issue every few days," recalled **Marcia Adams,** a Red Head from 1975–77. "Lynnea [Sjoquist] became quite adept at removing the tire and changing the axle, which kept us on schedule for the better. Some of the mechanics we encountered along the way were a bit dumbstruck when we showed up at their garage requesting packed bearing service."

Adams' teammate **Marsha Tate** remembers one "Murphy's Law" trip when it seemed that everything that could go wrong did go wrong.

"First of all, our car had broken down and was in the shop in St. Louis, Missouri, and we had a game in the southern part of the state," Tate said. "Our coach could not find a vehicle large enough to carry the team, our duffel bags, uniforms, and our four bags of basketballs, so he rented a U-Haul, and we rode in the back of it. Well, down the road, the tie rod fell out of the U-Haul, and we had to be towed into the next town, Peculiar, Missouri. As we hung out at a gas station trying to figure out how we were going to make it to our game in Dora, Missouri, a very nice man offered to take us in his Bronco. We piled into that Bronco, and some of us laid across the ball bags in the back. Oh, but that was not the end of our adventures. We then had a flat on the Bronco. An hour after the game was to start, we entered the gym to a packed crowd still waiting on us! Whatever we had to endure to make a game, we played hard and put on the show for the fans."

Red Heads "Big Red" gets a tow after a breakdown, circa 1975-76. Marilyn "Ralph" Nelson, Linda Jones and Kay O'Bryan get in the picture.

As you might expect when playing a schedule that starts in the fall and ends in the spring, winter weather was a frequent foe of the road warriors.

"In late February, we had to drive for five-and-a-half hours up a mountain pass to get to our game in Othello, Washington," recalled Red Head Carolyn Wooldridge about a 1976 incident involving a limo that the team affectionately called "Big Red." "It was snowing all the way. It was really pretty, but it was snowing so hard that we needed to put on chains. But Coach didn't want to chain 'Big Red' up, and we ended up getting stuck. So, we had to get out and push Red up the hill for about a mile. We were really tired and cold. A guy finally stopped and helped us put chains on the car."

Snow caused travel headaches for barnstorming teams, but also provided opportunities for play, as Southern Belle Dianne Kirkland experienced in South Dakota, winter of 1969-70.

"We traveled through many snowstorms over the years," said "Peps" Neuman about her travels during a career that spanned more than a quarter century with four teams. "We often would stop and dig out stuck vehicles, so we could clear the road. Sometimes, the whole team would get out to push to help stranded drivers on their way."

The Red Heads load up to head out to the next town, despite snow storm, circa 1956-57.

Southern Belles' limo after heavy snow storm in South Dakota, 1970

Car trouble wasn't the only reason the barnstormers had to take to foot on the road. Coaches often would stop the vehicle, let the girls out, drive two miles, park on the shoulder of the road, and wait for the players to run to catch up. This was called "roadwork." A coach with the Southern Belles added a new twist to roadwork, as recalled by **Lenna Carey**, who spent the '70-'71 season with the Southern Belles.

"Coach [Chuck] Plummer joined us about midway of the schedule," said Carey. "He was always smiling, chewing his gum, and fun to travel with. One afternoon as we traveled a winding mountain highway, Coach Plummer pulled over, pointed out a highway far below, and offered a ten dollar bill to any player that could beat the limo to that point. Linda Shanks, our team center, immediately jumped from the limo and down the steep side. After driving several minutes, Coach realized this was not the same road. We returned to the starting point and called Shanks back up the mountainside. She finally returned, scratched and scraped, but in good humor. I don't know if she was paid or not."

Humor often helped to diffuse tension on the road, especially following a frustrating loss, as **Cindy "Pecos" Roybal,** who played and coached with the Red Heads (1971–72) recalls.

"Once when I was coaching, we were traveling late at night after a game that we had just lost in Gunnison, Colorado. I was upset 'cause I felt the girls didn't play up to their potential. We also were driving very slow and cautiously because it was snowing, when all of a sudden we hear a *thud*. We got out of the van and removed a six-point buck from the road. I then had my male assistant take the wheel. Shortly afterwards another *thud*, and we move another buck out of our way! By this time I was upset (it was a wonder the van was okay), so I took over the driving duties. About 15 minutes later — you guessed it — another *thud*! Now we remove a 10-point buck! As we got back in the van, a voice from the back says, 'Coach, can I say something?' I answered reluctantly, 'Go ahead.' She said 'If we could have used all the points you coaches got, we would have *won* the game!' We all just laughed and enjoyed the rest of the trip."

When the barnstormers weren't sleeping on the road or fighting the weather, they had hours to pass until they reached their destination. Music was a favorite way of passing the time.

"Being from the Nashville area, folks assumed I was a country western music fan, so when it was my turn to control the radio, I always selected a country music station," recalled Red Head Brenda Moon. Some of the more popular songs for the road warriors were Dave Dudley's "Six Days on the Road" and Roger Miller's "King of the Road." "Since these were usually easy sing-a-long songs, we would often use our pretend microphones and join in. Now for full confession — when I joined the Red Heads, I did not like country western music at all! I would start shaking my red hair all over anytime I heard 'These Boots Are Made for Walking,' 'Good Vibrations,' 'I Heard It Through the Grapevine,' or anything by Elvis or the Beatles when they came blasting (as much as it could) out of our little AM radio speaker."

Red Heads Donna "Spanky" Losier playing guitar with Brenda Ragan, Chuck Plummer, Pam McAnally create some Christmas spirit, December 1968.

Accompanied on the guitar by **Donna "Spanky" Losier**, a Red Head from 1967–78, sing-a-longs were a staple of the team's road trips. "We all had fun laughing and singing," said Losier, "and it certainly helped pass the time in the limo."

The Red Heads weren't professional singers, but observers sometimes thought they were, said **Carolyn Gooch**, who played from 1968–70. "A lot of people thought we were a band. We would pull up in our 31-

Above: Red Heads Peggy Lawson, Hazel Vickers and Kay Kirkpatrick on back of their bus, circa 37-38

foot stretch limo. Seven redheaded women got out of the car. Someone would ask, 'Y'all a band?' We would reply, 'No, we're a basketball team.'"

The challenge of making it to the next game on time sometimes involved driving faster than the legal speed limit. Texas Cowgirl **Ginny Hill**, who played from 1959–63, shared driving duties and was ticketed many times.

"Sometimes we had to travel all night to get to the next game," Hill said. "Being one of the drivers, I got more than my share of speeding tickets. I never had to pay them, but the minute I started living in Minnesota and transferred my license from North Dakota to Minnesota, I found out I had too many tickets! After I told them that I was doing part-time driving for the Texas Cowgirls, they let me go and dropped all the tickets."

Travel outside the contiguous United States brought a welcome change from the routine of driving between games but was not without its share of unwanted excitement. Kathleen Ethington recalled an account mother Kay Kirkpatrick told her.

Left: Red Heads Peggy Lawson and Kay Kirkpatrick in front of venue before game, circa 37-38

"The Red Heads spent time in the Philippines in 1940, where they played exhibition games throughout the islands for several months. … World War II was beginning to brew, and international unrest was growing. … The U.S. State Department issued the warning for all U.S. citizens to leave the Philippines because of an imminent threat of invasion from the Japanese. The islands were filled with people who were loyal to the Japanese, and Pedro, the Red Heads' Philippine sponsor, was fearful that the women could be targeted to be used as propaganda since they were a 'high profile' group. … Mother quickly got the players together and told the team members to stay put while she left to contact Pedro to enlist his help to get the team off the islands. When Mother found Pedro, he told Mother to go back to the hotel and get the other team members to pack their things and wait for him to help them get home.

"When mother got to the hotel, the team wasn't there. A note was left saying they were going out for a while to get their last round of visiting in before leaving. Mother waited with her packed bags at the hotel. Pedro showed up by evening and told mother that they needed to be ready to leave around midnight, as transportation he had arranged would take them to a ship leaving for the U.S.

"Mom told him about the girls leaving, and Pedro said he would find the girls and bring them back to the hotel. Pedro returned a few hours later in the wee hours of the morning, but he didn't have the team with him. He said he had looked all over but had been unable to locate them. He told Mother she needed to leave with him to get to the waiting boat he had arranged, that he would find the rest of the team and get them to the ship so they could all travel home together. Mother got to the ship and discovered all would be leaving the Philippines on a cattle boat with a minesweeper leading the way. Several hours later, the team made it to the cattle boat and all left together.

"Pedro had arranged to get the women quietly from where they were to a larger ship on a small boat that was a ship that contained a boatload of cattle. That was a great 'cover' to get them safely off the islands without being noticed. Mother remembered seeing Pedro standing quietly on the shore as she got on that smaller boat, alone in the dark. Mother often recounted how the Red Heads arrived on a luxury commercial ship, only to leave quietly on a cattle boat with a minesweeper leading the way."

Another Red Head on the Philippines trip, **Hazel Smith**, found a bright side to the less-than-luxurious travel arrangements heading home. About the rough seas, she told her daughters that the experience gave her the best "sea legs." Regarding traveling on a ship with a bunch of men, she said, "the odds were great!"

All American Red Heads pose with sponsor Pedro (back row, center, surname unknown) in the Philippines during their 1940 tour of the island nation. Standing, L-R: Eleanor Liach, Ruth Osborn, Gladys Lommler, Pedro, Hazel Smith, Kay Kirkpatrick and Peggy Lawson. The three men in front are unidentified.

Red Heads aboard a "puddle jumper" during Alaska tour, 1976-77. L-R: Gretchen Pinz, Charlotte Adams, Rhonda Waters, Barb Hostert, Wanda England and Marsha Tate.

During the Red Heads' trip to Alaska to play for servicemen at military bases, the team went from island to island in the Aleutian chain by seaplane. "On one occasion, as the plane took off and became airborne, one engine went out," said Jessie Banks. "The pilot told us he was turning around, and we would be able to land where we departed. Well, we landed okay, but not before the other engine went out before we got to the dock. I do believe we were a little scared. Of course, they had to come and get us by boat."

Brenda Moon recalled the flight to Point Barrow, Alaska, near the Arctic Circle. "We flew in a small seaplane. In fact, it was so small that there were just enough seats for the players, and Coach had to sit in the co-pilot chair! And if that wasn't scary enough for someone that had flown just a handful of times (all due to Red Head travels), as we were flying over the mountains heading north to Barrow, the pilot said something like, 'Over there is where Will Rogers was killed when his plane, similar to this one we are in, crashed.' Boy, did my ears perk up and my heart was nearly pounding out of my chest."

Sandy Mann remembered the ground transportation arrangements during the Alaska trip to Point Barrow, near the Arctic Circle. "They hauled us from place to place in a military ambulance, one of those trucks with two benches in the back and straps to hold onto. It was daylight 24 hours a day now, and everywhere we went there were little kids running behind the truck after us. The kids would be playing outside at 3 or 4 o'clock in the morning, I asked a guy, 'Don't they ever sleep?' He laughed and said, 'When they want to.'"

Life on the road for the pioneers of women's basketball wasn't only about the time spent traveling and sharing a station wagon, van, or limo. The road also meant sharing hotel and motel rooms, double beds, restaurant tables and diner booths — in other words, sharing life with their extended family, united as sisters by love of a game — a love that may have been thicker than blood.

CHAPTER SIX

Sisterhood of the Traveling Basketball Players

Spending every day for over six months with the same six women might put a strain on some relationships. But for the barnstorming pioneers of women's basketball, the shared experiences of togetherness seemed to be a glue that bound the women together not only as teammates, but also as friends.

"The camaraderie of a team that travels in a station wagon and is on the road almost every day is amazing," said **Debra Parashak**, who was an All American Red Head from 1975–77. "For those two years, my teammates were my best friends."

Perhaps the fact that the girls had so much in common even before they met made their bonding not only easier, but also inevitable.

"Many of us girls were from rural areas and were pretty naïve," said All American Red Head Brenda Moon about her teammates in the '60s. "One year we stayed in downtown Chicago and had some time to explore. From our hotel, we could see an X-rated movie theater right on the main street, and since none of us had never seen an X-rated movie, we decided to be adventurous and check it out. A group of us walked to the theater, bought our tickets, and went inside. Almost immediately we knew something was different about this theater, so we all sat on the back row and tried to look inconspicuous. To our surprise, it really wasn't a movie theater like we were accustomed to, but rather more like a peep show. We exited as quickly and quietly as possible, laughing all the way back to the hotel. At least our black jackets sort of blended in with the guys wearing the black topcoats!"

Most of the destinations on the barnstormers' itineraries weren't metropolises like Chicago but were small towns and villages. But the opportunities for getting in trouble were just as numerous. One incident in Georgia involved old-fashioned horseplay.

"One night, we were waiting to go to the game in Homerville, Georgia," said Sandy Mann, who played for the Red Heads and the Southern Belles. "Dressed in our uniforms and warmups, **Mickey Gay, Glenda Ledbetter,** and I were outside, by the swimming pool. Only three feet away was a wading pool for kids. Let me say that all of this was a perfect recipe — for disaster.

"I was standing and bouncing on the diving board when I caught a strange movement out of the corner of my eye. Then I saw that Glenda had grabbed Mickey by the shoulders (they were occupying the small space between the two pools, with Mickey's back to the kiddie pool). Glenda was pushing then pulling Mickey to and fro, as if she was going to push Mickey into the pool. I opened my mouth to scold them and say, 'Coach will kill all of us if we get wet!' Well, before I could scream at them, Glenda's hand slipped and into the pool Mickey went. The next thing I saw was Glenda's back as she ran toward the motel room, that long ponytail bouncing as she ran.

"I looked at Mickey and she was standing in the middle of the kiddy pool *on one foot*. I convinced her that she had to put that dry foot down and walk out, which she did. We ran to the room. The next few minutes were spent with us trying to squeeze as much water as possible out of Mickey's warmups, shoes, and socks.

"When we got to the gym, we had to walk all the way across the court to get to our dressing room. We gathered around Mickey and walked, as a unit, across the court, hiding her from the coach. Every step we took, we could hear ol' Mick's squish, squish, squish. About halfway across I looked behind us, and there was a set of Mickey's wet footprints as far as I could see. I can't tell you how many times Mickey fell that night but it was a *lot*."

Speaking of wet uniforms, one of the common experiences of all the barnstorming teams was having to wash their own uniforms out in their hotel room after the game.

"I don't know what I was thinking would happen about getting our suits washed for each game, but after the first game, we all had to wash our suits either in a lavatory or bathtub," said Sue Petzold of the Southern Belles. "Then, we had to hang them up on hangers in order to get them dry by the next morning. When we arrived at the motel for the game that night, we had to iron our suits. Within the week, we were broken in fairly quickly on first-hand washing and ironing our suits."

When they weren't horsing around at the pool or washing their uniforms, the girls spent much of their hotel/motel time doing what young girls do — singing and dancing. The Red Heads of the early '70s even had their own traveling band, remembers Lynn Holst.

"I had my guitar. **Jeanne Oehlman** did some mean picking on her banjo, and **Kathy Tipton** could clog and make the ground rumble. We'd start playing that old Cajun 'Crawdad' Song ('You get a line, I'll get a pole, we'll go fishin' in the crawfish hole'). "We would go on and play that a long time. We couldn't play in the car, but did in the rooms or outside the motels."

Willa Faye Mason remembered a song the Red Heads came up with during the 1948–49 season to announce their arrival into a new town.

"We used to sing this a lot traveling around the country, even waiting to check in at a hotel for the night because the Red Heads had arrived:

(Sung to the tune of "Notre Dame Victory March")
Oh, we are the Red Heads, pretty and trim
We've come to town to play ball and win
Send seven girls out on the floor,
There'll be laughter and passing
and shooting galore
We want all you people to know
We do our best to put on our show
And whether we win or whether we lose
We hope to return to your town again"

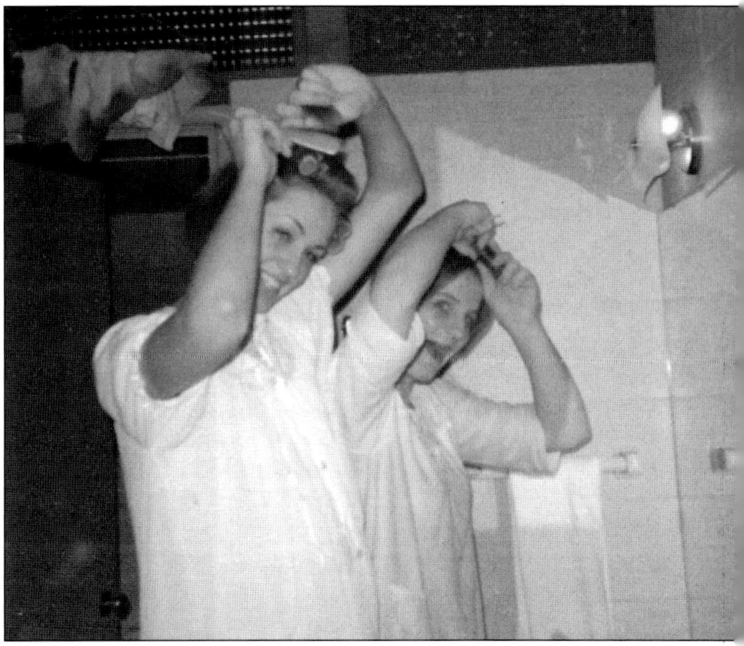

Red Heads Brenda Moon and Charlotte "Sweetie" Adams doing their hair prior to a game, 1967-68 season

Card games were another popular pastime for barnstormers. Lorene "Butch" Moore of the Red Heads introduced her teammates to what would become their favorite game — blackjack.

"It didn't matter where we were — in the car, in the locker room, or in the motel room — we played blackjack," said Jolene Ammons.

Brenda Moon recalled some of the low-stakes poker games she and her Red Heads teammates of the '60s enjoyed.

"Coach [Moore] was almost always up for a penny poker game, as were many of the girls. Everyone kept their little stash of pennies from game-to-game. The dealer would declare the game for each hand, such as five-card stud or seven-card draw, and what was to be declared as wild, so we were often making up silly versions of poker. There was always lots of laughter and joking around. And it was always fun breaking in the rookies to our unorthodox penny poker games."

For the most part, the overnight accommodations for the barnstormers were more austere than today's pro hoops stars enjoy.

"The hotels and motels we stayed in weren't as nice as they are today — in fact, some of them were downright bad, but we stayed, anyway," said "Goose" Garroutte of the Arkansas Travelers. "Some towns were so small they didn't have a motel at all, so we might stay in a boardinghouse. We got used to the travel routine — we were young, so it didn't bother us."

Garroutte remembers one memorable incident that occurred when the team was staying on a military base.

"We would stay in guest houses on the base. One time Hazel [Walker] and I were rooming together. After our game, we had gone to bed. All of a sudden, Hazel asked me if I was asleep, then she asked me if I'd go to the bathroom with her. I said, 'Hazel, what in the world is wrong with you?' She jumped up and ran out in the hall, and started screaming at me, 'Goose, there's a man under my bed!' I jumped up and joined her in the hall. The man started yelling, 'If you want me out from

Cramped quarters sometimes created a slumber-party liked atmosphere for the Red Heads and other barnstormers. Top bunk: Marilyn Nelson and Deb Parashak. Bottom: Kay O'Bryan, Connie Howe, Patty Bruce and Linda Jones. Circa 1975-76.

under this bed, you are gonna have to help me!' He was stuck. We left him under there until the MPs could get there and arrest him."

For some barnstormers, just finding any accommodations was a challenge, thanks to Jim Crow. After her career with the Texas Cowgirls during the '50s and early '60s, Linda Yearby was asked to leave the court to coach the Harlem Queens, an all-black women's team. "I witnessed firsthand the slap of discrimination in my players' faces," Yearby said. "I would have to go into restaurants and hotels first and ask if it was okay for my team to enter for a meal or to rest their heads at night."

When it came to dining on the road, the long distances between towns meant that meal stops often had to be kept short. To speed up service, sometimes the girls took matters into their own hands.

"I remember when we would all walk into a restaurant," said **Mary Alice Carpenter**, who played for the Red Heads during the 1966–67 season. "We virtually lived in them for seven months, so one of the players would usually go right up and grab the coffee pot and started filling all the others cups up, so the waitresses wouldn't have to worry about it. Sometimes, we would even help start another pot. The waitresses really liked that."

Betty Springer, who joined the Red Heads for a season beginning in 1963, said another way the team got to make the most of their meal stop was to eat dessert while their meals were being prepared. "We … learned to order dessert first. If we didn't, we didn't get dessert."

Traveling the country as a barnstormer meant getting used to the regional differences in menus.

"I ate oatmeal in New York, which was great," said Debbie Smith. "However, they didn't have grits or sweet tea in the North! I sure missed my grits and sweet tea."

Dining at fast food restaurants wasn't an option during the early years of barnstorming, and when those eateries began to be common, many teams didn't stop there because it was felt it would be bad for the image of professional athletes to eat there. But "Peps" Neuman found a way around the prohibition.

"Restaurants like McDonald's were still relatively new, and while I liked their food, they weren't a classy 'sit down' type of restaurant at that time. However, the team would park the limousine at a sit-down restaurant, and a teammate and I would walk to a McDonald's — sometimes a few blocks away, other times many blocks. With food in the bag and change in our pocket, we ate our meal on the way back to the limo, then sat in the eight-door limousine, and waited for the rest of the team to finish eating at the restaurant."

Whether on a plate or in a bag, restaurant food isn't like home cooking. The barnstormers welcomed those occasions when the schedule permitted them to enjoy a special treat.

"[Coach Orwell Moore] always tried to play at least one game close to every girl's home town at some point during the season," said Brenda Moon of the Red Heads, "and when time allowed, that girl's family would have all of us over for a real home-cooked meal."

Carolyn Grantham remembered the time it was her family's chance to host her and her Red Head teammates in 1966 in Norman Park, Georgia.

"After the game my mother had prepared a meal for the team. We ate in the cafeteria of the school. She invited some close friends, and we had a delicious meal. Mama really worked hard on that meal. Good ole Southern cooking for us for southern Georgia girls. The girls who weren't from

Georgia enjoyed it also. After the meal, all of us girls gathered around the piano. My favorite song is 'How Great Thou Art.' All of the girls knew the song because we had sung it in the car plenty of times a cappella. This time we had music, and the people there could not believe what they heard — it was like seven redheaded angels had descended from the heavens."

The mother of Red Head Sheryl Wood offered a good taste of home for the team in the '70s.

"We played at my former high school, Lawrence High," Wood said. "We looked and looked for a hotel room but could find none. It was in November, around Thanksgiving and two players' birthdays. My mom was bound and determined that we were going to be treated like royalty, so she housed the entire team overnight and made a full Thanksgiving dinner for the team to enjoy. In addition, she and my sister-in-law made two birthday cakes for the birthday girls. After that, the players affectionately called my childhood home 'The Wood Inn.'"

But opportunities to enjoy home were rare. Being away from home was especially difficult for the barnstormers during the holidays. **Lucy Thomason** of the Southern Belles remembers how the team made the best of the situation at Christmas 1970.

"We were in Charleston, West Virginia, and we stayed at the Daniel Boone Hotel. The hotel was built in 1929 by a group of Charleston citizens to provide an elegant center for hosting politicians and visiting dignitaries in the bustling capital city. The hotel was beautiful. We were a bit nostalgic because our busy touring schedule did not allow time for the Belles to make it home to their families for Christmas. So, we decided to make the best of it. Sandy Mann … came to our rescue and was instrumental in finding the Belles a Christmas tree. I believe she talked an employee at the hotel out of it. Having a tree did seem to make the holiday season a bit easier."

Letters from home helped ease the homesickness, although getting mail required some creative planning, since the team was rarely in the same town two nights in a row.

"Our game schedule was planned for at least one month in advance," Red Head Janet Cox remembers. "The players could send their schedule home, which allowed loved ones to write to us in advance. We would go to the post office in each town to collect our mail and also send out our letters and post cards."

Mail sometimes included special treats other than letters.

"There were the occasional 'care packages' that moms would send to the post office of one of the towns where we would be playing on a weekday," said Brenda Moon. "These care packages, as was any

Southern Belles Linda Shanks and Dianne "Kirk" Kirkland celebrate Christmas on the road, 1970.

Red Heads Brenda "Brooksie" O'Bryan, Lynn Holst and Mary Leasure acquired special Christmas pajamas to help them get in the spirit of the season, December 1972.

personal mail we received, was marked 'Hold for pickup by the All American Red Heads' and the post office would always be our first stop when we arrived at a new game town. No such thing as emails, cell phones, or texting, just old-fashioned letters. Moms would send enough goodies to share, and most of the time the girls did share.

Veteran players often took the younger ones under their wings and helped them with the transition to life on the road.

"Sandy Mann kept a watchful eye on the rookie players," said Lenna Carey, a Southern Belle during the 1970-71 season. "There were many times I shared problems going on at home, feelings of homesickness, and my faith with her. She was always a good listener and counselor, our surrogate mother and guardian angel."

Red Heads hang out at a soda shop during 1967-68 season. L-R: Mary Parsons, Sandy Mann, Charlotte "Sweetie" Adams, Pat Overman and Carolyn Linzay, with Brenda Hubbard in back.

Mann knew firsthand what a powerful emotion homesickness could be.

"At one point, during my second year with the Red Heads, I had developed a severe case of homesickness. ... One teammate was having the same problem. One day we had the bright idea of running away *to* home. Ben Overman was the coach at the time. Knowing it would be hard to outsmart Ben, much planning went into our little venture.

"We packed our belongings, waited till we knew Ben was taking a nap, called a taxi, and we were 'on the lam!' We went rushing into the bus station, and I told the clerk, 'We need two tickets on the first bus outta here, and we don't care where it's going.' The lady looked at me kind of funny, but she sold me the tickets.

"We nervously paced about the station, obviously in distress, as we knew full well that if Ben found out, he'd be coming to get us. Well, it wasn't very long till Ben came rushing through the door. He looked frazzled. His hair was in disarray. He had his overcoat on and shoes, but no socks. He 'herded' us over to a corner and started talking to us in, low tones.

"He calmly counseled with us, and reassured us. We finally came to our senses and agreed to go back with him."

But this wasn't the end of "the runaway Red Heads story."

"On the way back to the motel (I was sitting in the front seat with Ben), the cops pulled us over. They asked Ben to get out of the vehicle. He stood at the back of the car, trying to convince them that everything is 'legit.' One of the cops opened the driver's door and leaned in, taking a look at us. He asked me, 'Do y'all know this guy? I told him that we did, and they let Ben go.

"Poor Ben took the whole thing very well. I guess he understood how very homesick we would sometimes be."

"The runaway Red Heads story" is symbolic of the emotional lows that come from six months of one-night stands, 40,000 miles of two-lane roads, and hundreds of hurried meals in small-town diners. The sisterhood that emerged from those shared experiences helped the pioneers of women's basketball get through the tough times. Because camaraderie triumphed over discouragement, the barnstormers got to see things and meet people that most would never have seen or met had they not chosen the life of a pioneer of women's basketball.

CHAPTER SEVEN

See the USA in a Limo

According to Brenda Ragan, who spent a season traveling with the All American Red Heads in 1968–69, owner and coach Orwell Moore loved America. "Coach Moore told us when we were not playing basketball to see America."

On the rare off days during the season, the pioneers of women's basketball did indeed see America—its landmarks, its natural beauty, and its variety of people, including a few celebrities along the way.

"Playing with the Red Heads not only provided me with two more years of playing basketball, but also with a multitude of additional memories and experiences," said Debra Parashak. "Without the Red Heads, I probably would never have seen Graceland, petted Secretariat, met the Seattle Supersonics and the San Francisco 49ers, been interviewed on TV, gotten caught in a blizzard, seen the Bicentennial Wagon Train, traveled through 35 states (plus Mexico and Canada) in eight months (a total of 45,758 miles by car), or played basketball both in a barn and on a battleship."

Elvera "Peps" Neuman's experiences in traveling with the Texas Cowgirls and three other teams for over a quarter of a century mirrored those of Red Head players.

"We would travel the country many times, visiting such places as Gettysburg, Niagara Falls, Mount Rushmore, and the Naismith Memorial Basketball Hall of Fame. In Washington, D.C., we visited the grave of President John F. Kennedy and the changing of the guards. In Florida, we

Jo Darrow, Coach Bernard Cowden and Lucy Peters of the Ozark Hill Billies at Billy the Kid's grave at Fort Sumner, New Mexico, 1938-39.

Ozark Hill Billies Danny Daniels, Tex Nabors, Phyllis White and Nota McCain pose at Pipestone Pass, 10 miles south of Butte, Montana, 1938-39.

Nota Lee McCain of the Ozark Hill Billies takes to the water during down time in Corpus Christi, Texas, 1939-40.

Danny Daniels and Jo Darrow of the Ozark Hill Billies with Native Americans, 1938-39

Gene Love, Darlene Nabors, Beth Lively, Lorene Daniels and Nota McCain of the Red Heads on antique military cannon.

went to Disney World, saw many attractions, and went deep-sea fishing. But we also saw things that weren't so nice, such as the segregation in the South during the Jim Crow era."

Perhaps one reason many of the barnstormers relished the opportunity is that many of them had very limited previous travel experience.

"Until my time as an All American Red Head, I hadn't been outside the borders of Tennessee and Kentucky," said Brenda Moon. "As I learned firsthand crisscrossing the highways and back roads of the USA, there are so many amazing things to see and people to meet. Those experiences lit an ever-burning fire in my soul, and I have loved traveling ever since. Because of my Red Head travels, plus a little from my post-basketball career and leisure travels, I feel fortunate to have truly 'visited' every one of the states, not just passed through them. We are truly blessed to live in such a beautiful part of the world."

The barnstormers soon learned that being a pro basketball player carried with it a certain amount of celebrity status.

"Something … that stands out in my mind is how much the fans loved and appreciated us," said Southern Belle Dianne Kirkland. "We never got tired of the standing ovations after the games or signing autographs for the fans and young ballplayers. Sometimes, we would have an escort of police cars and fans waiting to escort us into their town. That made us feel very special."

"We were always in the spotlight — doing interviews, being on TV, and making personal appearances — if you were shy, this team brought it out of you," said Red Head Carolyn Gooch.

That celebrity status opened the door for brushes with some big-time celebrities on the occasions when the teams' travels took them to places where the show business elite hung out. According to Red Head Mary Alice Carpenter, while in Los Angeles, the team appeared on Art Linkletter's "House Party" TV show, then watched the taping of "The Red Skelton Show" next door.

Sandy Mann remembers the time the Red Heads appeared on the prime-time game show "I've Got a Secret" while in New York. For those not old enough to remember the game, a panel of four celebrities took turns asking yes/no questions of contestants, trying to guess what their secret was.

"I really didn't want to go," Mann said, "but the producers insisted that I come because I was the 'dribbler.' Then I found out that, not only did I have to go, but I also had to be a contestant, have 'the secret,' and do a dribbling routine. The show also flew a young man in. … My secret was that my team had played his team … and my team won.

"We arrived in New York City, and a lady called me and said, 'I need to pick you up so we can shop for you some clothes.' The show would be shown live, so we all went to pay phones to call home. There was a small room backstage that was high in the air. (During rehearsal) I'd go up there, put on the dress, come down some rickety stairs, out on stage, sit down, and go through the 'secret routine' with the young man and people who were standing in for the celebrity panel. … Every time I came down or went up those stairs, I passed by a fellow who was plunking around on a baby grand piano. After a couple of rounds, I realized that it was Neil Sedaka, one of my all-time favorite performers, sitting there playing that piano. I was so young and naive I didn't say a word to him. Grrrrrrrrr.

"Finally came the real thing and here I went. After the secret, which the panel did guess, I had to run backstage, off with that dress, run back out, and do my dribbling routine. The other four then joined me, and we did the 'Magic Circle' ball handling routine."

Because the Red Heads were playing several games in New York on that trip, they stayed for a few nights at the same hotel, the Hotel Knickerbocker, setting up a chance encounter that led to them being present for an unusual performance from future pop music stars. Sandy Mann continues the story:

"One night, we were waiting in the lobby, dressed out and in our warm-ups to go to the game. A man walked through the lobby, stopped, looked at us, and said, 'What's the deal?' We told him, and he said, 'I am the manager of the Peppermint Lounge, next door. When you get back from your game, you will be my guests at the lounge.'

"Well, us girls took him up on his invitation. We were already having a great time when the manager of Herman's Hermits came in and talked to the manager. He said that they had just flown in from England, first time in the U.S.A. They were on the way to California to film the television show 'Shindig' and had a long layover. He asked if they could set up and play a few songs. The manager said, 'Of course,' so we got to see Herman's Hermits' first appearance in this country."

While seeing Herman's Hermits impromptu performance was a treat, Jolene "Jo Jo" Ammons recalled the time when the Red Heads enjoyed a private performance from future stars.

"At one motel we stayed at, there was a rock 'n' roll group named the Grass Roots that were also staying there," Ammons said. "They were out in the courtyard playing their instruments, and we were practicing routines in the parking lot. We began to chat, and after our game and after their concert, they invited us to their suite, where they did another mini concert for us. Little did we know that the Grass Roots would become a famous band and sell over 20 million records."

Red Head Jolene "Jo Jo" Ammons with the Grass Roots outside their motel in 1968.

In the days before rock 'n' roll ruled the music scene, crooners like Bing Crosby and Lena Horne were superstars. It was Horne's recording of "Careless Love" that spawned Red Head legend Gene "Careless" Love's nickname. She told daughter Barbara Hagerman about the trip to Hollywood in the '40s when she got 'up close and personal' with two of the biggest stars in entertainment at the time.

"[Gene] saw the footprints and handprints of the stars in concrete at Grauman's Chinese Theater in Hollywood and got hugged by Bob Hope. A friend of hers was a friend of Bob's brother — and they

The Red Heads meet Bob Hope while in Hollywood, 1945-46. L-R: Gene "Careless" Love, Hope, Toby McGee, Lorene Daniels, Allegra Winters and Mary Alice Hatcher.

were able to get passes into the studio where Hope, Bing Crosby, and Dorothy Lamour were filming scenes for 'Road to Rio.'"

Ammons and the Red Heads also appeared on "The Mike Douglas Show" while they were in Cleveland. During that show, she taught Betty White to spin a basketball on her finger.

Basketball frequently gave the barnstormers opportunities to meet not only celebrities from entertainment, but also from sports.

"We took advantage of the opportunity to go to the different NBA arenas and see some of our favorite players that we had only seen on TV," said "Peps" Neuman. "Our schedule even gave us an opportunity to see the Boston Celtics at the old Boston Garden. I was really thrilled to meet and have my picture taken with one of my idols, Meadowlark Lemon of the Harlem Globetrotters. Later in the year, they gave us free tickets to their games when our schedule allowed."

But many of the pioneers of women's basketball believe that the most rewarding encounters they had on the road were the ones in which *they* played the role of celebrity. Sandy Mann related the story of a trip to Alaska when her team played several games at Point Barrow in front of audiences consisting primarily of Eskimos.

"We were in Barrow for three days to play three games. That first day, someone told us, 'If no one kills a whale, you will have a packed gym every night. It will be packed, with the same people for each game.' Well, we were very lucky because no one brought in a whale, and we had a packed house, standing room only, for all three games.

"When we walked into the gym for that first game, we had the most wonderful surprise waiting for us. The elders of the tribe were seated on folding chairs at mid court, wearing their finest clothing. They were there to perform a ceremony in our honor. These beautiful people have a custom of telling stories through dance. They each stood, one at a time, and told their story for us. I have never in my life felt more honored than I did at that moment. They were facing us as we sat on the bench watching them.

Sandy Mann of the Red Heads with two young Eskimo fans, 1967.

Red Heads Brenda Moon, Charlotte "Sweetie" Adams, Sandy Mann and Carolyn Linzay with Eskimo children. The Red Heads were popular with the young Eskimo children during their trip to Alaska in 1967.

"A reporter sat down on the bench by me. He leaned over and whispered to me 'You might want to pass the word down to your coach that they might come over and invite him to join them in a dance. Tell him that, if they do, he should get out there because it would insult them if he refused.' He then added that, actually, they might invite all of us to join them in the dance.

"Well, they did indeed invite us to join them, which we did. What a thrill! This is one of the most amazing things that has ever happened to me."

Red Head Sandy Mann signing autographs in Alaska for Eskimo children, Spring 1967.

The airport at Barrow, Mann remembers, was nothing more than a small building with a few tables and file cabinets.

"While we were at the airport, waiting for our plane, all the kids were there, squeezed into that little building with us. We had to climb up on tables and file cabinets, or anything that we could find, to try to stay above them, as they pulled at us and our clothing. It must have been how the Beatles felt with their fans. We were signing autographs for them, at the same time trying not to be 'pulled under.' We literally made a run for our plane as they chased us. They actually pulled the belt off of one of the girls' coats — I think it was Brenda Moon. We barely made it into the door of that plane. Whew!"

The Barrow story is one of many examples of how travel not only allowed the barnstormers to experience new sights, but also the variety of cultures that make up the populace of the USA.

Southern Belle Dianne Kirkland shows off a pair of crawfish in Louisana, 1970-71.

"There was the time in Louisiana we had a rare day off," said Southern Belle Lenna Carey. "The locals invited us to a genuine Cajun *boucherie* (a communal hog butchering), complete with a band and dancing. We were allowed to experience every aspect of cooking authentic Cajun, from crawfish to barbecue. Nothing was wasted. Even the blood was made into pudding. (No, thank you). Most remaining parts of the hog were tossed into a great boiling pot and stirred with a long wooden paddle. As I began to stir the pot, the hog head came to the surface, and I was done. The crawfish and barbeque was amazing, and the time spent with these families was unforgettable."

Red Head Janet Cox summed up her experiences during a season with the team in 1968–69. "We partied with The Monkees, played against the San Francisco 49ers, saw the Grand Canyon, gambled at casinos in Las Vegas, visited American Indian reservations for charity exhibition games, and entertained in small-town America night after night. We were a novelty, a sensation, and often times treated like celebrities."

Debra Parashak compared life as a barnstormer with today's women's pro basketball players.

"While the professional women's teams may get better pay now, I doubt that these women get to have these kinds of travel experiences, nor do I think they have the opportunity for the same kind of camaraderie that I and my Red Head teammates shared. After all, dyeing each other's hair red is certainly a bonding experience."

CHAPTER EIGHT

Show Biz Basketball

It's been said that sports has many of the same entertainment elements that are present in theater and movies — there are favorites and underdogs, heroes and villains. There is action, along with demonstrations of physical skill and talent. A beautifully-executed 22-foot jump shot that finds nothing but net is sometimes called "string music." For some, that kind of string music is just as pleasing as listening to a solo from a violin virtuoso.

C.M. "Ole" Olson recognized the entertainment value of sports. As player/owner/coach of Olson's Terrible Swedes men's pro basketball team in the '20s, he knew the kind of reaction from fans that one of his innovative backhand passes provoked. When he put two women's barnstorming teams on the road in the '30s, beginning with the All American Red Heads, Olson was determined that his teams would give the paying customers more than just a compelling sports event. His players were not just athletes — they were in *show business.*

"Playing basketball was only part of the job," said Glenda Ledbetter, who also played for the Southern Belles. "We were there to entertain."

Many of the show biz elements employed by the Red Heads happened during the competition. Trick plays were given names — Red Runner, Big Red, and Shotgun, to name a few, according to **Gail Marks** — and were worked into the offense as the game went along. Two of the most popular of the Red Heads' trick plays were conceived when Ole Olson noticed the response of fans to 5-foot-1 **Allegra "Stubby" Winters** and 6-foot-4 Gene "Careless" Love during the '50s.

"Stubby and Gene would have cameras flashing whenever they stood next to each other," said Stubby's brother James. "Olson saw this and incorporated a couple of new 'crowd pleasers.'"

One of those plays had Stubby dribbling to the hoop, her man guarding her. Gene would step between her and her man and open her legs to allow Stubby to bend down a bit and go between Gene's legs while dribbling. She would come out in front of Gene, her man blocked by Gene, and have an easy layup.

James Winters described another Red Head crowd-pleasing play.

"[Stubby] and Gene would also perform the first 'Piggyback' play ever done by any of the Red Heads. Stubby and teammate Ruth Haines would pass the ball back and forth as they dribbled down the court — little problem since 6-foot-4 Love attracted most of the defenders under the basket. Stubby passed to Haines as they got near Gene, just before Gene bent down and Stubby quickly climbed on her shoulders. From her perch on Love's shoulders, Stubby took a final pass from

The original "Piggyback" play as originated by Allegra "Stubby" Winters and Gene "Careless" Love, 1945-46. The Piggyback play was a crowd pleaser for the Red Heads for decades.

Red Head Lorene "Butch" Moore faking out opposing player, circa 1953.

Red Heads Gene "Careless" Love posing with referee and opposing player circa 1945.

Haines and dropped the ball in the basket. The Piggyback play brought roars from the crowd and left the defenders shaking their heads, wondering how they ever could have defended that play."

The Piggyback play was reprised by many Red Heads throughout the years, especially whenever there was a great disparity in height between two players.

Like the legendary barnstorming Harlem Globetrotters, the Red Heads, Southern Belles, Cowgirls, and others weaved a generous amount of comedy in with the basketball action. Like the Trotters, the teams usually had a designated comedian who took the lead in generating the laughs. The comedian had to be a bit of a ham.

"When the game started, I would introduce the team," said "Jo Jo" Ammons, who coached the Red Heads and Arkansas Lassies, in addition to a enjoying a long playing career. "After I introduced a couple of players, the comedian would be strutting on the end line making her presence known, as if to say 'What about me?' I asked her to get back in line. She would be the last one introduced."

While the team comedian earned a lot of laughs, the players who filled the role accepted it as a serious responsibility and an honor.

Dianne Kirkland wasn't sure her personality was suited to the role of comedian, but she thrived as comic during her two seasons as a Southern Belle.

"Every night, I would lead the show and entertain our fans, a task I initially was not too certain about," Kirkland recalls. "As time passed, I became experienced and comfortable with that role, and I served as Team Comedienne both years and learned to really enjoy it."

"I was the team comedian my second year," said Red Head Ruth Simmons. "This was a big responsibility. Spanky (Losier) was retiring, and she nominated me as the primary candidate. She taught me everything I needed to know, from crowd-pleasing antics to referee ridicule. And, of course, the 'passing of the torch' — the All American Red Head 'Krazy Kit.' The Krazy Kit is like Felix the Cat's bag of tricks. It was a hard shell case, red and blue with white stars. Inside the kit was a sparkly white sequin top hat, a round satin red, white and blue powder puff — about the size of a tambourine — and a whistle."

While the bag of props helped the comedian get laughs, it was up to the comedian to learn to use the bag of tricks effectively. "The magic is not in the kit," continued Simmons, "the *magic* is in the player using the *things* in the kit. What a privilege!"

When Gene "Careless" Love was comedian of the Red Heads, she made it a point to learn something before each game about their opponents that she could turn into a laugh.

"With the tune 'Careless Love' playing in the background, she'd always have a word with each referee — and any short balding ref always got a kiss, with an overload of red lipstick, on his bald head," said daughter Barbara Hagerman. "The opposing center often received a kiss on the cheek or forehead — much to the delight of the audience. It was also not unusual for her to take the opposing center by the hand and lead him to the water cooler — all the while the rest of her team had the men scrambling."

Dianne "Kirk" Kirkland of the Southern Belles takes the lead in clowning during the 1970-71 season with Sue Petzold (left) and Linda Shanks looking on.

While Georgia Washington waits at the foul line, Red Head Glenda "Twinkles" Ledbetter decides it's time to help the referee with his shoelaces.

Becky Harp recalls some of the antics of Red Head clown **Pat Overman**. "I can still see her pulling up the ref's pants leg or giving him a stiff kick in the backside as he bent over to pick up a ball she had cleverly put near her foot on purpose."

Red Head comedian Sue "Rosie Red" Whitten with fans, circa 1973

Red Head and Southern Belle comedian Glenda "Twinkles" Ledbetter said that "chatter" was a big part of the game.

"We talked to the guys we were playing, the refs, and the crowd. We called the guys 'Curly' or 'Smiley' or anything to get the crowd's attention. When the guys had the basketball up over their head, we pretended to tickle them. I was the clown, so I dealt the ref misery, such as following him step-by-step down the court, hiding the ball, and making faces behind his back!"

Red Head **Sue Whitten**, who played from 1971–74, told about an occasion when clowning almost went too far.

"Despite being a bit more from the South than a Connecticut Yankee, I was naïve about the value of Stetson cowboy hats. So, after a time-out, I ran up the bleachers to the top row, asked this cowboy if I could borrow his hat. I didn't wait for an answer and ran back down and inbounded the ball wearing a white Stetson hat, about ten-gallon size. The crowd couldn't see a thing but sneakers and red and white striped socks. The ball went through the guy's legs and my teammate *nailed it*!

Lynn Holst and Brenda O'Bryan of the Red Heads perform a team juggling routine during a halftime performance. The two also did a synchronized double dribbling act.

"I then pulled the infamous 'dust-off-the-hat routine,' where I put it on the floor, jump up, bend my knees with my feet together like I was going to stomp on it, then at the last moment spread my feet, and come down straddling the hat. I don't think I've ever seen a cowboy move that fast without a horse.

"Coach Jack didn't know I was going to do that one. I think it scared the Texas 'cow dung' clear out of his pants, since that hat cost more than I was paid each month."

Pre-game warmups and halftime provided opportunities for the pioneers of women's basketball to exhibit their skills with a variety of ball handling, passing, and shooting exhibitions. Elvera "Peps" Neuman recalled showing off before Arkansas Gems games.

"Before the Gems games started, the team had a special warm-up routine that eventually led to shooting free throws and different shots," Neuman said. "I would shoot half-court shots over my head with my back to the basket, making a good percentage. It was

Red Heads Brenda "Brooksie" Brooks goes in for layup before sellout crowd with Charlotte "Sweetie" Adams, 1971-72 season.

such a long shot, and the way I shot it, they were proclaiming me 'the Happy Hooker' in reference to an adult movie of the '70s." During the Gems' halftime show Neuman's display included stunts such as dribbling with her knees, dribbling two balls at once, and a glow ball act that was performed in the dark.

At the peak of their popularity, the Red Heads had two and sometimes three teams on the road at the same time. Best friends Lynn Holst and Brenda "Brooksie" O'Bryan developed a halftime act on their own to ensure that they'd be placed on the same traveling team for the 1970–71 season.

"Teammate Lynn Holst Thomas and I became friends my second year on the road, even though we were on different squads as there were three traveling the country that season," said O'Bryan. "We thought that it would be cool to play on the same team the next year, but you never knew what team Coach Orwell Moore would put you on. We thought and thought on how we could make sure to be on the same team and decided to invent a new halftime act. Lynn decided to come up for the summer, so we could work on one. We finally decided on trying a double dribbling act. We worked all that summer in the heat, sweating our buns off, to get it perfected. We would both dribble the same exact routine and then she would go between my legs while dribbling, and I would be dribbling at the same time." Coach Orwell Moore liked the act when they showed it to him at training camp, Thomas and O'Bryan were put on the same team, and a double dribbling act became a fixture in the Red Heads' halftime show from that time on.

Another halftime fixture for the barnstormers was their own version of the Globetrotters' "Magic Circle." Aaronette Eiffling of the Red Heads described their version of the routine.

"We each had our little specialty. We would all form a circle about 15 feet in diameter. Around the back, through the legs, a high step, and pass the ball under the knee, and then high step with the other leg. … Someone would turn their back to another teammate, stick out their butt, and the other player would bounce the ball off her butt. And, of course, the spin the ball in the finger and go under her arm and come back to stating position still spinning on her finger."

While the Globetrotters' "Magic Circle" is performed to the familiar whistling of "Sweet Georgia Brown," the Texas Cowgirls had their own theme music during their dramatic entrance onto the court, according to **Harlean Hudson**, who played for the team from 1959–64.

"Our routine was to come on court to the music of 'Orange Blossom Special,' wearing western hats, vests, and guns. Then we would go into a circle and do ball handling to the music of 'The Happy Whistler.'"

If basketball is indeed entertainment, then the gymnasiums and arenas the teams played in were theaters and the courts were stages. The barnstormers played in some of the best arenas in the country, but also in some of the worst. Carolyn Wooldridge recalled the time during the 1975–76 season that the Red Heads literally played in a barn.

"We once played in a barn in Freetown, Indiana, that was made of tin, painted blue. The barn was very small, with bleachers only on one side. The top of each free throw circle, which is now the three-point line, was in the middle of the gym. The floor was tile of some sort. It was very different. We were shooting from half court most of the night and taking free shots from half court. The crowd was very small, as was the town. We played a 2:30 game, which was most unusual, but the crowd was very excited to see us play. We found this particular gym to be the most unusual we played at all season. It was the true definition of 'barnstorming.'"

And then there was the time in 1975 in Acuna, Mexico, when the Red Heads played in a bullfighting arena, complete with residual dust from the most recent bullfight.

"The floor was just concrete with dull painted lines for the free throw lane," said **Kay O'Bryan**. "It was a really dusty, dirty floor, and we would slip and slide whenever we tried to stop or change directions. I think we could have written our names on the floor and have read it from the stands. The walls in front of the stands were concrete and about six to seven feet high. They showed us the door through which the bulls entered. (No, they didn't release any bulls that night). The gym had small, wooden backboards to shoot on."

The Texas Cowgirls' 1960 trip to Alaska to play for servicemen found them playing at Northeast Cape, 18 miles from the Soviet Union. The venue awaiting them there was less than conventional, said Ginny Hill.

"To make a gym for us to play, they had to make room in the hanger, pushing back the planes, helicopters, and fire engines. The audience had to sit on those to watch the game. We had a huge helicopter for our dressing room."

Helen Onson told her family about the time she and her teammates with Helen Stephens Olympic Co-Eds played during a snowstorm in Crow Agency, Montana. Needing to keep the players and spectators warm, a large potbelly stove was situated in the middle of the court.

Of course, the normal venue for the barnstormers was the local high school gymnasium in the small towns that dominated their schedules. But sometimes the pioneers of women's basketball got to play in the most well-known arenas in the country.

"One of [Red Head Nellie Marlow's] greatest memories was playing at Madison Square Garden in New York City," said daughter Bernie Hudgens King. "'The Garden' was one of the most famous sports arenas in the world, and my mom thought that was the grandest place. She said playing there made her feel like she was a movie star."

"We traveled with and played preliminary games to Harlem Globetrotters, as well as NBA teams like the Philadelphia 76ers, Los Angeles Lakers, and others," said **Bernice Holladay**, a member of the Texas Cowgirls from 1962–65.

Playing in arenas that were home to multiple sports did have its drawbacks, according to Willa Faye "Red" Mason of the Red Heads.

"The largest place I ever played was the Chicago Stadium, home of the Chicago Bulls of the NBA and the Black Hawks of the National Hockey League. The basketball court was installed right over the ice. When we were warming up before the game, one of the girls muffed the ball on a layup and went to go after the ball, which had rolled off the hardwood court. She didn't realize that there was ice underneath, and when she stepped off that court and onto the ice, her feet went flying higher than her head. She even got a concussion out of it."

Of course, thanks to the efforts of the pioneers of women's basketball, the day came when women playing in NBA arenas was no longer a novelty. The story of the transition from barnstorming basketball to today's professional leagues will be told in Chapter Nine.

Red Heads Barb "Gabby" Hostert and Sheryl "Woody" Wood doing double dribble routine, 77-78 season

CHAPTER NINE

You've Come a Long Way, Baby

"No person in the United States shall, on the basis of sex, be excluded from participation in, be denied the benefits of, or be subjected to discrimination under any education program or activity receiving federal financial assistance."

A portion of a broader bill passed by Congress in 1972 amending the Civil Rights Act of 1964, the legislation that has come to commonly be called Title IX had a profound impact on any educational institution that wanted to receive federal funding. As related to sports, local school systems, colleges, and universities could no longer relegate women's sports to footnote status. In the years immediately following passage of Title IX, opportunities for females to participate in sports increased dramatically.

One woman who didn't let the lack of women's college basketball programs deter her was **Cyndi Meserve Bona.** A high school star in Maine, she chose to attend Pratt College in Brooklyn to major in fashion design, even though the school had no girls' basketball team. When she saw a sign in an elevator announcing a basketball meeting, she decided to attend.

"When I walked into Room 101, there were a lot of guys already sitting at desk, and a couple of coaches standing at the front of the room," said Cyndi. "The 6-foot-5 coach asked me if I was there for the cheerleading meeting, which he said was the next night. I replied, 'No, I'm here to play basketball!'" Because Pratt didn't offer women's basketball in 1974, according to Title IX, Pratt had to allow her to try out for the men's team. She made the team and gained national attention by becoming the first woman to play on a men's college sports team.

Cyndi Meserve (front row, far right) and Pratt Institute team, 1974

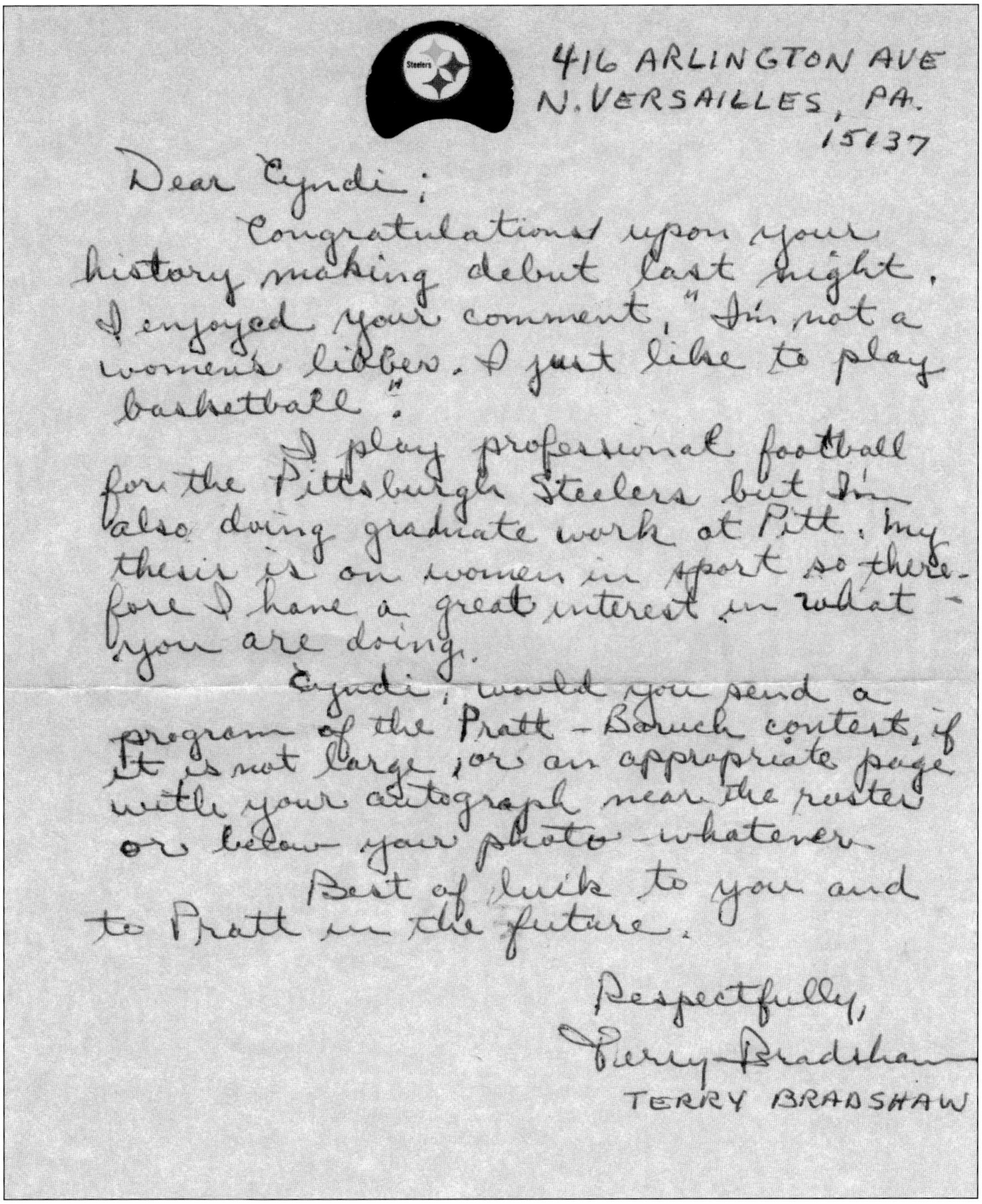

416 ARLINGTON AVE
N. VERSAILLES, PA.
15137

Dear Cyndi:

Congratulations upon your history making debut last night. I enjoyed your comment, "I'm not a women's libber. I just like to play basketball".

I play professional football for the Pittsburgh Steelers but I'm also doing graduate work at Pitt. My thesis is on women in sport so therefore I have a great interest in what you are doing.

Cyndi, would you send a program of the Pratt - Baruch contest, if it is not large, or an appropriate page with your autograph near the roster or below your photo - whatever.

Best of luck to you and to Pratt in the future.

Respectfully,
Terry Bradshaw
TERRY BRADSHAW

Letter from Pittsburgh Steeler quarterback Terry Bradshaw to Cyndi Meserve, congratulating her on becoming the first woman to play on a men's college team.

According to author Barbara Winslow's article "The Impact of Title IX," published in 2010 by the Gilder Lehrman Institute of American History, the percentage of female varsity athletes in high schools jumped from 7 percent to 41.5 percent in two decades after the law was enacted. Because of the law, colleges and universities were required not only to offer more sports opportunities for females, but also to increase their funding for scholarships and overall budgets for women's sports.

In terms of the impact on the sport of basketball, a 2008 study indicated that nearly 99 percent of colleges and universities offered women's basketball, making it the most popular varsity sport offered for females. The effect Title IX had on barnstorming basketball became apparent as the decade of the 1970s unfolded. Ruth Simmons was one female athlete who benefited from the leveling of the court.

"Girls sports in high school in the '70s was just unfolding," Simmons said. "My freshman year was the first season ever for girls' basketball — eight games. My senior year, we were state runner-up with a 23–1 record. Not too shabby.

"After high school and racking up all kind of awards, I wanted to keep playing, so off to college I went. Title IX had really kicked in by now and scholarships gave female student athletes an opportunity to pursue their dreams."

Simmons left college to play two seasons with the All American Red Heads, then returned to college with the goal of completing her education, but when an injury created an opening with the Red Heads for Simmons to return, she jumped at the chance. "I went back to school with the idea a college education, and that piece of paper would prove my existence of growth, discipline, and knowledge. I had already gotten it. My life experiences on the road with the All American Red Heads was a degree in itself."

With professional basketball no longer the only option for girls who wanted to play basketball after high school, filling out rosters with talented players became harder for barnstorming teams. As the '70s progressed, it became evident that the days of women's barnstorming teams were numbered.

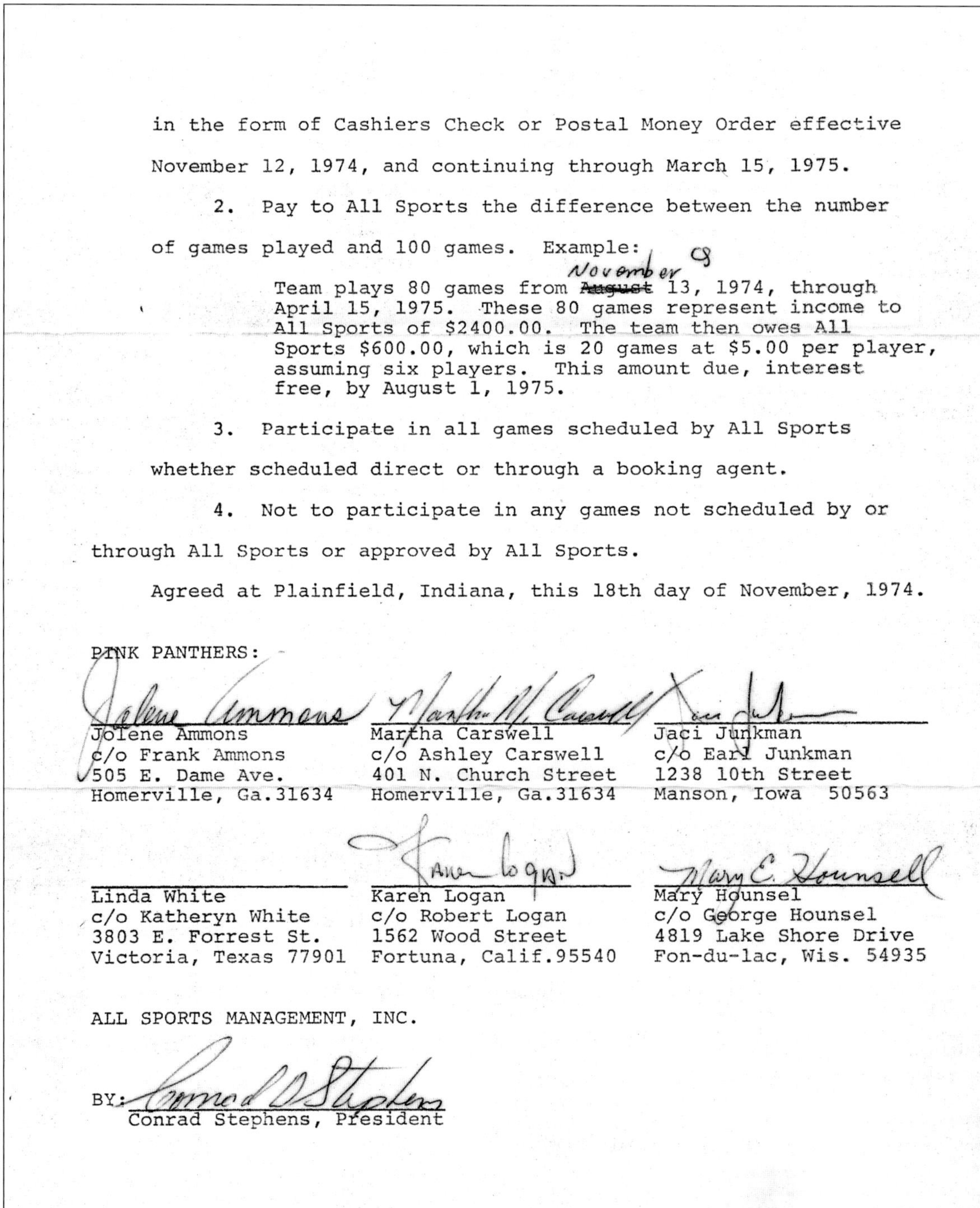

in the form of Cashiers Check or Postal Money Order effective November 12, 1974, and continuing through March 15, 1975.

2. Pay to All Sports the difference between the number of games played and 100 games. Example:

Team plays 80 games from ~~August~~ November 13, 1974, through April 15, 1975. These 80 games represent income to All Sports of $2400.00. The team then owes All Sports $600.00, which is 20 games at $5.00 per player, assuming six players. This amount due, interest free, by August 1, 1975.

3. Participate in all games scheduled by All Sports whether scheduled direct or through a booking agent.

4. Not to participate in any games not scheduled by or through All Sports or approved by All Sports.

Agreed at Plainfield, Indiana, this 18th day of November, 1974.

PINK PANTHERS:

Jolene Ammons c/o Frank Ammons 505 E. Dame Ave. Homerville, Ga.31634	Martha Carswell c/o Ashley Carswell 401 N. Church Street Homerville, Ga.31634	Jaci Junkman c/o Earl Junkman 1238 10th Street Manson, Iowa 50563
Linda White c/o Katheryn White 3803 E. Forrest St. Victoria, Texas 77901	Karen Logan c/o Robert Logan 1562 Wood Street Fortuna, Calif.95540	Mary Hounsel c/o George Hounsel 4819 Lake Shore Drive Fon-du-lac, Wis. 54935

ALL SPORTS MANAGEMENT, INC.

BY: Conrad Stephens, President

Portion of contract between Jolene Ammons, Karen Logan, Mary Hounsell and other with the WPBA Pink Panthers, 1974

Pink Panthers (L-R) Jackie Junkman, Karen Logan, Linda White, Jolene "Jo Jo" Ammons, 1974. Logan and Ammons were former barnstormers with the Red Heads.

The Red Heads, who at one time had three teams on the road, were down to one team by the end of the decade. "Jo Jo" Ammons saw the handwriting on the wall, as did others.

"Towards the end of my career with the Red Heads, I was contacted by Lee Bakunin," related Ammons. "I had never heard of him. He just asked me for a few minutes of his time. He had seen an article in *Sports Illustrated* on the All American Red Heads. He was very impressed and thought he might be the person to take women's basketball to the next level—a professional basketball league. It would be like the early days of the NBA. Some growing pains, for sure, but with the passage of Title IX, it was time … I was very excited. He also spoke with others. [Red Head teammates] Karen Logan and **Mary Hounsell** both liked the idea enough that we all decided to give it a try."

Ammons, Logan, and Hounsell went to Phoenix in the fall of 1975 to join the Phoenix Pink Panthers, who were to be a team in the proposed Women's Professional Basketball Association. Another team in the start-up league was the Arkansas Lassies, featuring owner/coach/player Linda Yearby. The WPBA teams had to barnstorm at first to gain an audience.

The Pink Panthers moved to Indianapolis, never having gained traction in Phoenix and in search of more revenue in an Indiana market with a long-running affection for basketball. The WPBA never got off the ground, but the Panthers did play a memorable exhibition game against the Lassies in January 1975.

"I played in my first professional women's basketball game against another women's team," said Ammons. "After thousands of games as a professional basketball player, this was going to be a first for me and probably a first in history. You might think we felt more relaxed because we weren't playing men. But it was the opposite—it was a lot more intense. We wanted to make sure we did everything right and probably tried too hard to be perfect. We ended up losing the game 65–63."

Although that game provided a glimpse into the future of women's professional basketball, it turned out to be the last game for the Pink Panthers. Ammons joined up with Yearby and joined the

Lassies as coach and, eventually, part owner of the team. She joined the team in Ionia, Michigan, at their home base, ready to start barnstorming again.

"It was apparent that the days of barnstorming teams were coming down to the end," said Ammons. "I don't remember how many games we played, but it was not a full schedule—maybe four or five a week." The roomy limousines that Ammons was accustomed to traveling in with the Red Heads were replaced by a station wagon. "In 1976, I realized it was time for me move on. I dissolved the partnership and left. This time I hung up my shoes, with no regrets."

The WBPA wasn't the only women's pro league trying to get off the ground in the mid-1970s, and the Lassies wanted in on this one, too. According to Linda Yearby, Red Heads owner Orwell Moore saw the potential for a women's hoops league and partnered with Yearby.

"[Moore] saw the future as well and wanted in. He would leave his barnstorming team on the road but would create another team for his own league. Initially called the NGBL (National Girls Basketball League), Orwell soon realized his gaffe in judgment and renamed it NWBL, changing Girls to Women." Moore was to be president of the league and Yearby the vice president, but like the WBPA, the NWBL never got off a shot in league play. Yearby and Ammons carried on with the Lassies.

The launch in 1978 of the Women's Professional Basketball League (WBL) marked the first time a women's pro league actually started play. The first player signed to play in the WBL was Iowa girls' high school star **Molly Bolin** by the Iowa Cornets, with the signing taking place with much "hoopla" at the office of Governor Robert Ray. The first player drafted by a WBL team was **Althea Gwyn** of Queens College in New York City by the New York Stars.

Bolin was tagged with the nickname "Machine Gun Molly," a nod to the frequency she put the ball through the hoop. She topped the 50-point/game mark four times, including a league record 54 in 1980. Her 54 would be the unofficial record for a single game in women's professional league play, topping the 51 scored by Riquna Williams in the WNBA. While Williams was aided by eight three-point baskets in her 51-point game, none of Bolin's 50-point efforts included a three-pointer.

1977-78 Queens College team photo, with Althea Gwyn (#31) and Donna Geils (Orender) #21. Gwyn and Geils both played in the Women's Professional Basketball League; Orender went to to serve as second president of the WNBA.

"We had a lot of challenges to overcome that very first season," Bolin said, "including our coach being fired before the season started, and we did actually barnstorm throughout Iowa, playing our home games in multiple cities across the state."

After the Cornets folded, Bolin finished her WBL career with the San Francisco Pioneers.

"None of the scoring records I set during the WBL have been officially recognized," Bolin lamented. "The hardest part … is being nearly forgotten in the progression of the sport we helped start."

Gwyn played all three seasons of the WBL's existence, with three different teams, emblematic of the instability of the league, which finally threw in the towel after the 1981 season.

Struggling to turn a profit, league owners did what they could to market the league's stars. Bolin was featured in pinup-style publicity shots and did a commercial in a hot tub. Twins Kaye and Faye Young appeared as Wrigley's Doublemint Twins and in yogurt commercials.

"Someone had decided if the rest of us wore make-up, we, too, would be offered commercials," Gwyn said. "I remember letting the 'make-up artist' try her skills on me, and the result was awful. She tried to use the same coloring and haircut that she used on the twins! I told her, 'Get this s*** off of my face.' Disaster!"

Molly Bolin of the WBL Iowa Cornets at free throw line, 1978-79 season.

Cardte Hicks played on her high school's boys' basketball team in San Pedro, California. Her incredible vertical leap allowed her to dunk the ball, even though she stood only 5-foot-7. Though not a blood relative, she did have a noteworthy basketball pedigree since her godfather was Wilt Chamberlain.

Hicks played all three of the WBL's seasons, then played on both men's and women's teams in Europe. She tried out for the WNBA's first season, making it to the last cut before breaking her knee and ending her career.

While the WBL was struggling to survive three seasons, the All American Red Heads were still hanging on by a thread, continuing to barnstorm despite defections of key players to the WBL. The team traveled the entire season with only five players. "Yes, only five players all year — no substitutes," said Gail Marks about the 1978–79 season, which saw the Red Heads win an astounding 127 out of 143 games. "Our sneakers never dried out."

One of the players who played for the Red Heads during that season was Gwen Reed, who jumped to the WBL's New York Stars the next season. She went through the tryout without her contact lenses or glasses — both lost by the airline en route to the tryout. She wasn't optimistic about her chances of making the team.

"I knew that there was no way I could have been chosen," Reed said. "I don't think I had sunk even one basket during the tryouts. I got close, but could not focus without my contacts or glasses. To my surprise, there was a contract waiting for me to sign when I got home from my return flight."

The WBL wasn't the first pro league to take flight briefly, only to crash, and it wasn't the last. The Ladies Professional Basketball Association was organized with six teams lined up for its inaugural season (1980–81) but only played five games before throwing in the towel; three of the six teams never played a game. The Women's American Basketball Association (WABA) technically finished their first season after starting in 1984, but most of the league's teams didn't last through the schedule. The first attempt at a women's summer league, the Women's Basketball Association (WBA), played brief schedules during from 1992–95.

The American Basketball League (ABL) made a go of it for two seasons, 1996–98, with stars such as Dawn Staley, Katie Smith, and Yolanda Griffith. But the launch of the Women's National Basketball Association (WNBA) in 1997 proved too much for the ABL to overcome.

More attempts at pro leagues never got off the runway.

The ABL, which played a traditional cold-weather schedule, paid better salaries in the beginning and was deemed by many to be the superior league athletically compared to its summer rival. But the WNBA had a big advantage over the ABL and other failed leagues — the backing of the National Basketball Association. With NBA ownership of many teams in the beginning, the financial resources to keep the league afloat during its first few seasons were there, allowing time to build a brand and a fan base. Although eight WNBA teams in 2016 are "sister teams" of NBA clubs, others are independently owned and operated. There have been some relocations and some teams have folded, but the league

"Machine Gun" Molly Bolin is featured on a poster for the Southern California Breeze of the LBPA, 1980-81.

has operated in relative stability compared to its predecessors. High-profile corporate sponsorships and broadcast rights agreements have helped ensure the viability of the league for the foreseeable future.

It's likely that most WNBA players today don't know a lot about the pioneers of women's basketball and what they did to help bring women's hoops to the masses. The probably have no clue who Kay Kirkpatrick, "Goose" Garroutte, Hazel Walker, and Linda Yearby were, or what they did to prove that women can not only play basketball at a high level but also do it profitably. Ask them who was Ole Olson, Orwell Moore, Dempsey Hovland, or any of the other entrepreneurs who invested hundreds of thousands of dollars and hundreds of thousands of miles into building a sport that could, more than a half century later, stand on its own. Most likely, you'll get an empty stare.

Hopefully, this volume enlightens readers of all ages about these little-known figures in sports history. They are the Babe Ruths, Jim Browns, Gordie Howes, Joe Louises and Arnold Palmers of their sport. They helped make women's basketball viable, popular, and profitable.

The pioneers of women's basketball deserve to be recognized — and to be thanked.

Barnstorming America

Biographies of the Pioneers of Women's Basketball

Hazel Walker's Arkansas Travelers. Walker and Frances "Goose" Garroutte are third and fourth from right, respectively.

Katherine "Kay" Kirkpatrick

CAREER 1936-40
ALL AMERICAN RED HEADS

As told by Kathleen Ethington, daughter

Kay Kirkpatrick, one of the original All American Red Heads, 1936-40

Mother developed her basketball abilities with the help of her brothers, Hubert and Milton. They all attended Baylor at the same time and both brothers played basketball for Baylor. Hubert would become the first All-American from Baylor. They shot 500 baskets a day from the free-throw line distance to hone their skills. Her ability to hit the basket consistently became extraordinary, based on her discipline.

Mother played basketball for Holt's Sporting Goods Store in Waco, Texas for two seasons (1934 and 1935) while attending Baylor University. During the state playoffs in the 1935 season, she was selected as an All-American from the state of Texas.

In putting the first women's professional basketball team together, Mr. C.M. Olson interviewed Kay as a possible candidate for that first team, one of many candidates he had interviewed in various states. When he returned to Cassville, Missouri he began contacting the women he had interviewed. All the first women selected had been named All-Americans in their home states.

C.M. Olson reached out to recruit her for the new team he was forming. When he first contacted Kay, she was unsure about joining. Her parents wanted her to finish school before she made any decisions about playing women's basketball. Mr. Olson informed his associates that he wanted the girl from Texas on his team, so they contacted her a second time and Mother decided to go ahead and play.

She packed her bags on Christmas Eve, 1936 and became a part of that first professional women's basketball team.

She spoke about how men would react to playing basketball against a group of women. She said the men's teams they played would usually start out being polite and reserved until they saw that the women were serious contenders. Most of the men would then leave their manners and begin to play "head-to-head" against the women to the best of their ability.

Those early days of basketball consisted of playing doubleheaders and traveling town to town. These were the years of the Great Depression, where inspiration and opportunity were in short supply. Those formative years of the Red Heads team served as a symbol of hope to people everywhere to have faith and not give up. People watched a group of women who weren't supposed to compete athletically play basketball on a national stage, game after game, against men. Not only did they play against the opposite sex, they held their own and won the majority of their games. This was a working model for people to witness — women accomplishing an "unheard of feat" during very difficult times. People began to believe that if a group of women could play against the odds and perform well, they could have hope that conditions would improve and get better.

The team worked approximately six months out of the year. Before each season began, they would get together and practice for about a week before hitting the road. Kay worked especially hard, and her effort was rewarded. She was consistently the highest scorer on the team and she seldom missed a free throw.

Mother mentioned that on numerous occasions, the team would have to have a police escort to assist them to depart a town after they defeated the local men's team. Some audiences would become very upset when they witnessed a group of women athletes beat their local men's team. Mother recalled one time in particular in the Detroit area where local police officers formed a line for the women as they exited the arena to get into their bus and leave after the men's team suffered a humiliating defeat at the hands of the Red Heads. Usually the local police would escort them to the outskirts of whatever city they were in. This occurred more in the larger cities than the smaller venues, but it occurred frequently in the beginning.

One of Mother's favorite experiences was the period the Red Heads spent in the Philippines in 1940, where they played exhibition games throughout the islands for several months. The women were celebrities throughout the islands and people turned out in large numbers to watch them compete against men. They filled large stadiums and played to sellout crowds as well as smaller venues in rural areas. The throngs came to watch the phenomena of "the battle between female versus male."

World War II was beginning to brew and international unrest was growing. In 1940 the U.S. State Department issued the warning for all U.S. citizens to leave the Philippines because of an imminent threat of invasion from the Japanese. The islands were filled with people who were loyal to the Japanese and Pedro, the Red Heads' Philippine sponsor, was fearful that the women could be targeted to be used as propaganda, since they were a "high profile" group.

After the State Department's order for all Americans to leave the islands due to the reliable information of a Japanese invasion, Mother quickly got the players together and told the team members to stay put while she left to contact Pedro, their Philippine sponsor, to enlist his help to get the team off the islands. When Mother found Pedro, he told mother to go back to the hotel and get the other team members to pack their things and wait for him to help them get home.

When mother got to the hotel, the team wasn't there. A note was left saying they were going out for a while to get their last round of visiting in before leaving. Mother waited with her packed bags at the hotel. Pedro showed up by evening and told mother that they needed to be ready to leave around midnight, as transportation he had arranged would take them to a ship leaving for the U.S.

Mom told him about the girls leaving and Pedro said he would find the girls and bring them back to the hotel. Pedro returned a few hours later in the wee hours of the morning, but he didn't have the team with him. He said he had looked all over but had been unable to locate them. He told Mother she needed to leave with him to get to the waiting boat he had arranged; that he would find the rest of the team and get them to the ship so they could all travel home together.

Mother got to the ship and discovered all would be leaving the Philippines on a cattle boat with a minesweeper leading the way. Several hours later, the team made it to the cattle boat and all left together.

Pedro had arranged to get the women quietly from where they were to a larger ship on a small boat that was a ship that contained a boatload of cattle. That was a great "cover" to get them safely off the islands without being noticed. Mother remembered seeing Pedro standing quietly on the shore as she got on that smaller boat, alone in the dark.

The Red Heads' fate was in his hands. Mother was very close to Pedro and his huge, extended family. She laughingly said that Pedro could stand under her arm and he had enough children to make several basketball teams. He was a wealthy businessman who loved basketball.

When Pedro took mother to the small boat late that night, Mother said that as she was getting ready to get on the small transport boat, Pedro asked her to do something for him. He handed her a satchel and asked her to take that with her and keep it for him until he could liquidate some of his proper-

Kay Kirkpatrick shows off her ball spining skills, late 1930s.

ties and livestock and get his family safely to the States. Mother asked him what was inside and he told her that it contained some valuables that he had been able to put together on short notice that he wanted to get out of the country before the Japanese invaded the islands.

Mother opened the satchel and could see large amounts of cash neatly sectioned off with rubber bands and several bags of precious stones. She said Philippine men loved showing their wealth with diamonds, rubies and emeralds. Mother was overwhelmed. She told Pedro she would love to help him, but didn't feel she could take the responsibility of getting his assets to the United States safely. Mother later found out that Pedro and all members of his family were victims of the Japanese when they invaded the islands; they never got to leave.

Mother often recounted how the Red Heads arrived on a luxury commercial ship only to leave quietly on a cattle boat with a minesweeper leading the way.

Peggy Lawson

Career 1936-40
All American Red Heads

As told by Peggy Lawson to daughter, Mary Kay Pfeiffer

Peggy was to the 1930s what Sue Bird is to women's basketball today. If there was a basketball game of national importance being played, Peggy was probably on one of the teams.

I was born near Eufaula, Oklahoma and I started playing basketball on the high school team when I was in seventh grade. When I was a junior, the district decided a basketball player could only play four years, so I coached the grade girls' team.

The last six weeks of my senior year, an independent women's basketball team in Wetumka, Oklahoma, owned by oil rich Indians, the Walkers, asked me to come and play with them in the National Tournament in Wichita, Kansas.

After my graduation I was invited by the American Business College of Des Moines, Iowa, whose scouts had seen me play in Wichita, to go to Canada with them to play a five-game basketball series with Canada's leading team, "The Edmonton Grads." Our Wetumka coach, Boots Wadley, talked me into going and I took my first train ride.

The Grads were simply known as the best team in the world. They would sometimes get in open cockpit Fokker VII airplanes and follow the train tracks below as navigation just to get to a basketball game. They also would go 27-0 in four Olympics (womens basketball was an exhibition sport at the time) and held a 147-game winning streak. They bested our team in the North American Championships.

The following year, the Walkers in Wetumka signed on the best players they could find, among them Hazel Vickers-Cone and the Dunford twins, Lera and Vera. We traveled all over the northwest playing the number one independent teams in the land. I played forward and made All-American at the Women's Basketball National AAU tournament in Wichita Kansas. The Tulsa Stenos (Stenographers) with Hazel Walker beat us in the national finals. The Indians got divorced and the team disbanded.

Tulsa liked what they saw in me and I was invited to go to Tulsa Business College and to play basketball with the Tulsa Stenos. Hazel Walker would leave Tulsa and move on to the El Dorado Lions. We defeated the same Lions in the national tournament in Wichita and I made All-American as a guard.

Peggy Lawson (left) and Gladys Lommler pose in their jackets promoting owner C.M. Olson's beauty salons, circa 1937.

That summer, when our season was over, the Stenos went to play a series of basketball games with the Grads in Edmonton, Alberta Canada. We traveled by car, and I saw Pike's Peak for the first time. The Grads again beat us for the North American championship.

The Stenos disbanded that year, but I stayed the summer in Tulsa to continue with Business College.

That fall I was contacted by a team in Houston, Texas to come there to play basketball. Vicki Cone and Helen Goodwin were there, as were the red-headed Dunford twins — Vera and Lera — who stood six feet tall. All the other girls I already knew.

The team never materialized. C.M. Olson, who owned men's professional teams, had started corresponding with the Dunford twins about coming to Cassville, Missouri, as he was organizing a women's professional basketball team, calling them the All American Red Heads. Vera decided to get married and Lera was devastated because she would be separated from her twin sister. So Vicki and I began corresponding with Olson in Lera's name and completed the deal. He knew nothing about it until we were all in Cassville and playing. I went home to see my folks, then took the bus to Cassville, arriving late at night at the hotel bus station. I was met by Wilbur Surface and Pete Pettigrew. Wilbur was to be our coach and Pete played on Olson's men's team, "The Terrible Swedes."

The Red Heads played men's teams, by men's rules, playing every night for six months a year over a period over four years. We played in every state in the United States except Florida. Wilbur was our coach for all but one of those years.

Olson and his wife, Doyle, owned five beauty salons in Missouri and Arkansas and in the summer I worked as an apprentice in the Cassville shop. After the third summer, I went to Kansas City for tests and received my operator's license. On April 17, 1940 we sailed for the Philippine Islands. We lived there and played men's teams until August of that year. I had arrived in Long Beach, California on August 29 and was married two days later to Wilbur Surface.

Vinia Hobbs (Poe)

CAREER 1938-41
OZARK HILL BILLIES

As told by Brenda Uhlich, daughter

Ozark Hill Billies, 1938-39. L-R: Jo Darrow, Vinia Nobbs, Nota Lee McCain, Joe Statovich, Eleanor "Ace" Laich, Danny Daniels and Lucy Peters. Statovich, the lone male on the team, played briefly with the Hill Billies but left the team when they got to the west coast.

Vinia Hobbs had the great fortune for playing for one of the most prestigious coaches in the history of women's basketball, Bertha Teague, at Byng High School in Ada, Oklahoma. She started at Byng in the eighth grade.

Vinia was one of the players that was on Teague's team during its 98-game winning streak between 1936 and 1939. During that time, it was not unheard of for Vinia to score 15 or more points in a game. In 1938 she scored an amazing 518 points and was named All State.

It was during this time that Ole Olson would go to watch the Byng school team and became impressed with Vinia's play. Bertha Teague was known to recommend her better players to Olson to join his traveling teams so that the girls could continue to play basketball and become professionals and get paid for doing so.

In the fall of '38, Vinia joined the Ozark Hill Billies.

Some of Vinia's high school teammates would also go to play for the Hill Billies and the All American Red Heads, including Nora Muncrief and Lorene Daniels.

In January of 1940, the Hill Billies would take on Olson's other team, the All American Red Heads. The Red Heads were much bigger and considered faster. The Red Heads were also much more popular than the "backwoods" girls of the Ozarks. Despite this, Vinia and her teammates gave the Red Heads a run for their money, losing by a scant two points in a second overtime.

Hazel Smith (Marks)

CAREER 1938-41
ALL AMERICAN RED HEADS

As told by Jeanie Marks and Kathy Marks Lasseter, daughters

Our mother, Hazel Smith, loved basketball.

Hazel was recruited by Ole Olson directly from Branford High School in Branford, Connecticut to the Red Heads.

While still in high school, she played for the famous East Haven Jeffs, alongside another All American Red Head, Eleanor Laich. Hazel was named the greatest women's basketball player by the Associated Press, where she was commonly referred to as the "Queen of the New England Courts."

The Red Heads played men's teams throughout U.S. and abroad. When Hazel joined the Red Heads, she quickly showed that she belonged on the same court as the men they played. She was six feet tall and could pick up a basketball in each hand at the same time off the floor. This was a stunt usually only performed by men.

A natural brunette, as were many of her teammates, Hazel had to use henna hair color to match the hair of the other Red Heads.

Hazel and the other Red Heads enjoyed many wonderful experiences, traveling all over the country and competing against men. Their barnstorming travels took them to many tourist attractions and landmarks. One of her favorite destinations was the Painted Desert in Arizona, where she obtained a sample of the famous multicolored sand as a souvenir. Hazel also told great stories about the Brown Derby Restaurant in Beverly Hills, California, the famous hangout of Hollywood celebrities. The team hobnobbed with many of the most famous personalities of the day, including Bing Crosby, one of the most popular crooners at the time. The team was introduced to many dignitaries throughout their travels.

While playing in Manila, Philippines, war broke out in the Pacific. The U.S. mandated the All American Red Heads return home to the mainland in America. The long trip on a cargo ship back

Red Heads, spring 1940, on ship to Phillipines. Kay Kirkpatrick, Peggy Lawson, Eleanor "Ace" Laich, Gladys Lommler, Hazel Smith, Ruth Osborn, Lila Blue, Ole Olson

to the U.S. was quite the experience, with very rough seas. But Mother had a sense of humor about the voyage, saying she had the best "sea legs" ever since! She joked about traveling on a ship full of men, saying "the odds were great!"

Mother loved basketball and followed the sport after her playing career was over. In an era when most women knew little about sports, she was way ahead of her time — she knew more about the game than anyone. As we were growing up, when our dates came to pick us up, they loved talking sports, especially basketball, with our mother. They would have preferred to stay, rather than take us out. Funny, but TRUE!!!!

Helen Onson

CAREER 1938-39
STARS OF THE WORLD, CO-EDS, OZARK HILL BILLIES

As told by Bob Knutson, nephew

Helen Onson was born in 1915 in Two Harbors, Minnesota. Her father was a logger and her mother was a cook at the logging camp.

She played basketball and was the only cheerleader in high school, graduating in 1933. She worked in a clothing store after high school, then began working at the Oneida County Courthouse while continuing to stay active in women's sports.

In 1937, Grover Cleveland Alexander's "Stars of the World" played at the Memorial Building in Rhinelander. A player was injured, and Helen was asked to join the team in Chippewa Falls, Wisconsin.

Helen's family wasn't happy about her decision to leave home to join a traveling basketball team and refused to lend her money for train fare or meals. A friend's mother lent her money for train fare for the 100-mile trip. When at the train station in Chippewa Falls, she found a quarter under the bench, enough to pay for her first meal with the team.

Grover Cleveland Alexander's team was booked by Abe Saperstein, owner of the Harlem Globetrotters. Due to Saperstein's busy schedule, Helen's first day with the Stars of the World was a hectic one. They played a doubleheader in Chippewa Falls in the afternoon, then traveled to Mondovi, Wisconsin for an evening game.

Helen Onson, Ozark Hill Billies

In 1938 Helen played for Helen Stephens Olympic Co-Eds — another team booked by Saperstein. Both teams had to perform all of the acts of the Globetrotters. Helen Stephens won the 100-meter event in the 1936 Berlin Olympics and played for the Red Heads for a season. Helen Onson traveled the United States and Canada with these teams and developed lifelong friendships with Abe Saperstein, until his death in 1966, and Helen Stephens, who died in 1994.

Helen Onson had many stories to tell about her barnstorming days. Once the Co-Eds played during a snowstorm in Crow Agency, Montana. A large potbelly stove was in the middle of the floor of the court, and the teams had to play around it. Tragedy struck while the team was playing a game in Hedley, British Columbia, as a large landslide crushed a nearby mine cabin with a miner and his girlfriend in the cabin. While still in Canada, the Co-Eds' driver, Ham Olive, paid off provincial police so that the team could play on Sunday, as it was against the law.

Heading back into the United States and down to Minneapolis, the team raised $1000 for charity in what came to be known as the "Minnesota milk game." The Co-Eds got their photo on a Wheaties box, but they couldn't enjoy the honor very much, since there wasn't enough room in the car to take any cereal with them.

They would even cause concern with safety at games. It wasn't common for women to play competitive sports against men, much less beat them. The women got to get on a bus to leave for the next game, but the humiliated men had to stay behind and explain to their family, friends and neighbors how they could lose to the 'weaker' sex. One restaurant owner in Colorado threw the team out of his establishment, saying he "didn't want any trouble."

As with the other teams of the day, the Co-Eds played against men's teams. The girls often would recruit a local woman athlete and make her a member of the team for the day, with the goal of making the hometown girl look good against their male opponents.

Helen Onson joined the Ozark Hill Billies for the 1938–39 season, finishing her career.

Nota Lee McCain

CAREER 1938-40
OZARK HILL BILLIES

As told by Nota Lee McCain

Nota Lee McCain, Ozark Hill Billies, 1938-39

I was born in a little town southwestern Oklahoma called Benson, population 300 or so. I never did have a doll when I was an itty-bitty one — it was always a ball — although I never did to get play basketball in school until I was in the eighth grade. They didn't have a basketball goal outside for girls back then.

We played in a weekend tournament in Cordell, Oklahoma and we won. The superintendent's sister, Helen Onson, played on one of Ole Olson's teams and knew about me. Soon Mr. Olson called and asked if I wanted to play for the Ozark Hill Billies.

My parents didn't want me to play, especially my Daddy. But when they saw how badly I wanted to go they finally gave in. They came to watch us play the Red Heads, Ole's most famous team. The Red Heads barely beat us.

Bernard Cowden was the coach when I played. For the first season we had a man on our team for a while named Joe Statovich who played a little. Joe was just a bunch of show — he could handle the ball and jump real well, but not much else. He looked like a tailless monkey. He played with us until he got to California, then quit us, having made it to the west coast.

I liked the Northwest better than any place we traveled. One time we were going up all those big hills in Idaho and we pulled off the road to look at the scenery. As we were looking, along came a kid on a motorcycle who wanted to take all us girls riding. None of the other girls wanted to ride with him, but I did, so I crawled on behind him off we went. When we got back Coach Cowden chewed me up a lot, saying, "Darn fool, you could've been killed on that thing."

I was the type of gal who was raised up with a bunch of boys and never did fit in with gals well. I wasn't one of their favorites, that's for sure, probably because I didn't join in with them in all the things females liked to do. But if I stood in one place and shot the ball and someone would pass it back to me, I would shoot it again. Once I hit 49 in a row.

Nora Muncrief

CAREER 1939-41

OZARK HILL BILLIES

As told by Alan and Melinda Jo Isaacs, grandson and wife

Nora Muncrief, Ozark Hill Billies, 1939-40

In 1939, Nora Muncrief graduated from Byng High School in Ada, Oklahoma.

Prior to her years as a Hill Billie, Nora would play basketball under future Hall of Famer Bertha Teague at Byng from 1936-39, where they were state champions. When she started high school she was much shorter than her sister, Dora, who also played. Yet in one year she grew a foot and made the All State team. Nora had the opportunity to play for a coach who compiled an astounding 1,157–115 record over four decades, including 27 consecutive undefeated seasons in league play.

Nora had the right attitude. "We never had a fear of losing a game, because we never lost and didn't know what losing felt like," she said. Yet they would learn what it was like when they lost their 99th game, the first game of the '39 season. "We didn't practice very much and they beat us by one point."

Upon graduating, she would have gone to college, but there was no basketball around the area. Ms. Teague wrote a letter to the All American Red Heads owner, Ole Olson, telling him that Nora had the skills that Olson was looking for.

She made 80 dollars a month — very good pay for the day. Traveling through 38 states, they played almost every day. Some nights they played the same team twice. The Hill Billies played a total of 150 games between November and April.

One night they even played Olson's other famous team, The All American Red Heads, in Shawnee. The Hill Billies lost by two points.

Nora's sister Dora wanted Nora to play with her down in Galveston, Texas but Nora had a two-year contract with Olson. After the two years was over, Nora got married and retired from professional basketball, just before her own brother, Bob Muncrief, began his Major League baseball career. Bob pitched in two World Series — with the St. Louis Browns and the Cleveland Indians.

Lorene "Danny" Daniels (Wilkes)

CAREER 1938-50

OZARK HILL BILLIES AND ALL AMERICAN RED HEADS

As told by Cindy Wilkes Thoren, daughter

Growing up on a farm in the 1920s and '30s was not easy. Most farmers didn't have money to hire "hands" so their children were put to work. And work they did — hard work. My mother was a farmer's kid and, as the oldest, she knew all the chores that had to be done — milking cows, feeding chickens, slopping hogs, planting peanuts and cotton and picking them in harvest — not to mention the household chores!

A respite from the work was school, and her favorite class was physical education. Lorene chose basketball to study and played under one of the finest high school coaches ever – Byng's Hall of Famer Bertha Frank Teague. She was playing for Mrs. Teague when they won an AAU championship.

One day in 1938 Ole Olson came out to the farmhouse — a white, four-room structure with porches on two sides, a porch swing and an outhouse in the back. He was looking for Lorene Daniels to play basketball for his Ozark Hill Billies. Undoubtedly, he heard of her from Mrs. Teague. The family pointed out to the back 40 and said he would find her there. She was planting peanuts — walking the planter behind the horse. When Mr. Olson saw her he said, "I have to have her on my team. That girl can work!"

The 1938–39 Ozark Hill Billies at Coach Bernard Cowden's house in Oklahoma City. L-R: Lucy Peters, Vinia Hobbs, Eleanor "Ace" Laich, Jo Darrow, Lorene "Danny" Daniels, Nota McCain.

Mom left the peanut field and joined the Hill Billies, along with her classmate, Vinia Hobbs.

The next several years would fulfill that farm girl's dreams of travel, fame and fun — as well as the work it took to be a successful pro basketball player. She had a beautiful, long shot that, while worth only two points at the time, should have been worth three.

She eventually joined the All American Red Heads after that team had returned from the Philippines and most had retired. At one point Mom became captain of the Red Heads.

Since the trademark of the Red Heads was their red hair, she dyed her hair — much to my grandmother's chagrin. Mom brought many of her teammates out to the house to visit. Like teens at a slumber party, they would dye each other's hair with henna and sit in front of the gas stove to dry it and set the color. The heat made the red color brighter.

According to my aunt, postcards and letters arrived every Thursday and Danny would come home during the summer hiatus, bringing boxes to stash away that would become Christmas gifts later in the year.

Genevieve "Gene" Love

Career 1939-49
All American Red Heads

As told by Barbara Hagerman, daughter

My mother was a small town girl from Louisiana. She was the oldest child of four — two boys and two girls. Her life wasn't easy in rural Louisiana prior to and during the Depression, but they had a good life. She told stories of riding a horse to town to stay with her grandparents on Sunday so she could go to school during the week. The kids would steal apples and get sick, and then go fishing instead. The usual rural life.

Her family has always been tall. All of the men were 6-foot-4 or more. Mom inherited that trait, standing 6-foot-4 herself. In addition her sister, daughter, cousins, etc. are almost all tall — many topping 6 feet, including the females.

Mom played basketball at Olla-Standard High School. Although they had an indoor gym, many of their games and practice sessions were played on outdoor courts because the boys got the gym.

In college, she and her roommate saw the ads for a traveling women's basketball team — the All American Red Heads. They couldn't afford to go to the game, but thought traveling and playing basketball sounded great. So they wrote to the coach, C.M. Olson and requested opportunity to try out for the team.

Much to their surprise, Olson showed up and was impressed enough that he asked to accompany Mom back to Olla to ask her daddy if she could become a member of the All American Red Heads. They went into Monroe to get a picture taken of Mom in the Red Head uniform. A picture of her palming a basketball in each hand is her first publicity shot taken. Olson later sent money for her to travel to Cassville, Missouri — home base of the Red Heads — and join the team. And thus a career began.

She began traveling with her teammates throughout the U.S. Their schedule was grueling. They traveled and played nights and Sunday afternoons for roughly six months a year. Each of the seven team members carried only one suitcase, a makeup kit and a uniform bag. They and the male driver traveled in a stretch limousine, staying in hotels every night. Their salaries started at $250 a month each and went as high as $1,000 a month — good pay for the time. They also received a food allowance.

Gene "Careless" Love (right) and Darlene Nabors standing in front of their 'bus' in North Carolina.

My Mom hated her birth name Genevieve, so she went by Gene — Gene Love. And Lena Horne's "Careless Love" was a popular tune of the time. And so was born "Careless Love."

At each game, she learned something beforehand about their opponents — something that later was parlayed into something funny. And with the tune "Careless Love" playing in the background, she'd always have a word with each referee — and any short balding ref always got a kiss, with an overload of red lipstick, on his bald head. The opposing center often received a kiss on the cheek or forehead — much to the delight of the audience. It was also not unusual for her to take the opposing center by the hand and lead him to the water cooler — all the while the rest of her team had the men scrambling. Another favorite stunt was for "Stubby" Winters, another Red Head teammate — although a relatively short one at all of 5-foot-1 — to dribble the ball thru the legs of Mom. The men chasing Stubby were stopped in their tracks. Another famous stunt had Stubby jumping on the back of Careless Love and sending the ball sailing thru the basket. The audience loved it all. Despite all the high jinks, the Red Heads won more than 70% of their games.

Between games their lives were pretty mundane. They'd check into a hotel, maybe do laundry, shampoo, apply henna, go sightseeing, shopping, out to eat or to the movies. They were often joined by members of the opposing teams on their outings.

They once played the preliminary game for the Boston Celtics. They visited Niagara Falls on both the U.S. and Canadian sides and crossed Lake Michigan on a ferry while ice chunks floated by. She was proud to say she'd been to every state that was part of the United States at the time (prior 1959) except Maine. She was able to see the presidents on Mount Rushmore in South Dakota and visited Mexico four times — entering at four different points. She saw "Careless Love" singer Lena Horne perform in Las Vegas. She saw the footprints and handprints of the stars in concrete at Grauman's Chinese theater in Hollywood and got hugged by Bob Hope. A friend of hers was a friend of Bob's brother — and they were able to get passes into the studio where Hope, Bing Crosby and Dorothy Lamour were filming scenes for "Road to Rio" (released in 1947).

Mom's stories of her experiences on the road went on and on. Once they were in Portland, Oregon and the lights went off in their part of the city. Since they couldn't play, they went down the road to see the Sons of the Pioneers performing. Then they took a ferry across Puget Sound into Vancouver, British Columbia to sightsee. They fed seagulls by throwing pieces of bread into the air.

She never said too much about it, but on Sunday, December 7, 1941 they were in Indiana playing a game and noticed that somewhere in the middle of it people starting getting up and leaving, and there was a lot of talking. Of course, the news about the attack on Pearl Harbor interrupted the game that night.

The Red Heads came off the road during World War II. Mom returned to Louisiana and worked in the bus station and later for Georgia Pacific Railroad, in Monroe, Louisiana. They resumed playing in the fall of 1945, and Mom continued to play until the spring of 1949.

She later was featured on a promotional picture for a new team just starting up, the Texas Cowgirls, but Mom ended up not playing any more professional basketball.

Marvalee Jo Darrow

CAREER 1938-42

OZARK HILL BILLIES AND ALL AMERICAN RED HEADS

As told by family in obituary

Hill Billies Joe Statovich and Jo Darrow at Manley Cabins near Ole Olson's home in Cassville, Missouri, 1938-39.

Marvalee Jo Darrow was born on June 6, 1921 in Vinson, Oklahoma and raised as one of six children to a cotton farmer during the Great Depression. She worked very hard and long hours on the farm.

Jo was an exceptionally good student and an outstanding athlete.

She held the record in Harmon County for throwing a softball the greatest distance. During her time, there weren't any sports other than basketball that ladies could enjoy. After graduating from high school, she enrolled and attended Mangum, Oklahoma Junior College. During her short stay at Mangum Junior College she was contacted by a representative of the famous Ozark Hill Billies basketball team.

Her daddy would not give in to her going off and playing ball and not getting her education. Jo promised Daddy everything "But just let me go. I promise I will finish school."

After several days, it is believed that her Momma stepped in and made a decision that Jo was going to go play ball.

Everyone of this small town was so excited, because this was such an honor for someone from this small community to enjoy. After about one year she joined the All American Red Heads.

When entering the court for introduction before the game, Jo led the team onto the court, spinning a basketball in each hand.

However, it was so sad that her family did not have the chance to see Jo play very many games as money was tight and the distance was so great that it was nearly impossible.

She continued playing for the Red Heads for four years before entering college and fulfilling her promise to her daddy.

Evelyn Turner, a.k.a. "Toby McGee"

CAREER 1939-49

ALL AMERICAN RED HEADS

As told by Evelyn Turner

I played basketball under the name "Toby" McGee. We had a mule when I was a kid. I was as stubborn as that ole mule so my Daddy started calling me by the name of the mule, Toby. It stuck with me.

I grew up in the sand hills of Oklahoma. I was last of 10 kids. There was lots of love, food and second-hand clothes, but little money for entertainment, so we had to create our own. We nailed a hoop on the barn. We chose up sides and played basketball. Since I was the youngest and smallest I had to concentrate on developing moves.

We had basketball in our little rural school, Ocina. It was too small for football, so we concentrated on basketball.

Students were allowed in the gym before school, recess, lunch hours and after school. Our family rode the second bus. This meant the bus would take one load of children home then come back for the second load. I spent my hours waiting for the bus on the basketball court. That second bus would help determine my destiny.

By the time I was a freshman I had grown to six feet tall. I had developed some talent so I made forward on the varsity team. We played three-division court, forward, center and guard. No player could leave the zone they were assigned to. The school did not furnish girl uniforms, so the mothers bought black satin material and made the suits. I got my first pair of real basketball shoes at this time.

I was a junior in 1939 when I went to live in Ozark to live with and play in Ozark High School, where my brother taught. The coach gave me the key to the gym, so I practiced up to three hours every day. I had grown to 6-foot-1 and had become an outstanding player. My senior year the rules for games had been changed to half court play with only forwards and guards.

During my senior year, I was recruited to play for the All American Red Heads. I had talked with Ole Olson many times by the telephone and through the mail about playing basketball for him. The first time I really saw him was when I rode the bus from my home to Cassville, Missouri when I was reporting to the team.

The bus pulled into this little town. There wasn't even a bus station — the bus pulled up to a drug store and the bus station was in the store. I kept looking for some big guy because he promised me he would meet me by the bus, but I was surprised to meet this little guy outside the store.

The little guy led us across the street to Doyle's beauty shop where Doyle was at the shop with three or four of the girls that had reported before me. She was applying henna to some of the girls' hair. That's when I met her and some of the girls that were there.

Once we hit the road, we played every night of the week and sometimes twice on Sundays or holidays. Each player was allowed a cosmetic bag, a regular bag and our uniform bag. When we traveled, the bags were carried on a rack on the top of the bus. We usually stayed in the town where we played, then traveled to our next game the following day. Each night after the game, the coach gave us a departure time for the next morning. It was up to each player to be in the hotel lobby with their three bags and ready to leave on time.

Red Heads, circa 1945-46, L-R: "Toby" McGee, Phyllis White, Darlene Nabors, Ruth Haines, unidentified, Margie Arrends, "Stubby" Winters, Coach Wilson Turner. McGee and Coach Turner married in 1947.

When I played high school basketball in Oklahoma only one person could play the full court. On our team, that one person was me, so playing a full court game for me with the Red Heads wasn't a big a adjustment. Playing men was a bit scary, but you got used to that, too.

One time we did play against a women's team and it was very boring. There was a team in Tennessee that had just won everything and their coach kept bugging Ole to play us. He finally gave in and scheduled a game against the Tennessee team. We played one half by girls' rules and the other half by men's rules. It wasn't even close — we were so much better it was embarrassing.

I was on the road with the team in December of 1941. We were eating breakfast somewhere, I don't remember where. I was sitting at the counter with a couple of the girls and they had the radio on when I heard President Roosevelt announce that we were going to war. It just sent chills all over your body. You could hear a pin drop in that restaurant.

We went on to play that night. It was very different — almost like being at a funeral. Everyone was quiet, almost in shock. We had a contract to play a ball game that night and we did. People came out to it, but it was so different than our normal games.

We kept playing for a while after Pearl Harbor, but soon the rationing of tires, gas and other supplies needed for the war effort meant we had to stop traveling. It was less than a full season after the war started that the team disbanded. Boeing Aircraft Company in Wichita, Kansas offered me a job and the opportunity to play on the "Boeing Bombshells," a team that traveled to military bases and played to entertain the troops.

After the war, the team was reunited in 1946. We had a new manager/coach that year. His name was Wilson Turner. He had played on one of Olson's men's teams, the Terrible Swedes. During the season, Wilson and I fell in love. We married after the season ended and made our home in Cassville, Mo. We lived about a mile from Doyle and Ole. They were guests in our house many times.

Allegra "Stubby" Winters

Career 1941-51

All American Red Heads, Arkansas Travelers

As told by James Winters, brother

Allegra was born ninth out of 12 children, growing up on a farm in Parkston South Dakota. She had a basketball in her hands when she knee high to a calf. She was fortunate being from such a large family, since she had four brothers to play basketball with. She became an outstanding athlete playing with her brothers, despite only standing 5-foot-1. Over the years, I read many articles that spoke of Stubby playing in high school. As her brother, I was never convinced that her high school even had a basketball team for girls — the high school stories may have been fabricated by the team for promotional reasons. But yes, she was that good a basketball player.

On the farm we had a big barn where we would store feed and hay for the animals. We had a hoop in the hayloft and that's where we would play in the long winters when everything was covered by snow.

We would play all day on the weekends, even though that barn was very cold, even for someone from the Dakotas. She developed a really good shot and became a great basketball player.

One day Ole Olson and the All American Red Heads came to play in this little town where we lived when she was in high school. That is how she became aware of the Red Heads.

When she graduated high school she contacted Olson, who invited her down to Cassville, Missouri for an interview and tryout. She was hired to play for the Ozark Hill Billies, which were then owned by former Red Head Ruth Osborn but whose games were still booked by Olson. She soon moved over to the Red Heads team. Despite her being the shortest Red Head thus far at 5-foot-1, her skills proved and that not only did she belong on the Red Heads with her pure basketball skills, she brought something more to the team that had not been seen on the court as of yet.

This is where she got the nickname "Stubby." She could literally stand under the arm of some of the players.

She became close friends with the tallest player to play for the team to date, Gene Love, who was 6-foot-4. Stubby and Gene would have cameras flashing whenever they stood next to each other.

Olson saw this and incorporated a couple of new "crowd pleasers." One of them would be when Stubby would dribble to the hoop, her man guarding her. Gene Love would step between her and her man and open her legs to allow Stubby to bend down a bit and go between Gene's legs while dribbling. She would come out in front of Gene, her man blocked by Gene and have an easy layup.

She and Gene would also perform the first "Piggyback play" ever done by any of the Red Heads. Stubby and teammate Ruth Haines would pass the ball back and forth as they dribbled down the court — little problem since 6-foot-4 Love attracted most of the defenders under the basket. Stubby passed to Haines as they got near Gene, just before Gene bent down and Stubby quickly climbed on her shoulders. From her perch on Love's shoulders, Stubby took a final pass from Haines and dropped the ball in the basket. The "Piggyback play" brought roars from the crowd and left the defenders shaking their heads, wondering how they ever could have defended that play.

Red Heads Allegra "Stubby" Winters, and Gene "Careless" Love demonstrate the short and tall of basketball players, circa 1945-46.

When they traveled out west to California they stopped in Hollywood. Stubby and her teammates would meet Bob Hope and Bing Crosby and other stars of the time.

She had to quit playing for the Red Heads during World War II as Olson would take them off the road due to war rationing of tires and gasoline. Stubby and Gene decided to do their part to support the United States during the war. They jumped in a car and headed to Wichita, Kansas and worked for the aircraft manufacturer, Cessna.

After the war, Olson asked them both to return to the Red Heads. Most of the team that she played with returned, as well as some who didn't dye their hair red, but wore wigs. This was the only time in the Red Heads history where a player was allowed to use a wig.

There was a new addition to the team — a very notable one. Anyone that knew anything about women's basketball knew the name Hazel Walker. Hazel, who was also part Cherokee, had decided to become a professional after being an All American for 10 years. She was a six-time national free throw champion as well as national champion as a player and coach. Hazel would take on all challengers to free throw competition during the halftime and rarely lost.

It was during this time that the players were paid extremely well for the season. Stubby would make a minimum $5,000 for the season, plus receive an envelope at the end of each week with an additional $5.00 in it for each win over the men during the preceding seven days.

During the '48-'49 season the team had an issue with Olson, who ended up letting the entire team go, having its schedule filled by his second team, the "Famous" Red Heads, with newly-hired coach Orwell Moore.

But Stubby's career didn't end there. Hazel had many years of basketball to go. She would create her own barnstorming team, the Arkansas Travelers. While they barnstormed like the Red Heads, there were no wigs and a bit less comedy. Yet, the Piggyback play would go on with Stubby.

After two seasons with the Travelers, Stubby retired from basketball and returned to the farm.

Lorene "Butch" Moore

CAREER 1947-58
ALL AMERICAN RED HEADS

As told by Jessie Banks, Jolene Ammons and "Spanky" Losier

As her teammate, Jessie Banks, I first met Butch in the spring of 1954. It was at a game I had gone to see when I was a senior in high school. Of course, I didn't know who she was, not even that she was Coach Moore's wife. Butch had been an English student of Orwell Moore in high school. They ended up falling in love (scandalous today, but the world was very different then) and got married before Orwell was hired to coach for the All American Red Heads and brought his young bride along with him to play.

The next time we met was at training camp in the fall of 1954. We stayed in this tiny motel in some little town in Arkansas. C.M. Olson still owned the team then and Orwell was coaching. We worked out in the local high school gym. When I first saw Butch run I thought, "Can this woman really play basketball?" I soon found out, the answer was yes! I was really amazed at her long-range shooting skill. If there was a three-point line in 1954, who knows how many points she would have scored? I have never seen anyone shoot from so far out and still make them.

Butch stood about 5-foot-7. She had long hair, which she put in a ponytail when she played. She was a kind person, but when she stepped on the court she was all business. If the men were doing something she didn't like, she let them know about it — even with the ponytail.

Butch was the general on the court. Once, when one of the guys was doing something to our center, Emo (Emogene Shelton), she told Emo to step aside when she was ready to do a backhand pass, which she could throw very hard. You can imagine where it went. Emo had no more problems that night.

Red Head Lorene "Butch" Moore and husband and Coach Orwell Moore, circa 1953.

At halftime and she would step up to the foul line and put on a free throw shooting exhibition. What was the big deal? She would shoot free throws on her knees. Most would have a hard time making one or two of 10 shots, but Butch would make 10 for 10.

On the rare occasions when we got behind and needed to catch up, we just started setting screens for Butch. It wasn't long before we caught up.

Along with being our teammate, Butch was our friend and mentor. She taught us so much about shooting and how the game of basketball was played. She also taught us how to play blackjack. It didn't matter where we were — in the car, in the locker room or in the motel room — we played blackjack. The other thing she could do was make a Coke last a whole trip from one town to another. We could never understand how anyone could like flat soda pop.

After she retired she would still hit that dusty road and fill in whenever a team needed another player.

Butch would also hit the road on occasion during a vacation with their kids. "Spanky" Losier was in her third season on the road in 1969–70, when the whole family caught up with them when they were out in Colorado. At the time the team was on its home stretch of the season. Lorene and family arrived in their beautiful blue Pontiac Bonneville with the white top. When we traveled, some of us got to ride with Butch or Coach in the car, since her kids wanted to ride in the limo with the rest of the girls.

It was great having Butch around again. She would help us with things that we needed to improve on and offered suggestions on how to recognize and add things to the comedy part of the game. This was a big help because our team at the time had just two veterans — the rest of the players were new. Butch got out on the court and showed the pivot how to keep the ball up behind her head when she stepped back to shoot. This was the Red Head way that the pivots shot to help prevent the defender from blocking the shot.

Butch also showed us that she could still shoot free throws on her knees — even 15 years after she retired. It was something else to see her out there after all these years and no practice, making it look so easy, swishing shot after shot.

Butch told stories about how things were back when she played — how the Red Heads traveled, how they were received by the townspeople, and the audiences they played for. The week went by quickly. It certainly was fun and educational. We always considered Butch a friend and teammate. We had the utmost respect for her. She was a woman who not only was the Red Heads' leading scorer and outstanding player, but was a class act on and off the court.

Years after her playing days were over, Orwell and Butch created a camp attended mostly by girls to enhance their basketball skills as well as other sports. It was called Camp Courage, located in Holly Springs, Mississippi.

Butch played a large part in Camp Courage from behind the scenes. You could feel her presence as she sat in the gift shop, watching every practice. Many times she would stop a counselor (a Red Head), telling her to keep a check on a camper that was developing a bad habit with shooting etc. She may have been retired from the court, but was always looking to help these girls have their dreams fulfilled.

For a Red Head, Butch was our mother away from home. She was warm and helpful to any of us that had a problem or needed some to talk with. The gift shop was manned by Butch and Theresa Corbin. They were always busy personalizing tee shirts and tank tops with the label machine. They would also make the Red Heads uniforms while in the store.

A woman we called Miss Carolyn and two of her daughters prepared the meals for the campers, with Butch overseeing this as well. The big walk-in cooler was full of candy bars for the gift shop, and some of the campers would get up in the middle of the night and sneak over to mess hall and take a few candy bars. Butch usually turned a blind eye. She would also handle the Friday night talent shows and awards given to campers who excelled in various activities during the week.

Butch lived and breathed the Red Heads all her life.

Willa Faye "Red" Mason

CAREER 1948-56
ALL AMERICAN RED HEADS

As told by Willa Faye Mason

I was an All-State basketball player at Siloam Springs, Arkansas High School for two years. I even had a boyfriend that was a cheerleader for the girls' basketball team. How's that for a switch?

My high school was only 60 miles from Cassville, Missouri, home base for the All American Red Heads. Ole Olson, the Red Heads' owner, had read about me in the newspapers and was watching me. He came to watch our team, which had made the state tournament three years in a row. He asked all three of our forwards — including me — to join the Red Heads.

I remember in the early days playing basketball in Indiana, which was often called "Basketball Heaven." I was accustomed to playing at a tempo that allowed me to shoot a lot of set shots. But in Indiana they were more into the fast break.

The Red Heads were a hit wherever we played. Often people would come up to us after the game and ask where the next game was and if they could come and watch us play again. We loved repeat customers.

The largest place I ever played was the Chicago Stadium, home of the Chicago Bulls of the NBA and the Black Hawks of the National Hockey League. The basketball court was installed right over the ice. When we were warming up before the game one of the girls muffed the ball on a layup and went to go after the ball, which had rolled off the hardwood court. She didn't realize that there was ice underneath, and when she stepped off that court and onto the ice her feet went flying higher than her head. She even got a concussion out of it.

Red Head Willa Faye "Red" Mason on an advertising poster, circa 1949

We also traveled north and played the University of Alaska in Fairbanks. They had never seen girls play basketball and didn't have a girls' basketball team. It was so packed that people were standing and we hardly had enough room to make layups. People were standing on the lines at each end of the gym. They loved us.

I was always surprised we would be booked to play on Christmas Eve and also on Christmas night. In the smaller towns it gave people something to do as a family after spending time together that day.

Playing night after night after night you encountered a variety of teams with different skills levels. You might play an AAU team that had a regular schedule that it was playing, or you might run into a team of just a bunch of local coaches getting together for a pickup game to see if they could beat a bunch of girls. The competition was different every night, and that was a challenge.

Some teams just tried their darndest to beat us and did not want us to win no matter what, especially the teams of men coaches. The coaches where in front of their peers, as well as the players they coached. They couldn't afford to look like fools. After all, we got to leave town 30 minutes after the game, but they had to coach the next day and explain to their players why they lost to a bunch of girls.

We even had a song we came up around with around 1948-49 season. We used to sing this a lot traveling around the country, even waiting to check in at a hotel for the night because the Red Heads had arrived:

Oh, we are the Red Heads, pretty and trim
We've come to town to play ball and win
Send seven girls out on the floor
There'll be laughter and passing and shooting galore
We want all you people to know
We do our best to put on our show
And whether we win or whether we lose
We hope to return to your town again

Dolores "Dody" Petersen (Clack)

CAREER 1950-53
ALL AMERICAN RED HEADS

As told by Jim Clack, son

Basketball was probably the most exciting thing that happened in the towns of Northern Minnesota. Seventy-five per cent of the town's population would show up at these games. Mom would shoot baskets every chance she got — through a rim on the side of a barn in the snow banks to lunch hours at the gym when the boys weren't using it.

In her senior year, the All American Red Heads came to play in Erskine, Mom's hometown. The girls' team got to play in a preliminary game, prior to the men's team playing the Red Heads. After the girls' game, the Red Heads coach, Orwell Moore, went up to her and asked if she ever thought of playing professional basketball and gave her the address of the owner of the team. About 10 days later, Mom got a red, white and blue-edged envelope in her family's mailbox. In the envelope was a letter inviting her to join the team the following October.

Seven players would be on the team, including the coach's wife, Lorene. The team traveled to all 48 states during her third season, 1952-53. The Red Heads made their way around the country in a DeSoto station wagon, playing games every day, with two on Sunday. The only exception was Christmas Day.

Her teammates called Mom "Dody." The men's teams they played against always wore green uniforms, trimmed in white, which contrasted with the red hair that was the trademark of the Red Heads.

Being the shortest member on the team at 5-foot-7, she got the privilege of being in on one of the Red Heads' crowd-please stunts, which they called "the Piggyback trick." Dody would hop up on the shoulders of another player, catch a pass and then put the ball in off the backboard while none of the men could reach her.

Her favorite moment was when the team headed back to Erskine, where they played in front of everyone she knew, including family and friends. She was also offered the opportunity to play for the famous Grand Rapids Chicks softball team, but did not play. This was the team that the movie "A League of their Own" was based on.

Dolores "Dody" Petersen palming two basketballs with arms outreached in skirted style Red Heads uniform, circa 1953

Mom played for three seasons before leaving the team and heading to college. Mom's days with the Red Heads made her realize that she could do anything she wanted if she set her mind to it.

Frances "Goose" Garroutte

CAREER 1951-67
ARKANSAS TRAVELERS

As told by Frances Garroutte

I'm from Van Buren, a little town in Arkansas. There were no divisions in girls' high school basketball in Arkansas in those days — we competed against the big schools as well as the small ones. There was the county tournament, then the district tournament, and then finally the state tournament. Our team ran drills, sprints and practiced until we were like a well-oiled machine. We won the state tournament three years in a row and at one time had a record of 106–1.

We even played again the Byng High School teams, coached by the legendary Bertha Teague. We beat them every time we played them. We had to travel there to play, since Bertha wouldn't bring her team to Arkansas to play us. Our coach wasn't afraid to play anybody — even on their home court.

Bertha was a really great coach whose teams had great players and put together some great winning streaks of their own. She felt they had players that could hold me to eight or nine points in a game. The first time we played down in Ada I scored 43.

When I got out of high school there were very few colleges that had women's basketball. There were Amateur Athletic Union (AAU) teams, including El Dorado and Wayland Baptist. I had a few letters to play AAU basketball, but they were all from up north. That's why I went into pro ball.

One of the players on the El Dorado team was Hazel Walker, who led the team to the national championship. After her amateur career, Hazel played for the All American Red Heads, but decided to start her own team — the Arkansas Travelers — in 1949. Hazel not only coached the team, but

Arkansas Traveler Frances "Goose" Garroutte, early 1950s

she owned it and still played. Hazel recruited me right out of high school. I played until the team came off the road.

On my first day in training camp, Walker and the other players were so impressed with my dribbling, as well as my other skills and abilities, that they started calling me "Goose" — a reference to the famous "Goose" Tatum, star of the Harlem Globetrotters. The nickname stuck with me for the rest of my career.

Hazel insisted in her rules being followed. One rule was "my players should look like a woman, act like a woman and play basketball like a man." We couldn't outmuscle the men, and we couldn't out jump them. But we could outshoot them. I practiced shooting for hours at a time, sometimes 500 shots a day.

The game we played with the Arkansas Travelers was a little different than that played by the Red Heads, who worked a lot of entertainment into their "show." We played more of a straight-up game.

We had a little bus that we traveled in, playing 90 to 100 games a season over 6 1/2 months. We traveled light — we were allowed only one suitcase, one makeup kit and a ball bag. The hotels and motels we stayed in weren't as nice as they are today — in fact some of them were downright bad, but we stayed anyway. Some towns were so small they didn't have a motel at all, so we might stay in a boardinghouse. We got used to the travel routine — we were young, so it didn't bother us.

We had to wash our own clothes on the road. We were lucky to get mail about four times a month. Hazel would make connection with someone from the team that we would be playing in a town a few weeks ahead of time and we let everyone know where to write. Mail days were a real treat.

The Travelers played every night, including a lot of doubleheaders. We would play one town at 6 o'clock and then drive 20 or 30 miles and play another game later that night. And if we had to go for 500 miles to the next game, we didn't sleep in a bed — we got in the car right after the game and started driving all night to the next game to do it all over again. In some cases we played a doubleheader in the same town. We would fill up the gym and play the game, then clear the people out and bring in all new fans for another game in the same place.

I averaged 45 to 50 points a night and I never had any problem shooting. That included not only shooting a basketball, but also a gun. We always carried a gun with us — Hazel kept the revolver right in her purse and carried it right into every gym we visited. Here we were, seven women on the road, and since we always got paid in cash, we always carried a lot of cash. No one was to mess with us. Both Hazel and I could handle the gun very well.

We played a lot of men's independent teams. Some times our opponent was a team made up of all the coaches of the surrounding area, which was a great drawing card. We also played all the service bases. And they played us hard. But the coaches teams were by far the worst, since they did not want to get beat in front of their kids by a bunch of women. Most of them were nice, but some of them did get nasty. Once I had a fist thrown at me that hit me — and that was from the principal of a high school. Things like that were just part of life on the road. Believe me, at the end of the six and a half months we were all ready for a vacation.

We were like celebrities when we went into town. In most small towns we were the only entertainment that they would have for a year. So we were a big deal when we came to town — like movie stars back then. Everybody wanted an autograph and to come up and talk to you. When we were down in Mexico, if we played at noon in a town, those crowds would follow us all day long before we even got to the gym to play ball.

We even played the House of David, a very famous men's barnstorming basketball team. It was great fun and the guys were really nice.

My first year with the Travelers was '51, Hazel's third year after leaving the El Dorado AAU team and her one season with the Red Heads. I played with the Travelers for 16 seasons. I was the coach and the business manager of the ballclub for the last five or six years. She got to where she wasn't traveling as much with us on the road. I drove the bus and did all the business end of it. And at that time it was just six of us. When Hazel showed up there would be seven of us and she would help sell the programs and do the business side.

The last three or four years Hazel didn't travel with us at all. Hazel and I were the only ones that ever drove. We just looked at the map at night, then took off the next day. There were no superhighways — just a bunch of little "pig trails" through the little towns. I think I traveled every pig trail in America!

Hazel knew all the generals and at one time the government was talking about sending us over to Europe to entertain the troops. We went a long way in the process of getting it all set to go and then Abe Saperstein, who owned the Trotters, put a stop to it. He told them that if we went over and play, he would never play another game on any of their bases. So that was the end of that.

But we still ended up playing on military bases a lot. We would stay in guest houses on the base. One time Hazel and I were rooming together. After our game we had gone to bed. All of a sudden, Hazel asked me if I was asleep, then she asked me if I'd go to the bathroom with her. I said, "Hazel, what in the world is wrong with you?" She jumped up and ran out in the hall, and started screaming at me, "Goose, there's a man under my bed!" I jumped up and joined her in the hall. The man started yelling, "If you want me out from under this bed you are gonna have to help me!" He was stuck. We left him under there until the MPs could get there and arrest him.

I don't understand how people say they lose their legs in the game today. We played every night, week after week. There was no such thing as losing your legs. I have played on sprained ankles, I have played with pneumonia. We had to, as it was only the seven of us. If you had a jammed finger or anything you just played through it.

In my 16 years we only missed one game and that's when the police shut down the highway due to a snowstorm in Colorado. I don't know how we even did it, looking back. It's kind of scary how we even made it to some of those games in the winter and bad weather.

Jessie Banks

Career 1954-59
All American Red Heads

As told by Jessie Banks

Orwell Moore, coach of the All American Red Heads, came to my high school in Lindsay, Oklahoma. Three of us seniors tried out. We just shot around. They were playing at a town nearby so he asked us to come over to the game. He later told me if I hadn't attended that game he wouldn't have considered me. The game was great. Afterwards we were invited to the locker room to meet the team. That is when I first met Lorene "Butch" and Orwell "Red" Moore. He told me then he was looking for taller girls but would let me know later that summer.

We had moved to Arkansas for Dad's job. Coach Moore called me and asked if I wanted to play for the All American Red Heads. Of course, I said yes. He later came down and brought uniforms so I could have my picture made. He said "Oh, by the way, I want you to learn to juggle."

The first week on the road was hard for me. I couldn't shoot very well, since I had only played defense in high school, and in six-on-six basketball, which we played, players couldn't move from the backcourt into the offensive end. So "Butch" — who was Coach Moore's wife and a star player — took me under her wing, so to speak, and worked with me after the game on shooting techniques. We spent so much time together that we became best friends.

I remember traveling in a station wagon with three riding in the front seat, three in the middle and two in the back. Luggage was on top, carefully loaded in order to get bags for eight people to fit, and covered with a large, heavy green tarp. Our uniform bags went behind the back seat.

I can recall playing on Indian Reservations in New Mexico. During the game the crowd just sat there quietly. They didn't laugh, cheer or anything. Coach Moore told us not to worry about it

Jessie Banks (second from left) with Red Heads teammates Zethel Keith, Katherine Pitcock, "Butch" Moore, Nellie Marlow, and Loraine Milligan, circa 1957

because they were enjoying the game. Sure enough, after the game they just talked on and on about how much they liked our game and wanted us to come back.

Another memory was our first trip to Alaska. Our mode of transportation was by seaplane, going from island to island. On one occasion, as the plane took off and became airborne, one engine went out. The pilot told us he was turning around and we would be able to land where we departed. Well, we landed okay, but not before the other engine went out before we got to the dock. I do believe we were a little scared. Of course they had to come and get us by boat. It wasn't long before another plane came to pick us up.

Nellie Marlow

Career 1955-57
All American Red Heads

As told by Bernie Hudgens King, daughter

Nellie Marlow was born and raised in Pearson, Georgia. She played high school basketball at Pearson High. Every time you would see this tall, lanky girl, she would have a basketball in her hand. Then one day, this man came to her, asking her to play for the All American Red Heads. It was the owner of the team, Orwell Moore. She really didn't know what to say.

My grandparents told Mom to go for it — this is a chance of a lifetime. And so she joined the Red Heads. Mom said she had very mixed emotions about her decision. On one hand, she was excited to play for the Red Heads, but on the other hand she was homesick.

Of course, becoming a Red Head meant that Mom had to become a redhead. Coach Moore expected all the players to dye hair their hair red. Because Mom's natural color was a very dark shade of black, she had a problem getting her hair to turn red.

Besides going from a brunette to a redhead, another transition Mom had to make was the style of basketball she played. Girls' high

Nellie Marlow of the All American Red Heads, circa 1956-57

school basketball in those days was still a half court game, six-on-six. But the Red Heads played against men and by men's rules, which meant running the full court.

Mom told us about a situation during one game where one of the men that they were playing against got very rough. He had been pushing her around and elbowing her all night. Lo and behold, my mother went up for a rebound with him and got outjumped. As he came down with the ball he elbowed her in the mouth and knocked two of her teeth out. My mother was NOT going to come out of the game for good. As the night went on, the coach let her come back in after she had begged him. She got the perfect opportunity to remind this player not to play dirty and what a man can do, a woman can do better. She got a rebound and when he came down she popped her knee up, sending him to the floor. As he lay on the floor with a bruised ego (among other things) she told him, "Don't ever elbow another lady in the mouth."

Our mother loved basketball and she would tell us about her high school years up to her professional years. She bragged about her teammates and how proud that she had the opportunity to play professional basketball for the All American Red Heads. She spoke often about her coach, Jessie Shelton — a very kind man, but very stern. Later she played under Coach Orwell Moore. He was very strict, even off the court. He insisted that his players would be ladies and act like ladies at all times.

One of Mom's greatest memories was playing at Madison Square Garden in New York City. "The Garden" was one of the most famous sports arenas in the world, and my mom thought that was the grandest place. She said playing there made her feel she like a movie star.

But despite Mom's time in the spotlight with the Red Heads, she never forgot her roots. She was proud of being from a small town in Georgia, and equally proud of her rearing. She had the greatest parents, who allowed her to live a dream few women would ever even get to imagine, never mind live. We, her kids are so proud of our mother and of the opportunity and privilege she had to play professional basketball.

Linda Yearby

Career 1956-76

Texas Cowgirls, Shooting Stars, Arkansas Lassies

As told by Linda Yearby

Always fascinated with the game of basketball, Linda began playing in earnest at the age of 8. Her four brothers found that her ability to get the ball in the basket made her a formidable opponent. When her nephew moved next door the challenge was even great, as he was much bigger and stronger than her brothers. By this time, she had made up her mind that basketball would always be a part of her life.

Linda had been a life-long sufferer of asthma, and her father attempted to discourage her from being so passionate about the game of basketball. Strong minded and vocal as well, Linda openly felt that if she was to meet her end, it might as well be on a basketball court, playing the game that she loved.

As a child, she became so good she was recruited by the eighth grade boys' basketball coach, Walter Parker. With Linda as the only female on the team, they enjoyed a 15-7 season. Despite being allowed to play on the boys' team, there was still some evidence of segregation as her uniform was a different color than the boys on the same team. To say she endured her share of razzing and name calling is putting it mildly. But her determination won out, and as a Midway Panther, she made headlines in November 1950 for her performance in invitational tournament; invitational due to the fact that, other than Coach Parker, no coach felt there should be a woman on a basketball team, despite the league allowing her to play. Yet the other coaches would not let themselves look bad and boycotted the tournament in fear that people would think they could not beat a team that had a girl on it.

In high school, girls' basketball was played only as part of physical education classes, with an annual class tournament always won by the class of which Linda was a member. The style was six-on-six, with the court broken into two zones. Each team consisted of three guards and three forwards.

As a forward, Linda was able to score, and score she did, racking up a whopping 103 points in two tournament games!

Graduating high school, Linda was as passionate about basketball as ever, so when the famous Texas Cowgirls traveled to a nearby town in her native Indiana, she was made an offer she couldn't refuse: With the Cowgirls' average of 180 games a season, traveling 40,000 miles, she would replace a member who had been injured. Linda would be on the team that would even be on the same bill as the Harlem Globetrotters, opening up for them many times on the road.

After a few seasons she became player/coach for five seasons. It was during this time the owner of the Cowgirls asked Linda to leave the court and take up coaching another one of their teams — the Harlem Queens. The queens were an all-black women's basketball team. While the team was successful on the court, Linda would witness firsthand the slap of discrimination in her players' faces. She would have to go in restaurants and hotels first and ask if it was okay for her team to enter for a meal or to rest their heads at night.

Linda left the Cowgirls and become part owner, player and coach of the Shooting Stars, alongside fellow Cowgirls player, Elvera "Peps" Neuman. The Stars would be on the road for just two years, playing a total of about 300 games before changing their name to the Arkansas Lassies, based on urging from a booking agent. Between the Cowgirls and Shooting Stars, Linda traveled to every state in the country but Hawaii, as well as overseas trips to Spain and Morocco.

They played on the military bases, representing the government as a USO show. "We were given $7.00 for food," she remembered. "We flew in Army planes, and we were hungry a great deal of the time, as everything was cooked in olive oil, which some of us weren't too happy about."

Arkansas Lassies program, featuring Linda Yearby, 1976

Owner

LINDA YEARBY

Linda Yearby is the original organizer of the Arkansas Lassies. Having played 17 years on the pro basketball circuit, playing 180 games a year, Ms. Yearby has undoubtedly played more professional basketball than any other female in the country. She is a pioneer of women's pro basketball, and in a very real sense is "The First Lady of Women's Professional Basketball".

When did it all start? "When I was in the eighth grade, I played with the boys on the seventh and eighth grade team. That was back about 1950. We won all the invitational tournaments, but it came time to play in the county tournament, and they wouldn't let me play. Our school lost. Then in high school, girls couldn't play sports, which was very disappointing."

Yearby's professional career began with the Texas Cowgirls. She was given star billing with the team, and was player-coach for five years. In 1960 she went to Spain and Morocco and played men's teams on army bases there.

Eleven years ago, she organized the Arkansas Lassies. Playing on a show team is "a play, eat, sleep and travel life," according to Linda. "It is a good education to see how other people live, and you do see a lot of people when you play in a different town and state almost every night."

Forming a women's stunt team was hard... "A lot of hamburgers... I started it on a shoestring... everything I do gets started on a shoestring and the shoestring just gets longer."

Originally from Chrisney, Indiana, Linda now resides in Ionia, Michigan.

WELCOME

NUMBER ONE IN WOMEN'S SPORTS

To an exciting evening of Arkansas Lassie Basketball

The Arkansas Lassies is the finest girls' professional basketball team in America. Basketball at its best is provided by this stunt team under the guidance of Linda Yearby and Jolene Ammons. The Lassies compete in a 180-games-a-year schedule in towns across the country. They travel over 60,000 miles during the season, playing six games a week. It's a tough schedule, but the players' enthusiasm for the game never fails.

Competition is unique because the Lassies play all male teams composed of local talent--teachers, businessmen, coaches and others are given the opportunity to match basketball skills against this team. The girls ask no favors; they play men's rules and they play to win. Like their male counterparts, the Harlem Globetrotters, the Arkansas Lassies are highly successful, winning about 80 percent of the time.

The Arkansas Lassies are dedicated performers and disciplined athletes; they love basketball. They mix comedy with good basketball and you get good entertainment!

* * *

Linda would eventually become the sole owner of the Lassies in the '70s. Her teams played upwards of 180 games a season across North America. Yet, after the passage of Title IX, she knew things were changing as well and she would have to be willing to change with the times.

In 1974, a start-up league named the WPBA (Women's Professional Basketball Association) was formed. Linda took her team and joined the league. Women would finally get the opportunity of their own league and play each other, instead of playing only men. One of the other teams in the league would be the Indianapolis Pink Panthers. This was a very formidable team with a lineup that consisted of several former All American Red Heads, including Jolene Ammons, Karen Logan and Mary Hounsell.

In January 1975, the Arkansas Lassies, out of Michigan, entertained the Indianapolis Pink Panthers while on their site search. While on this quest, a name change was in the offing, with the Michigan Robins was suggested, but the league never got off the ground due to lack of backing. Little did the prospective backers realize what opportunities they missed!

Another league was attempted around the same time. Orwell Moore, owner of the Red Heads, saw the future as well and wanted in. He would leave his barnstorming team on the road, but would create another team for his own league. Initially called the NGBL (National Girls Basketball League, Orwell soon realized his gaff in judgment and renamed it NWBL (changing Girls to Women). Times were a changin'. Linda was to be vice president of this league, while Orwell was president. They never played a game. So Linda carried on with the Lassies.

In 1975-76, Linda recruited one of the best ball handlers to ever play on the court, Jolene Ammons. Jolene would eventually become co-owner and coach. She also put on a dazzling halftime show with her ball handling skills.

But barnstorming was waning, and crowds were decreasing for almost all teams. Financial hardships hit the team and the partnership was dissolved after just one season.

Barbara Wells (Gwinn)

Career 1956-57
All American Red Heads

As told by Barbara Gwinn

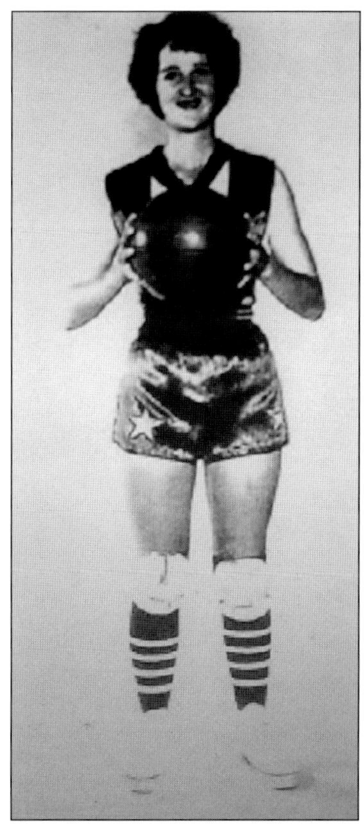

Barbara Wells Gwinn, who was still high school age when she played for the Red Heads, 1956-57

My dad and mom were divorced. My sisters, brother and I had to more or less raise ourselves. We lived with our Dad and he worked from sunup to sundown. He was a sharecropper and we had to help him in the fields, mostly in the cotton fields.

I had to go to school, work in the fields and do the things in the house that usually the mother does. Being the oldest of the siblings, I did the best I could at cooking, cleaning the house and watching over my brother and sisters.

I played high school basketball in Caraway, Arkansas. Little did I know, Coach Orwell Moore was watching me play. I had never heard of his women's basketball team, the All American Red Heads.

In 1956 I learned that they were no longer going to have a girls' basketball team in our school. Since basketball was the only enjoyment I had at the time, I chose to leave school.

A few months later when I was in the cotton field, my dad came to me and asked me if I wanted to play basketball. Well, he didn't have to ask me twice. He told me that he knows this man named Red Moore that has a girls' basketball team that travels and wants you to play for him. I met Coach Moore and his wife "Butch" and signed the contract to play on October 25, 1956. I was just 16 years old. My contract was for $150.00 a month and a $100.00 a month for meal expenses. That was good money in those days, and it sure beat chopping and picking cotton. Coach Moore and Butch gave me some luggage and some money to buy some clothes and other things that I needed.

I'll never forget the first game I played. It was at a school I had attended years before. My dad and family came to see me play. It was the second game my dad ever saw me play. Well, I made the first two points, then said to myself, "I can do this." I was so happy to be playing basketball again!

Our team had some problems during the year. One of the girls got hurt (broken arm) and had to leave the team and go home. Three more of the girls were let go for one reason or another. We got three new players. Butch stepped in to help us out until we could get the team filled. We finished the season out with five players. No one got any rest. I'm sure there were other teams like that.

After the basketball season was over I went back to Caraway and returned to school. I later joined the Women's Army Corps.

Shelby Tedder (Faulkner)

Career 1958-61
All American Red Heads

As told by Shelby Tedder Faulkner

I heard about the All American Red Heads by word of mouth. They were from Caraway, Arkansas, not far from my hometown of Light. I always knew about them.

It was my senior year at Greene County Tech High School in Paragould. I asked my coach if I might be able to play basketball for the All American Red Heads. He said, "Maybe." He must have really helped me, because soon Mr. Orwell Moore, owner and coach of the Red Heads, came to our house and asked me if I would like to play for them. Of course, I said "Yes!" After all, playing basketball was what I loved to do, and I wouldn't have to pick cotton anymore. My mom and dad were very happy for me as well.

We went up to the gym at Light, Arkansas for a tryout. I passed the tryout. I was working at Emerson Electric at the time. I told my boss, Peck Bryant, that I was going to be playing for the Red Heads, but needed to continue working until it was time to leave for practices. I didn't have a suitcase so I used all the money that I made at Emerson to buy one.

Red Head Shelby Tedder spins a basketball, circa 1959

My first week on the road was exciting! I hadn't ever been anywhere besides Light and Paragould, Arkansas. Also, getting to eat out in a restaurant was a treat. To me it was a dream come true! I loved every minute of it. And I didn't miss the cotton fields.

After most games we stayed in a motel, then left in the morning for the next town. But if the next booking was a long drive, we hit the road right after the game. Often we traveled 500 miles or more to the next game.

When we did stay in motels, we would have to wash our uniforms in the bathroom and hang them up to dry. The next day we would pack up everything and put our suitcases on top of the van. One time, during the winter, we got to the next game and had to wear our black suits instead of our usual red and white. My black uniform was frozen together! I had to pull it apart and put it on. Luckily, it dried out some when I ran up and down the gym floor.

A wintertime tradition for the Red Heads was playing in the snow. Coach Moore would just stop the van and let the girls get out and have snowball fights for fun. Since most of us were from the South, this was a treat. The girls picked a player whom they would literally roll over and over on their sides down the road. There normally wasn't much traffic on the two-lane highways when there was snow on the roads. Being the rookie on the team I was the one that got "rolled" in the snow.

One time the electricity was out in the town we were playing in. When we arrived at the gym we were surprised to see that the place was packed! The people patiently waited for the power to come on so they could watch the game. It was a very big deal that our team came to their town to play and they were not going to leave.

One of our players even knew Wilt Chamberlain and she made sure I got to shake hands with him at one of the pro games we attended.

Ginny Hill (Butz)

Career 1959-63
Texas Cowgirls

As told by Ginny Butz

Texas Cowgirl Ginny Hill, early 1960s

I grew up on a farm near Hesper, North Dakota. My dad saw to it that I had two basketball hoops — one outdoors for warm weather and one indoors in the haymow to use in the wintertime. For those of you who do not know what a haymow is, it is a part of the barn where hay is stored in winter. I would shoot hoops every chance possible, even during the heavy snows.

My high school only had two years of high school basketball for girls, 11th and 12th grades. When I was in the eighth grade they let me play on the boys team. We won all the regular season games, but when it came time for the tournament, they would not let me play.

The year after I graduated the Texas Cowgirls came to Maddock, North Dakota to play. As I was walking into the gym to watch the game I met the coach of the Texas Cowgirls (Shirley Dorow) and coach of the men's team they were playing in the hallway. The coach of the men's team knew me and said to the coach of the Cowgirls, "There is a gal that can play ball for you." She stopped me and asked, "Do you want to try out after the game?" I said, "Sure." I remember being nervous and not hitting many shots. But they evidently liked my ball handing, as well as the fact that I was left-handed and had a left-handed hook shot that was hard to stop.

Shortly after the try out I had a letter from Dempsey Hovland, the owner of the Cowgirls. Dempsey wanted me to join the team in Bismarck, as they were traveling with the Harlem Globetrotters for two weeks, playing the preliminary games. I wanted to very badly, but my folks wouldn't let me. By this time I had been out of high school a couple years — one year attending college and another coaching the Hesper boys grade school basketball team. I still had my heart set on playing for the Texas Cowgirls.

I finally got the approval of my parents, but I had no money to get to training camp. Dad told me to take the combine and go out around the slues to harvest flax. The money I got for the flax I could have to get to training camp. I managed to scrape up 60 bushels of flax at $4.00 a bushel, which was more than enough to get me into camp.

Much to my delight I made the team and signed a contract for a year. We trained for two solid months. I was so happy to get on the road. I was one of the taller gals, so I got to play center or forward. I liked the center position the best, since I could get my left-handed hook shot off easier in that position.

I got to do part-time driving for the team. I was doing three things I loved to do — drive, play basketball and travel.

In the fall of 1960 the Texas Cowgirls were sent overseas to play in Spain and Morocco for the Department of the Army. Then over Christmas and New Year's we went to Alaska for 15 days. We played for our servicemen on their bases. We even got to ride on a dog sled to return to our plane.

That was when we played at Northeast Cape, 18 miles from the Russian border. To make a gym for us to play they had to make room in the hanger, pushing back the planes, helicopters, and fire engines. The audience had to sit on those to watch the game. We had a huge helicopter for our dressing room.

The more games we played, the better I liked it, especially the doubleheaders. Sometimes we had to travel all night to get to the next game. Being one of the drivers, I got more than my share of speeding tickets. I never had to pay them, but the minute I started living in Minnesota and transferred my license from North Dakota to Minnesota, I found out I had too many tickets! After I told them that I was doing part-time driving for the Texas Cowgirls they let me go and dropped all the tickets.

Dempsey usually booked games in our hometowns once every year. It was fun playing against guys I had played with growing up. The whole team would stay at my mom and dad's. We had to get the cows milked before we went to our game.

Harlean Hudson

Career 1959-64
Texas Cowgirls

As told by Harlean Hudson

I started playing team basketball in the eighth grade at Milton, Iowa, a town of 500 people. In 1959 I graduated from high school and that year received "Honorable Mention" from the Iowa Girls Basketball Association. I received a letter from the owner of the Texas Cowgirls, Dempsey Hovland, asking if I would like to try out for the team. It didn't take me long to answer that letter!

When I arrived at camp, I found plenty of talented girls that also wanted to be on the team. I did make the cut and played with the Cowgirls for five seasons.

While in the States, we traveled in a Dodge Van equipped with a rack on top that held our luggage. We were allowed two pieces of luggage — one for personal and one for the gym.

Texas Cowgirl Harlean Hudson, early 1960s

We loved having a full schedule (a game every day). One 30-day month we had 32 games, including two doubleheaders. Sometimes the next day's game would be a long distance away. Once we drove 701 miles through a snowstorm to make it to the next game. We got there safely and on time, playing with only a couple of hours of sleep.

Our routine was to come on court to the music of "Orange Blossom Special" and be wearing western hats, vests and guns. Then we would go into a "circle" and do ball handling to the music of "The Happy Whistler."

Joyce "Jo" Eastman

Career 1961-69

Texas Cowgirls and All American Red Heads

As told by Joyce Eastman

I graduated from Lake Odessa High School in Michigan in 1958. I played basketball all through high school. I was fortunate enough to be on the first Lake Odessa team to compete against other schools, as it was not all that common.

After graduation I heard about a professional women's team that traveled around the country, playing men's team. I contacted the owner, who asked me to tryout with the team. Linda Yearby and another woman came to Lyons, Michigan to tryout a friend of mine, Kate, and me. We were asked to some shooting and ball handling. We were both sent letters later and told we were hired and to report to Beloit, Wisconsin. I was fortunate to make the team.

Texas Cowgirls "Joyce" Jo Eastman and Harlean Hudson practice spinning basketballs, with Carole Nicholes watching from the floor, circa 1962.

My first year with the Cowgirls, our uniforms were shorts and a shirt. We would come out before the game and do a circle warm up, much like the Globetrotters, with fancy ball handling done to music. We would then come out on the floor wearing cowboy hats, vests and guns. At halftime, I did a dribbling act, which also including juggling basketballs.

We did some wonderful traveling. We went to Morocco, as well as "North to Alaska" — as the old Johnny Horton song went — to help support the USO by playing for servicemen.

I became aware of the Air Force's motto — "Hurry up and wait." We would have to arrive at the hanger early, then sit or lay around until we were flown to the next base. These military planes weren't the fancy, comfortable aircraft like the commercial planes. They were tankers with seats on the side. They were VERY LOUD and VERY COLD.

The next year I heard about the All American Red Heads. I was asked to go the Caraway, Arkansas for a tryout. I made the second team, which meant we played most of our games in the western states.

I returned to the Cowgirls after just one year with the Red Heads because of a better salary offer. Upon my return I not only played, but also coached.

As a coach I was to guide the new players and make sure substitutions were done. Also, before the game I would go the men's dressing room and instruct them on what gags we were going to do and how they should respond.

On top of playing and coaching, I did a lot of driving as well. There were many nights that we drove all night to get to the next game. We would check in to a hotel, catch a few winks and go to the games.

I continued to play until 1969.

Georgia Washington

Career 1961-66
All American Red Heads

As told by Georgia Washington

My name is Georgia Washington. I grew up and attended school in a beautiful, rural area in north central Arkansas, in a town called Calico Rock. I played one and one-half of basketball in high school, and I loved it.

In 1961 the owner and coach of the All American Red Heads, Orwell Moore, asked a girl in nearby Ash Flat, "Who was the roughest girl you have ever played basketball against?" She answered, "Georgia Washington." I was in Washington state at the time, and Coach Moore contacted me and asked me if I would be interested in playing some professional basketball. The next thing I knew, I was an All American Red Head.

Coach Moore was a very unique man. To have the best basketball team, I always thought you would simply go out and look for the five best players you could find. That is not how he worked. He had a vision in his head and he would assemble it that way. It could be that sometimes he looked for a scorer; at other times for a person he felt would get the crowd into the game. On occasion he would look for a rough and tough player.

I was simply in the right place when he was looking for that player.

I played for the Red Heads for five years, and it was one of the greatest times of my life. Being an All American Red Head was an experience like none other. It strengthened my confidence in myself and affected, in a positive way, how I would meet the challenges that I would face in "life after basketball." I am so blessed to have been one of only 300 girls that actually played for the All American Red Heads.

Red Heads Georgia Washington (behind) and Pat Overman, circa 1962

We played against men only. I was 6-foot-2 and played pivot. We played every night, and twice on Sunday, to packed gyms of wonderfully enthusiastic fans. They loved us and we loved them. They paid hard-earned money to see us play. We were determined to give them their money's worth, even when we were feeling "under the weather."

After the game, the fans would come down on the court to be close to us, talk to us, and get our autograph. We appreciated them and enjoyed talking to them, so we stayed, as long as it took, to see each and every one of them. We were fans of them, as much as they were fans of us.

We played good, hard basketball and won most of our games. We played the first quarter straight up in order to show the men and the fans gathered on the sidelines that we could play with the best of them. However, we did add a great deal of show starting in the second quarter. We did lots of ball handling, passing and, to the delight of the crowd, our team clown dealt the referees a ton of grief.

We performed a half-time show that included dribbling routines, passing routines, trick shots, and a "magic circle," which featured a lot of skilled passing. While we were working hard to entertain the fans at halftime, the men were sitting on their bench, drinking water, wiping their brow of some sweat and catching their second wind to play us in the second half.

There were usually a lot of miles between our games. We averaged traveling 50,000 to 70,000 miles each season. Sometimes we had to travel all night to make it to our next game. On Sundays, with the doubleheaders, it was sometimes tough getting from the afternoon game to the night game on time.

Early in the season the coach would often stop, let us out on the highway, and we had to do "roadwork" — in other words, running. Motorists must have been puzzled to see five to eight red-headed girls, running down the side of the highway or freeway.

We often appeared on radio and television shows. Some of us were on "I've Got a Secret," "The Red Skelton Show," "What's My Line" and various other shows. It was a lot of fun, as well as educational.

I have many treasured friendships with teammates that have lasted throughout the years.

Bernice Holladay (Shafer)

CAREER 1962-65
TEXAS COWGIRLS

As told by Bernice Holladay Shafer

I was raised on a small dairy farm near Walkerville, Michigan and grew up loving all sports.

When I went to gym class one day, the coach asked me if I wanted to play forward or guard on the basketball team. Never seeing or playing a game, I asked an older girl what position she played. Suddenly, the coach threw me the basketball. I literally took the basketball and tucked it under my arm and ran towards the basket. That's all I knew about basketball. Fortunately for me, I was a quick learner.

When I was a senior the Texas Cowgirls came to a neighboring town and I had the privilege of seeing them play. My coach had talked to the team captain, Linda Yearby, about me and a couple of weeks later I received a letter from their owner, asking me to travel with the gals for one week.

I was one scared, bashful, little country girl traveling with those girls. WOW, were they good or what! That same week, I'd made up my mind that I was going to travel and become a Texas Cowgirl too. Up until then, I always thought I was going to become a policewoman!

After much thought, my parents finally told me I could go to training camp, but had to come home at spring time to help them farm. Deal or no deal, I was headed for training camp at South Beloit, Illinois. I was ready to travel and play too!

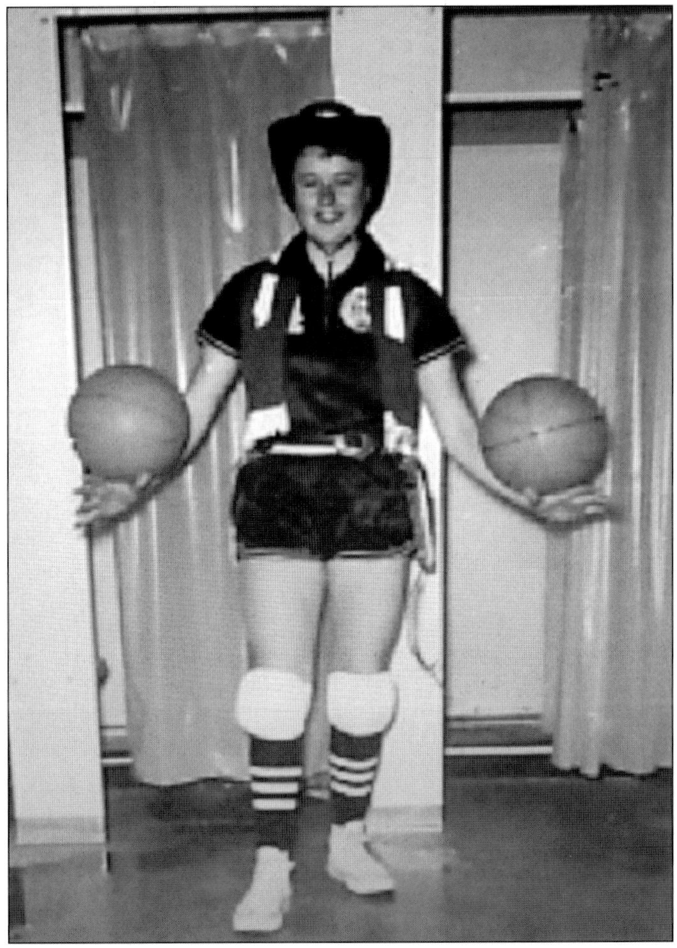

Texas Cowgirl Bernice Holladay, circa 1963

And travel and play we did. Washington, DC, New York City, west to Montana, the Indian res ervations, the Dakotas, Georgia, Kansas — we played in 36 states and seven provinces of Canada. We traveled with and played preliminary games to Harlem Globetrotters, as well as NBA teams like the Philadelphia 76ers, Los Angeles Lakers, and others. We played against men's teams, by men's rules, and won about 80 percent of our games. We averaged 230-250 games per season, traveling approximately 36,000-40,000 miles per year. What a life!

I thank the Lord and Savior for my ability and privilege of playing and for the friendships that developed with all the players and other farm gals on the team.

Pat Overman

CAREER 1962-73
ALL AMERICAN RED HEADS

As told by Pat Overman

I played high school basketball in northeast Missouri, making it to state tournament three times. I had enrolled in college having never seen the All American Red Heads play, but my coach had not only seen them play but also played against them. He suggested I find out more.

My first year with the Red Heads I spent a lot of time on the bench, along with a 6-foot-7 girl and Coach Ben Overman. He began coaching the year before I started playing with the Red Heads in 1962. He grew up in Caraway and was around the Red Heads, rolling the posters to be sent to towns on their schedule to promote the games. Eventually he became the coach, appointed by owner Orwell Moore.

There was an unwritten rule that players didn't go out on dates during the season, but after the season was over Ben came over to my house and we started a relationship. We were married that summer. Mr. Moore was a bit skeptical at first, even though he himself was married to a player.

Red Head Pat Overman shows off her ball spinning skills during a halftime show, circa 1968

After Ben and I got married we put a goal up in the backyard and I did nothing but play basketball. I learned tricks like spinning the ball. Then I played more basketball.

I put a lot of pressure on myself being married to the coach. I wanted my playing time to be because I earned it, not because I was Ben's wife. All my work in the backyard paid off, because I was a much better player that next season.

The Red Heads would play in any town that had a gymnasium and a post office. Many of those towns didn't have a motel, so we spent the night in another town. Often there wouldn't be a restaurant open after the game, so the people that booked us would prepare something for us to eat.

There was not much excitement in these little towns, so when you came to town as a barnstorming basketball player you were an instant celebrity. People watched everything we did, whether we were playing the game or in a restaurant eating.

Because of our hectic schedule, we had to watch our time closely in order to make it to the next game on time. When we got to a restaurant to eat the coach would tell us how much time we had. I didn't like to miss dessert, so I always ate my pie first.

When we walked into a game against a team of men, we always felt that we could outshoot any team. We couldn't outrun them, but we felt if we could control the tempo of the game, we could outshoot most teams. As a result, we didn't lose very often. And though we didn't like to lose, when we did we always did it professionally.

It always seemed we ended up around West Virginia at Christmas. Every season there were new girls that had never been away from home for Christmas. Most of these small towns closed up at Christmas. If the town knew we were coming, sometimes a church would do something special for us such as announce us during the morning mass or have a bit of special food for us. So sometimes we would go out and buy our own Christmas tree and buy fruit for presents and put the Christmas tree right up in our motel room.

Playing against men meant the games could get rough at times. Once when we played against the Boston Patriots football team I got my nose broken by an elbow to the face — one of the two times I got my nose broken. I only missed one game, even though I played on a sprained ankle quite often. When your team has only seven players, you don't have the luxury of missing games.

Shirley Beckman (Cheatum)

Career 1962-63
All American Red Heads

As told by Shirley Beckman Cheatum

At 6-foot-2, I was the tallest on my La Plata, Missouri High School team. I was working at a small frozen custard shop one day when Coach Ben Overman approached me and told me about the Red Heads. I was so excited. He wanted to know if there was a basketball court available and I told him about the open-air court that was at the church. The next day after I got off work we went to the church and laced them up, then went through a mini workout. The very next day I was offered a contract to play professional basketball.

Red Head Shirley Beckman, 1962

Boy was I flying high! But I was soon no longer the tallest player.

When I was playing, we traveled in a station wagon. Just think — Coach and seven players, with basketball gear, uniforms, warm-ups and then your meager clothing. Talk about closeness! But I was having the time of my life.

I only played basketball with the Red Heads one season, 1962-63. But what a whirlwind that was. We played a few games in Arkansas, Missouri and Tennessee, then we were off to Canada. While playing at Prince of Wales College, we were escorted onto the court by a bagpipe band — a first for me. We also played in Nova Scotia. Pretty exciting stuff for a country girl.

Red Heads owner Orwell Moore usually scheduled our games in the northeast before the winters became so harsh. We carried our luggage on top of the car, protecting it from the weather with a tarp. We took turns with the tarp, and when it was my turn it was really rough on the hands on those cold mornings.

After the northeastern swing we started working our way farther south. We spent Christmas in Gate City, Virginia, which happened to be the hometown of one of the players, Mickey Hendrix. We looked forward to playing in the girls' hometowns because it meant a home cooked meal, and by that time we were sick of restaurant food.

It was great at Mickey's home. On Christmas Eve the carolers came around, and we exchanged gifts. It was my first Christmas away from home. Homesick Mickey loved being home so much that she decided to leave the trail. We really hated going on without her.

Near the end of December we were in Cochran, Georgia. A girl named Peggy Padgett tried out for the team while we were in town. She joined us in Pineville, KY. While we were in Cleveland we appeared on "The Mike Douglas Show." Another guest on that show was Betty White.

Later, we headed for sunny California! It was amazing seeing large number of former Red Heads attending the games. We did a lot of sight seeing, if time allowed it, but not often enough. Our schedule meant that we sometimes traveled all night to make the next game and played with little sleep. Those games were rough, as were the doubleheaders. Our schedule also included personal appearances and interviews to promote the game. But sometimes that sponsor would thank us by taking us out for a meal.

Looking back, the life we lived on the road was a hard one. But I realize that what we did had a big impact on women's basketball. I guess that's why some refer to us as "the pioneers of women's basketball."

Mickey Hendricks (Childress)

Career 1962
All American Red Heads

Authored by Jolene Ammons

Mickey Hendricks of the Red Heads, 1962

Mickey was from Gate City Virginia. Coach Orwell Moore sent her a bus ticket to West Memphis Tennessee to catch another bus to training camp. Upon arriving, she saw another taller girl at the station. She went over and said, "You're a Red Head," even though the other didn't have any red hair. Sure enough, it was Jolene Ammons, who had just arrived for her rookie season as well. They both boarded the bus for training camp in Paragould, Arkansas and became roommates as well.

During training, they both ended up so sore, they didn't know which was more so. All of us thought we were in good shape prior to reporting. Wrong!! But we made it through the tough times of training and started the training games, learning the show routines and doing the halftime show.

While with the Red Heads Mickey played center and forward and had a fabulous hook shot.

Home cooked meals were a rarity on the road. As good as some restaurants can be, it becomes the same old day after day. The team was fortunate enough to be playing in Mickey's hometown on Christmas. Even though they lost the game 55-53, it was so very special. Her mother had a gift for each and every Red Head. A huge Southern feast was set up for all. Family and friends that were at the game were there as well. Red Heads and local community were coming together to share the good will of Christmas. Carolers even came to the door and all sang carols together.

Then, some of the players would call home. As great as it was being on the road and a Red Head, you could see how hearts were torn from players being away from their families, especially at Christmas. Tears would roll down their face as they talked to mothers, fathers and siblings. Mickey was blessed to be an All American Red Head, and even more so to be blessed to have a loving family.

When the station wagon pulled out the day after Christmas, it was a bit lighter in luggage. Mickey decided to remain behind with family, her playing days coming to an end, with no regrets.

Jolene "Jo Jo" Ammons

Playing/coaching/owner career 1962-76
All American Red Heads, Pink Panthers, Arkansas Lassies

As told by Jolene Ammons

My senior year of High School in Homerville, Georgia was 1960. I traveled over to Pearson, Georgia to try out for the Arkansas Travelers women's basketball team. I had seen the Travelers at a game before and told Hazel Walker I would like to play. She gave me another date they would be in the area. I was so I nervous, after changing into shorts and getting on the court, I looked back at the dressing room door and there was the entire team watching, including the world famous Hazel Walker. Hazel said to shoot a few free throws to loosen up. My first shot didn't come close to the rim. I missed the whole thing. She came over to me and told me to settle my nerves.

So, I did what I loved most, taking the ball and spinning it, doing some ball handling. She seemed to like what she saw. After that my confidence was restored. Later in the year she contacted me by phone to report to Little Rock for pictures and to be fitted for uniforms. We drove out that summer. Due to family issues I made a decision not play with the Travelers.

During the summer of 1962, Lurner Williams, who was a sports writer for the Atlanta Journal as well as a scout for the All American Red Heads, arranged a tryout. I did everything I knew how to do with a basketball. Having always been a fan of the Harlem Globetrotters, I knew how to do a lot of the ball handling, spinning, dribbling and some of the fancy passes. I wanted to impress Mr. Williams. I shot from close range as well as from what today is the three-point area. I played one on one with one of the guys. We took a breather, then I finished the tryout with more ball handling and my favorite, a spinning routine. Mr. Williams handed me Coach Moore's card, saying, "You're OK. Give me a couple of hours to give him a scouting report, and then you phone to work out details." Excitement doesn't even begin to describe my feelings.

I reported to training in October 1962. I was sitting in the bus station when a tall lady walking in my direction said, "You're one of the Red Heads reporting to training." In my mind I was thinking, "This is really great. I don't have red hair and someone recognizes me!" She turned out to be one as well and we became roommates during training. Her name was Mickey Hendrix, from Gate City, Virginia.

I never thought that I would be one of the shorter players. I was short in stature, but tall in attitude. Arriving in Caraway, Arkansas Coach Orwell Moore met the bus. His greeting wasn't "Hello" or "Welcome to the team," it was "The hair has to grow!" Very soon I had red hair.

My first game as a Red Head was in Strawberry, Arkansas. I twisted my ankle on the last day of training; it was quite painful. Coach Moore asked me to show him the corner of the court. I pointed to each corner. He said "I asked you to show me the corners," and he sent me off on a trot to each corner. The purpose of this was to teach me to play wide and not crowd the post. It's strange that I remember my first game, but I can't remember my last game.

Red Head great Jolene "Jo Jo" Ammons, mid 1960s

I was fairly lucky shooting long shots. Coach Moore would tell me to take a shot just as I crossed the center line.

Getting to know the players was a chore in itself. It's a new lifestyle, learning the do's and the don'ts. Washing uniforms by hand was a challenge. And it doesn't take long before one becomes a pro at dyeing hair red.

We traveled by station wagon, learning the routine of arranging the luggage on top of the vehicle, covered by a specially-made tarp. On freezing cold, snowy mornings, YUCK! Later we traveled in limos, which was a bit more comfortable that the station wagon.

Traveling around the country year after year I got to meet some special people.

We were invited to be on the Mike Douglas talk show. Betty White was a guest. We all did ball handling — our magic circle tricks. Betty was amazed at our ability. I did spin the ball, putting it on her finger.

At one motel we stayed at there was a rock 'n' roll group named the Grass Roots that were also staying there. They were out in the courtyard playing their instruments and we were practicing routines in the parking lot. We began to chat, and after our game and after their concert, they invited us to their suite, where they did another mini concert for us. Little did we know that the Grass Roots would become a famous band and sell over 20 million records.

On another occasion I worked at the John F. Kennedy basketball camp in Wahoo, Nebraska as a counselor. One of the campers was a late arrival and there was no room for her to bunk in, so she moved with me. She introduced herself as Reba McIntyre. She was my roommate for almost a week. At the end of the day she would play the guitar and sing. She was a great basketball player. Needless to say, she wasn't a bad singer, either.

A couple of times during my career the game was stopped and the game ball was presented to me. The first time was when I scored my 10,000th point. The owner, Orwell Moore, made the presentation. That basketball is at the Women's Basketball Hall of Fame (archived). The second time was at the 15,000-point mark. I've never been one to toot my own horn, but I was very humbled by the appreciation shown.

I ended my last two seasons as a player/coach, winning 357 and losing 46 for a winning percentage of 88.6.

Red Heads Jolene "Jo Jo" Ammons with Billie Jean King, circa 1974

Being player/coach, I also had to ensure that we checked in a motel. I would then call the sponsor, checking on how advance sales are going. If we had any interviews or personal appearances we had to make sure we scheduled our time appropriately. If sales were slow, we became our own promoters. We set out to go into the public right away, chatting with folks mostly as we walked along them down the little Main Streets in America. Seeing seven girls with red hair — some well over six feet tall — is a spectacle in itself. Plus, our limo was hard to miss and would attract many locals who wanted to go over and see it up close.

We always left for the gym an hour early to make sure we would arrive on time and get ready for the crowds by loosening up, working on plays and so on.

When the game started, I would introduce the team. After I introduced a couple of players, the comedian would be strutting on the end line making her presence known, as if to say "what about me?" I asked her to get back in line. She would be the last one introduced.

At halftime, the players entertained the crowd with their special show. Players would also sell programs at halftime. It was my job to settle the gate with the sponsor. We always got paid in cash. Can you imagine that today?

Western Union was our eighth player on the team. Receipts would be wired regularly when I checked in with headquarters. I would give them an update on the game — the result, the gate, injuries and anything else important. Once a month, I would get the next month's schedule.

While Christmas brought mixed emotions with some being homesick, we also had another Christmas almost every month. We would find out what town we would be in on a certain date and families were informed. They would send their mail to the post office and the sponsor would usually pick up the mail and deliver it to us at the game. It was one of our favorite days of the month.

Towards the end of my career with the Red Heads I was contacted by Lee Bakunin. I had never heard of him. He just asked me for a few minutes of his time. He had seen an article in Sports Illustrated on the All American Red Heads. He was very impressed and thought he might be the person to take women's basketball to the next level — a professional basketball league. It would be like the early days of the NBA. Some growing pains, for sure, but with the passage of Title IX, it was time. We would be touring as well, but for purposes of publicity.

I was very excited. He also spoke with others. Karen Logan and Mary Hounsell both like the idea enough that we all decided to give it a try.

In the fall of 1975, we all headed to Phoenix, which is where the team would be based out of and be called the Phoenix Pink Panthers. We even had our 'own' practice facility in a sense. It was the same gym where the NBA Phoenix Suns practiced. The players would even work out with us some and rebound for us. Can you imagine? NBA men rebounding for a women's professional team. We were earning their respect.

We stayed there for a bit and played a few games, yet money at the gate wasn't what we hoped it would be and Lee moved us to Indianapolis and our city name changed. I would be both player and coach, similar to my days with the Red Heads. We would stay with Conrad and Velma Stephens, who fully opened their home to us. They were just gracious people and I couldn't help but wonder that it had to be a strain of them for seven women to move into their house. Yet, they also believed in Lee's vision and wanted to be a part of it. We ate mostly at buffets and stuffed ourselves whenever we could, since their money was at a shortage.

The league would never really get off the ground, but a game was set up with another barnstorming team, the Arkansas Lassies. This was a team owned by Linda Yearby.

I played in my first professional women's basketball game against another women's team. After thousands of games as a professional basketball player, this was going to be a first for me and probably a first in history. You might think we felt more relaxed because we weren't playing men. But it was the opposite — it was a lot more intense. We wanted to make sure we did everything right, and probably tried too hard to be perfect. We ended up losing the game 65-63.

After that game we continued to travel. Lee called me about a competition on the ABC TV network called "The Superstars." It would feature some of the greatest women's athletes of many different sports. They would then get together and compete in sports other than what they were known for. We all went down to an event at the Astrodome, but when it came down to the competition, I was able to bring my mother down with me to Florida to watch. It meant the world to me to be able to show her how women's sports were growing and respected.

I had deferred to my teammate Karen Logan, and Karen would participate in "The Superstars." The Panthers would never play another game, and it was the last time I would see Karen.

Yet, even though the Panthers were done, I would end up getting another call. This time it was Linda Yearby of the Lassies. She must have heard about the Panthers folding. She offered me the coaching job and taking the team on the road. I wasn't ready to hang my shoes up. It was my decision to be a player/coach. After reporting to the base camp of Ionia, Michigan, we had the discussion of a partnership.

The team was already there when I arrived. I'm not sure if they had a training camp, but it was apparent that the days of barnstorming teams were coming down to the end. I don't remember how many games we played, but it was not a full schedule — maybe four or five a week. We drove from town to town in a station wagon and I also did the driving.

In 1976, I realized it was time for me move on. I dissolved the partnership, and left. This time I hung up my shoes, with no regrets.

Elvera "Peps" Neuman

Career 1962-88

Texas Cowgirls, Shooting Stars, Arkansas Lassies, Arkansas Gems

As told by Elvera Neuman

In 1962 the Eden Valley High School Annual came out. I was a senior and it stated that my plans for after school were playing women's professional basketball. At the time many remembered the remark of the superintendent of the school — a remark that in today's society would have him labeled as a "male chauvinist pig." He was quoted as saying, "Can you imagine — that Neuman girl wants to play professional basketball?"

I was about to embark on a career that would last for 26 years My desire to play basketball when I was a kid in school knew no boundaries. While I was still in high school I would organize six-on-six games for my town to play other towns. I had to lobby the school to form a team and was able to convince a school advisor to start a team.

One game we had a blizzard and my dad would not allow me to drive the tractor to get to the game. But that wouldn't stop me. I simply walked.

Right before I graduated from Eden Valley High School in Minnesota in 1962, I was contacted by the Texas Cowgirls to try out for them. I not only made the team, I ended up becoming a coach.

I got the nickname 'Peps' because I had a lot of pep and was alway drinking Pepsi-Cola instead of water. The name Peps stuck with me throughout my long career.

As a rookie with the Cowgirls, we had training camp in a gym with a tile floor. I'd run over 100 laps around the gym, with each step pounding on that hard floor. I eventually got shin splints. They didn't know how to treat it, so I would have extra hot whirlpools at the schools and they would take tape and wrap it tightly all the way up from the top of my ankle to below the knees. It put a strain on my muscles and I would get tape burns from pulling the tape off every night, as there was no foam wraps or spray. They even brought in another player. I thought my basketball career was going to end after only three months, but the good Lord helped me through it. The only way I knew I had shin splints was because I was limping as I was walking around in a new pair of penny loafer shoes and I could hear my clip-clapping when I walked. Thank God for Christmastime, when we got some rest and my health got better.

It took a lot of courage to leave the comforts of home, friends and family, but the adventure was worth it. We didn't have cell phones, etc., so when I did get back home, my relatives and friends would love to hear our stories.

Being a farm girl, I was naive but knew how to work and was always active and anxious to play basketball and experience the adventures of travel. In the early 1960s when I started my career, there weren't many motels, so we had to stay in hotels. They had only one bathroom, with a single toilet, sink and bathtub at the end of the hallway to accommodate all of the people on that floor. Nowadays I couldn't stay unless I had my own private bathroom in my room. We didn't have TV or radio and our rooms, but in later years, we bought a little portable one and then bought a small record player and played vinyl records on it.

To fill the time I would write a lot of letters to my family and friends. When we would have mail call, I would get 10-20 letters in return. Another way I enjoyed passing the time on the road was exploring the towns we stayed in on foot. One of my teammates who was also a farm girl and I would often wake up early get up and walk around the town, even though the stores were closed.

One of the ways we saved money was by not eating much. The team captain would ask us every day if we ate. The saying back then on the road was, "No eat, no play, no pay."

That first year we weren't allowed to eat at fast food restaurants such as McDonald's. We weren't allowed to eat at a place like McDonald's because we were professional athletes. Restaurants like McDonald's were still relatively new and while I liked their food they weren't a classy 'sit down' type of restaurant at that time. However, the team would park the limousine at a sit-down restaurant and a teammate and I would walk to a McDonald's — sometimes a few blocks away, other times many blocks. With food in the bag and change in our pocket, we ate our meal on the way back to the limo, then sat in the eight-door limousine and waited for the rest of the team to finish eating at the restaurant.

After two years with the Cowgirls I decided I wanted a career in basketball, so three teammates and I formed the Shooting Stars. A booking agent persuaded us change the name to the Arkansas Lassies because it was more feminine and easier to book.

When we pulled into town, people would tell each other that we had arrived and showed us great respect. On the basketball floor we had mutual respect for the men's teams we played, for the referees who were donating their time, and the people in the audience who were part of our stunts. We liked it when the guys showed up with a dunk or a good play.

We played by the old men's rules — a jump ball at the beginning of each quarter and a free throw on every foul. There was no three-point line and no shot clock. We used a men's regulation basketball — not the slightly smaller women's ball.

A banner year for me on the court was in 1969, when I scored 108 points in a game at Mount Clemens, Michigan in the Detroit area. I scored over 80 points in a game many times that year.

Arkansas Gems owner, coach and player Elvera "Peps" Neuman, circa 1970

In 1973, after having basketball partners for quite a few years, I decided to be the sole owner and booking agent so I could run the business and basketball show the way I wanted to. Since it was a new start, a new name was in order. We were now called the Arkansas Gems. Ironically, none of the players were from Arkansas. I recruited mostly in the Midwest, but because I had put my heart, sweat and soul into the Arkansas name, most people I worked with would remember the name Arkansas.

I created Peps Sports Incorporated for the office that scheduled and took care of the Gems business, located near Eden Valley. The Gems practices were at the Eden Valley High School gym and training camp was at the Elvera Neuman farm near Eden Valley until we moved the Peps Sports Incorporated office to Clearwater, Minnesota in 1977. We would still use the Eden Valley gym for training and practice.

I made it a point to book our games so that we could gain new experiences and see new territory. We wanted to go west, so I booked a tour to California and the west coast, I also booked a tour to the South — Texas, New Mexico, the gulf coast and and Florida. We even took five to seven days off as a vacation in Florida, since a lot of the high schools had basketball playoffs and a lot of the gyms were in use. Then we would book games up the east coast to New York, and all of New England, then to the Midwest before getting back in Minnesota at the end of April. Traveling with the team was great fun, since it was like traveling with family. I wouldn't have traveled alone.

Before the Gems games started, the team had a special warm-ups routine that eventually led to shooting free throws and different shots. I would shoot half court shots over my head with my back to the basket, making a good percentage. It was such a long shot and the way I shot it, they were proclaiming me "The Happy Hooker" in reference to an adult movie of the '70s. We had a halftime show where I did a basketball handling routine, some dribbling with my knees, spinning a basketball and dribbling two basketballs around and through my legs and the glow ball act, where the lights were turned off and I did a basketball routine in the dark. I did the basketball and comedy show with the help of my special teammates. As Frank Sinatra sang, "I did it my way."

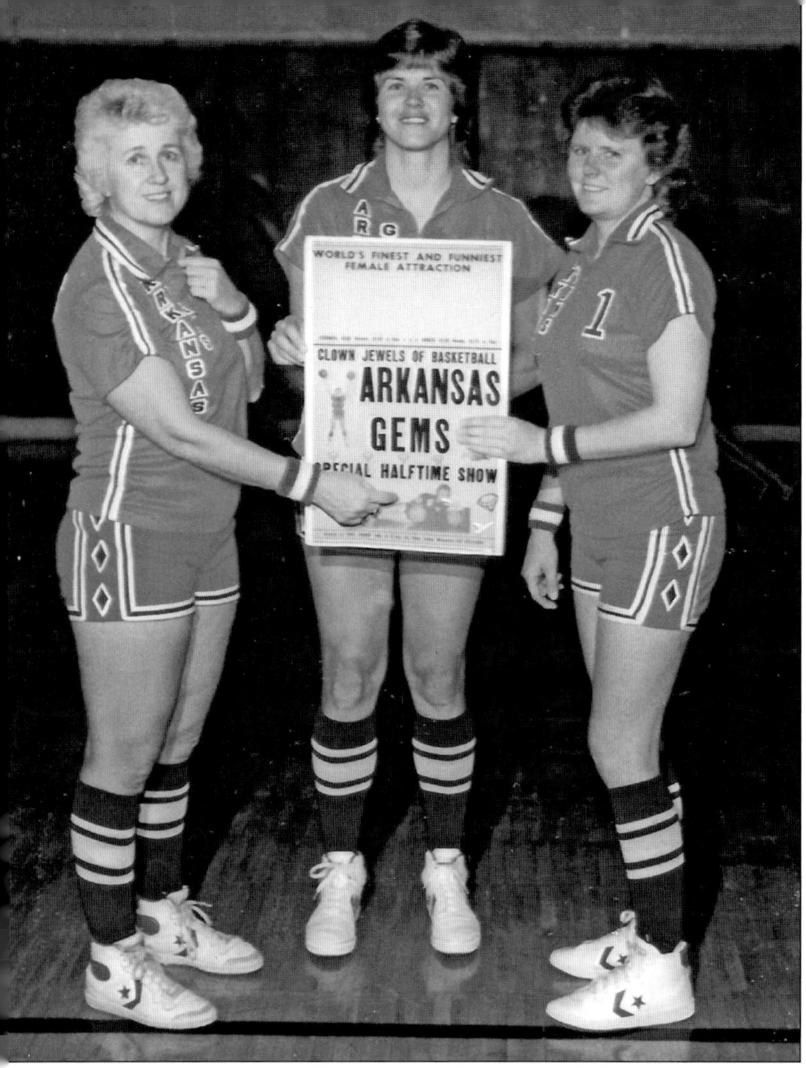

Arkansas Gems (L-R) Elvera "Peps" Neuman, Judy Oelrich and Vicky Nelson, circa 1980s

In 1982 we played against Lawrence Taylor and the rest of the New York Giants football team at a college in New York City. We all had our hair done for the big game. After introductions each of us received a beautiful bouquet of roses from the different Giants players. In 1983 the rest of the Gems and I did a 20-minute special halftime show at an exhibition game between the North Carolina Tar Heels and the Yugoslavia Olympic team at Chapel Hill, North Carolina. This featured Michael Jordan and other greats while being coach by Coach Dean Smith. We had a game the night before in New York state, then drove all night to get to Chapel Hill. We were tired, but what a great experience! Two days later we had a game in New York state again.

Between 1983–88 we would perform at armed forces bases across the United States. Playing and touring the different bases was unique. If the game time was 7 o'clock, it started precisely at 7 o'clock — not a few minutes early, not a few minutes late.

A big experience was playing the New York prisons. Luckily we had toured Alcatraz outside of San Francisco. They had told us about the life of a prisoner. It put us at ease when we played in the prisons. We had to be searched and locked in a room until the inmates were marched into their seats. We then we went in and played basketball and did our show. We were the first women's team allowed inside the walls of Sonoma prison for hardened criminals. We did go into the audience and tease the inmates with my fun-filled jokes. I understand the guards were worried that one of the inmates would take us hostage or harm us. I never gave it a second thought until after we were done with our game and gone to the next game. Actually all of the inmates were very much gentlemen towards us.

When we played in Nebraska and my front tooth cap fell off during practice. I went to a teacher's desk, got some super glue and glued it back in until I could see a dentist.

In New York City we left the car parked on the street with our mascot — the cat — in it, so we could eat breakfast around the corner. When we came back the window was smashed and they had robbed the van, but the thieves didn't take the cat or anything behind the cat, thank God.

Our Suburban caught on fire outside of St. Louis from a wheel bearing that I had just fixed. It ended up burning our money for three games, some uniforms, clothes, souvenir pennants, programs etc. We got a lot of luggage and more out, but when I went to go back in, they wouldn't let me get inside the car, afraid I'd get smoke inhalation, burned or that the vehicle was going to blow up. It created a bit of a hardship for us. At that time I didn't have a credit card, and even though I had plenty of money in the bank in Minnesota, no one would rent or sell me a vehicle without cash or a credit card. Friends and family drove down and picked us up.

We traveled through many snowstorms over the years. We often would stop and dig out stuck vehicles so we could clear the road. Sometimes the whole team would get out push to help stranded drivers on their way.

We would travel the country many times, visiting such places as Gettysburg, Niagara Falls, Mount Rushmore and the Naismith Memorial Basketball Hall of Fame**.** In Washington, DC, we visited the grave of President John F. Kennedy's and the changing of the guards. In Florida we went to Disneyworld, saw many attractions and went deep sea fishing. But we also saw things that weren't so nice, such as the segregation in the South during the Jim Crow era.

We also took advantage of the opportunity to go to the different NBA arenas and see some of our favorite players that we had only seen on TV (Minnesota didn't have an NBA team at that time). Our schedule even gave us an opportunity to see the Boston Celtics at the old Boston Garden. I was really thrilled to meet and have my picture taken with one of my idols, Meadowlark Lemon of the Harlem Globetrotters. Later in the year they gave us free tickets to their games when our schedule allowed.

Wherever we went with our team jackets on, people would stop us on the street and ask for autographs, since they thought we were famous. The best compliment a person can give someone is asking for an autograph, so no matter how busy I was I always tried to accommodate them.

Unfortunately, no accurate records were kept of the games when I played basketball against men's teams from 1962 to 1988. I played over 3,300 games scored over 120,000 points. If there had been three-point line back then I would have scored a lot more. When our schedule took us close to our teammates' families' or friends' homes, we were honored to enjoy their hospitality. We enjoyed great conversation and delicious home-cooked meals.

None of us barnstormers got rich financially, but the experiences we enjoyed and the friendships we built are priceless. Teammates like Judy Oelrich, Marli Wilt and Vicky Nelson helped make this a reality for many years.

"Remember, think women's basketball!"

Bessie Shelton (Elliott)

Career 1962-64
All American Red Heads

As told by Bessie Shelton Elliott to Jolene Ammons

Bessie Shelton of the Red Heads, circa 1963

When I joined the All America Red Heads in 1962, we were in Ash Flat, Arkansas, just prior to heading to Canada for nearly a month. We played at Prince of Wales College, where we were escorted on to the court by a bagpipe band, dressed in kilts and the works. After the Canada swing we headed south into New England, where we played two doubleheaders in two days, winning all four games.

We did a bit of everything. We played at Ft. Bragg military base, then headed to Cleveland to be on the Mike Douglas Show. Some games were so far apart we would have to travel all night and most of the next day just to get into town in time to change into our uniforms and play once again.

During my second season, one of the most somber moments in U.S. history happened when I was on the road.

It was November 22, 1963. My teammates and I were traveling on the road when across the little AM radio was a special news bulletin. President Kennedy had been assassinated in Dallas. Seven normally very talkative women became very silent, a tear flowing down more than one face. We were out to play basketball and entertain local townsfolk. Never did we think we would hear that the President of the United States had been murdered.

After we checked in, we sought out TVs and became glued to them until it was time to head to the game. The crowd at the game was very quiet and somber. It was an empty feeling playing that night.

The town we played in that fateful day? Ironically, it was Whitehouse, Ohio.

Before I retired at the end of the season, we played in my hometown of Ardmore, Oklahoma. My family was there, including my brother, Jessie, who had coached the Red Heads several seasons previously, and my sister Emogene, who also played for them.

It was topped off with a 54-53 win over the local men.

Sandy Mann

CAREER 1963-71
ALL AMERICAN RED HEADS AND SOUTHERN BELLES

As told by Sandy Mann

I was in the seventh grade when the All American Red Heads came to our school in Desha, Arkansas and played. I went home from that game and said to my parents, "If you will put a basketball goal up in the backyard, and get me a basketball, I'm going to play with the Red Heads." They did, and I did.

Although I thought I was grown, I really was a baby, fresh out of high school, when I showed up in training camp in Caraway, Arkansas that day. I will never forget standing in the motel room, as the door opens and in walks a girl that is 6-foot-7 (Lee Kaschmitter). I was so green that I didn't even know that girls grew to be 6-feet-7 inches tall. She had to duck down to get in the door. Now that was an eye opener.

While we trained in Caraway, we stayed at the Jami-Bee Motel in Jonesboro, Arkansas. The Jami-Bee had a little coffee shop. These were the years when you put a nickel in the jukebox and played and danced to some of the greatest songs of the day — the same songs we heard on Dick Clark's "American Bandstand." One season Betty Springer, Glenda Ledbetter and I spent a lot of time listening to their jukebox. Betty was simply wild about The Village Stompers song "Washington Square." Like a time machine, my mind takes me back to 1963, when that song was at the top of the charts. We all liked it, but Springer was just crazy about it.

In later years we would travel in four-door stretch limos. However, let me tell you, that first year there was no such thing. We traveled in a "funeral family car," I kid you not. It was one of those old gray Cadillacs that had the front seat, and backseat, which was way back there and, out of the back of the front seat, you pulled two little jump seats out, and that's what two of us had to sit on. It was so cold in that thing that ice would freeze on the INSIDE of the back windows. We would stuff Kleenex all around those windows, trying to stay warm. Yessirree, that was barnstorming in 1963!

There were only six of us on the team, and "the Big'un," as we called Lee, fell during a scrimmage game in training camp, and injured her knee. This left five of us and we hit the road.

Red Heads Sandy Mann, Jolene "Jo Jo" Ammons in front of Whitey, fall of 1966

We did not have a single "sub" and we loved it. No sitting on the bench for us. There were three of us who were rookies, 18 years old and right out of high school. We came to play ball, and play ball we did. We played the west coast that year and, of course, played every night and twice on Sunday.

After each game, we would stand on the court, making ourselves available to the crowd. A lot of them wanted to come down, visit with us, and get our autograph.

The crowd saw 32 minutes of glamour and fun. What they didn't see was hours upon hours of traveling thousands of miles. Up more than half the night, ironing, washing uniforms out by hand, doing our hair — the usual stuff that you do at home — then sleeping in the car the next day as we traveled on to the next town.

Sometimes there would be too many miles to make it to the next game. On those occasions we would pack to "travel after the game." We went to the gym, instead of a motel, when we arrived in town. This meant working out all afternoon right at the gym. Ironing our uniforms on somebody's suitcase, if you could find a plug-in somewhere in the gym. Then we'd load up after the game and travel most of the night in order to be close enough to make it to tomorrow night's game on time. Whew!

At one point, during my second year with the Red Heads, I had developed a severe case of homesickness. My family was an extremely close one, and in spite of how very much I loved playing basketball and "barnstorming," I missed them dearly. One teammate was having the same problem.

One day we had the bright idea of running away "to" home. Ben Overman was the coach at the time. Knowing it would be hard to outsmart Ben, much planning went into our little venture.

We packed our belongings, waited till we knew Ben was taking a nap, called a taxi and we were "on the lam!" We went rushing into the bus station and I told the clerk, "We need two tickets on the first bus outta here, and we don't care where it's going." The lady looked at me kind of funny but she sold me the tickets.

We nervously paced about the station, obviously in distress, as we knew full well that if Ben found out he'd be coming to get us. Well, it wasn't very long till Ben came rushing through the door. He looked frazzled. His hair was in disarray. He had his overcoat on and shoes, but no socks. He "herded" us over to a corner and started talking to us in low tones.

He calmly counseled with us, and reassured us. We finally came to our senses and agreed to go back with him. You probably would expect that this would be where the story ends. Nope, 'fraid not.

On the way back to the motel (I was sitting in the front seat with Ben) the cops pulled us over. They asked Ben to get out of the vehicle. He stood at the back of the car, trying to convince them that everything is "legit."

One of the cops opened the driver's door and leaned in, taking a look at us. He asked me, "Do ya'll know this guy?" I told him that we did, and they let Ben go.

I shudder to think about the outcome of our "adventure" if the kid in that front seat had said, "we've never seen this guy before."

Poor Ben took the whole thing very well. I guess he understood how very homesick we would sometimes be.

As a Red Head, one season we went to Prince Rupert Canada and stayed for three days and played three games. The folks there were so good to us. They took us out on a fishing boat, into the open waters of the ocean.

Then we boarded a ship and traveled over to Alaska and up its coast. We would get off in a different town each day and play a game, then move on the next day. Some of our traveling was by amphibious planes, also. There was Ketchikan, Sitka, Juneau, Fairbanks and Anchorage. Beginning with Anchorage, it started being daylight a big part of the night. Up to this point it was beautiful, shirtsleeve weather, no snow or ice.

Next we flew to the top of the world, Point Barrow. From there we saw Alaska as I had imagined it to be — solid ice, a frozen land.

Barrow was a very small village and the airport was just a little building with a few tables and file cabinets. Except for a two story building, which was the hotel, the village was made up of small huts. One little building served as a café. The nearby Arctic Ocean was frozen solid, and we saw people riding by on dog sleds.

They hauled us from place to place in a military ambulance, one of those trucks with two benches in the back and straps to hold onto. It was daylight 24 hours a day now, and everywhere we went there were little kids running behind the truck after us. The kids would be playing outside at 3 or 4 o'clock in the morning, I asked a guy "don't they ever sleep?" He laughed and said, "When they want to." The kids were always feeling our hair, as they had never seen red hair.

We were in Barrow for three days to play three games. That first day, someone told us, "If no one kills a whale, you will have a packed gym every night. It will be packed, with the same people, for each game." Well, we were very lucky because no one brought in a whale, and we had a packed house, standing room only, for all three games.

When we walked into the gym for that first game, we had the most wonderful surprise waiting for us. The elders of the tribe were seated on folding chairs at mid court, wearing their finest clothing. They were there to perform a ceremony, in our honor.

These beautiful people have a custom of telling stories, through dance. They each stood, one at a time, and told their story for us. I have never, in my life felt more honored than I did at that moment. They were facing us, as we sat on the bench watching them. A reporter sat down on the bench by me. He leaned over and whispered to me, "You might want to pass the word down to your coach, that they might come over and invite him to join them in a dance. Tell him that, if they do, he should get out there, because it would insult them if he refused." He then added that, actually, they might invite all of us to join them in the dance.

Well, they did indeed invite us to join them, which we did. What a thrill! This is one of the most amazing things that has ever happened to me. Then the reporter asked me if I would like to have a souvenir from Barrow. Of course, I said that I would. He said that he knew and an older man, an artist, who did beautiful etchings. He said, "He is retired but I think I can get him to make you something."

At our third game he brought me the most amazing gift. It was a thin, dark gray object, about seven inches long and four inches wide. It had ripples running through it. On the face of it was a bear, standing on land that came up to a point (Point Barrow). Below was a man going by on a dogsled. The artist had signed it, Willie Sielak. Actually, the material he used was the hard palate from a whale's mouth.

While we were at the airport, waiting for our plane, all the kids were there, squeezed into that little building with us. We had to climb up on tables and file cabinets, or anything that we could find, to try to stay above them, as they pulled at us and our clothing. It must have been how the Beatles felt with their fans. We were signing autographs for them, at the same time trying not to be "pulled under."

We literally "made a run" for our plane as they chased us. They actually pulled the belt off of one of the girls' coat — I think it was Brenda Moon. We barely made it into the door of that plane. Whew!

This was just one, of many great experiences that I had while barnstorming this great country, playing basketball and having a wonderful time doing it. I can honestly say that I wouldn't trade being an All American Red Head, for anything.

One year we had the opportunity to appear on "I've Got a Secret," which was a popular game show at that time. Steve Allen was the host. I really didn't want to go, but the producers insisted that I come because I was the "dribbler." Then I found out that, not only did I have to go, but I had to be on the panel, have "the secret" and do a dribbling routine.

The show also flew a young man in. He was on the panel with me, and my secret was that my team had played his team … and my team won.

We arrived in New York City, and a lady called me and said, "I need to pick you up so we can shop for you some clothes. The show would be shown live so we all went to pay phones to call home. There was a small room backstage that was high in the air. I'd go up there, put on the dress, come down some rickety stairs, out on stage, sit down and go through the "secret routine" with the young man and people who were standing in for the celebrity panel. Whew!

Every time I came down or went up those stairs I passed by a fellow who was plunking around on a baby grand piano. After a couple of rounds I realized that it was Neil Sedaka, one of my all time favorite performers, sitting there playing that piano. I was so young and naive I didn't say a word to him. Grrrrrrrrr.

Finally came the real thing and here I went. After the secret, which the panel did guess, I had to run backstage, off with that dress, run back out and do my dribbling routine. The other four then joined me and we did the "Magic Circle" ball handling routine.

Also while in New York City we stayed at the Hotel Knickerbocker. Each night we would play a game in a different borough.

Red Head Sandy Mann with 1960 Heisman Trophy winner and Boston Patriots football player Joe Bellino, 1966-67

One night, we were waiting in the lobby, dressed out and in our warm-ups, to go to the game. A man walked through the lobby, stopped, looked at us, and said, "What's the deal"? We told him and he said, "I am the manager of the Peppermint Lounge, next door. When you get back from your game, you will be my guests at the lounge."

Well us girls took him up on his invitation. We were already having a great time when the manager of Herman's Hermits came in and talked to the manager. He said that they had just flown in from England, first time in the U.S.A. They were on the way to California to film the television show "Shindig" and had a long layover. He asked if they could set up and play a few songs. The manager said of course, so we got to see Herman's Hermits first appearance in this country.

I also played for the Southern Belles for two seasons. It was a great women's professional basketball team. Once we checked into a motel in Medicine Lodge, Kansas. When we woke up the next morning there had been a blizzard. The first thing I noticed was a pile of snow INSIDE the door. It had snowed so hard that it had blown under the door. The snow was chest deep. We were so lucky to be right next door to a café. However, we did have to wade quite a distance to get there, which was difficult in snow that was chest-deep. Of course we had a game scheduled, in another town, for that night. Although we players tried to convince the coach that it was futile, let alone dangerous, to travel he insisted on leaving. You couldn't even see the roads, just the top of the road signs. We didn't make it out of town. There were choppers dropping hay to livestock. It really was a bad situation. The coach had to turn around and go back to the motel where we checked BACK in. This was one of the few times that we ever missed a game.

As we traveled around the country, playing basketball, we usually knew our upcoming schedule only about a month ahead of time. I recall one time we were hearing on the news, in advance of playing in Watervliet, Michigan, that there was a serial killer operating in that area. Now we were pretty worried about that, because the owner sent out promotional items like posters and prints of individual players to the folks who had booked us into a town and they would be put in the front windows of stores. We could just imagine that certain individual getting one of our posters and deciding which one of us he would grab. We decided that we did not want to spend the night in that town so we packed to travel after the game. It turned out that we weren't the only ones concerned about our safety. The police met us at the gym, escorted us to our dressing room, and locked us in. They guarded the door and were very "present" during the game and halftime show. We were also "locked in" during halftime. Then, of course, we were escorted to our vehicle, after the game. We traveled right on out of there.

One night, we were waiting to go to the game in Homerville, Georgia, which is the hometown of the outstanding pro basketball player, Jolene Ammons. Dressed in our uniforms and warm-ups, Mickey Gay, Glenda Ledbetter and I were outside, by the swimming pool. Only three feet away was a wading pool for kids. Let me say that all of this was a perfect recipe — for disaster.

I was standing and bouncing on the diving board when I caught a strange movement out of the corner of my eye. Then I saw that Glenda had grabbed Mickey by the shoulders (they were occupying the small space between the two pools, with Mickey's back to the kiddy pool). Glenda was pushing then pulling Mickey to and fro, as if she was going to push Mickey into the pool. I opened my mouth, to scold them and say "coach will kill all of us if we get wet!"

Well, before I could scream at them, Glenda's hand slipped and INTO THE POOL Mickey went. The next thing I saw was Glenda's back as she ran toward the motel room, that long ponytail bouncing as she ran.

I looked at Mickey and she was standing in the middle of the kiddy pool ON ONE FOOT. I convinced her that she had to put that dry foot down and walk out, which she did. We ran to the room. The next few minutes were spent with us trying to squeeze as much water as possible out of Mickey's warm-ups, shoes and socks.

When we got to the gym we had to walk all the way across the court to get to our dressing room. We gathered around Mickey and walked, as a unit, across the court, hiding her the coach. Every step we took we could hear ole Mick's squish, squish, squish. About halfway across I looked behind us and there was a set of Mickey's wet footprints as far as I could see. I can't tell you how many times Mickey fell that night but it was a LOT.

This is just one of the wonderful times that we had while being paid to travel this country and do the thing that we loved most — playing basketball.

Glenda "Twinkles" Ledbetter (Litaker)

Career 1963-66
All American Red Heads and Southern Belles

As told by Glenda Ledbetter Litaker

My mom was my inspiration. She loved the game. Her team played full court. She played in a league after finishing school. The team was sponsored by a local factory and Mom excelled at it, according to friends and family who were there to see.

I played two years as an All American Red Head (1963-64 and 1964-65) and one as a Southern Belle. I was recruited to play with the Red Heads by Lurner Williams. He wrote for the Savannah Morning News and on the side scouted for Orwell Moore, owner of the All American Red Heads. After Orwell signed me, I came to Jonesboro, Arkansas by train, then took a taxi to the motel where we would stay during training camp. When I tried to open the motel room door, Sandy Mann opened it from the inside. It scared us both and we started to laugh, It was the beginning of a long friendship!

My first year we began training camp with six players but lost one to a knee injury before the season even started. That left us with five. To us it meant no one had to sit on the bench!

During the years we played small towns and big cities usually traveling two-lane roads. We played most every night and doubleheaders on Sundays. We loved it!

Playing basketball was only part of the job. We were there to entertain, so we had dribbling, ball handling routines, trick shots and a "Magic Circle." The trick shots included the Dipsy Doodle, Spin Shot, Knee Shot, Head Shot, Flip Shot and a Piggy Back Shot.

Some of these are self-explanatory, but the Dipsy Doodle was one of my halftime shots. I would stand facing the goal. Holding the basketball with both hands I would bend over, throw the ball back through my legs up to the basket.

"Chatter" was also part of the game. We talked to the guys we were playing, the refs and the crowd. We called the guys "Curly" or "Smiley" or anything to get the crowd's attention! When the guys had the basketball up over their head we pretended to tickle them. I was the "clown" so I dealt the ref misery, such as following him step by step down the court, hiding the ball and making faces behind his back!

Traveling on the road was always interesting. I was introduced to trying to walk on the snow and ice in Fort Smith, Arkansas. Betty Springer and I were walking down the street when both of my feet shot straight out. There I sat on the snow-covered sidewalk while my friend continued on as if she didn't know me. It was just the beginning of many memories about which I still laugh.

Driving through the mountains I couldn't figure out why some of the highways had swinging gates on the sides. When Coach said it was so they could close the roads I thought he was kidding! The fog in California was another experience. When we left the motel heading for the game we sometimes did a tour of the residential area.

Red Heads' funny gal Glenda "Twinkles" Ledbetter reverses roles with the officials, circa 1964

I considered myself so lucky! What other job in 1963 could I possibly have that paid me to play a game that I loved, travel through 48 of the 50 United States and parts of Canada. All of this while making friends and memories that would last a lifetime!

I wish I could have known that young lady who later became my mom. She would have been ecstatic to have the opportunity to barnstorm across the country! She encouraged me to follow my dreams, even though there were people who told her they would never allow their daughter to go. I did!

Betty Springer

Career 1963-64
All American Red Heads

As told by Betty Springer to Sandy Mann

My name is Betty Springer. I lived and attended school in Flint, Michigan. Basketball was my favorite activity. I was the captain of our team.

Later, while attending cosmetology school, I was playing ball in a league and met Shelby Tedder, who was a former All American Red Head. She suggested that I try out to play for the Red Heads. Shelby contacted Orwell Moore, owner of the All American Red Heads, and arranged a tryout for me. After the tryout, he signed me to a contract, and I began touring as a professional basketball player.

There were two teams that year, and I played on the west coast team. We played every night and twice on Sunday, and only against men. Playing bymen's rules, full court, was a new experience for me. Feeling like a "bird out of a cage," I absolutely loved it.

We played skilled, competitive basketball and won most of our games. It was exhibition basketball, however, so some show was included. We all participated in this, both during the game and at halftime.

Coach Moore gave everyone a nickname. He chose names that he felt fit each person. He told me that I had a lot of personality and "pizzazz." The next thing I knew I found myself being billed as "The Personality Gal."

We always played hard the first quarter, to show folks that we were skilled players. I played the wing position and had a good set shot. Then we started mixing in some show. I loved this. I would call the guy I was guarding shorty, curly or skinny. This was called "chatter" and Coach Moore told me that I had a knack for knowing what to say.

As far as the entertainment side of our game, our team "clown" was Glenda Ledbetter who, much to the crowd's delight, dealt the referees a great deal of grief. At halftime we entertained the crowd with the "Magic Circle," fancy passing, trick shots, dribbling and ball handling routines. I did a passing routine, juggling routine and a knee shot.

Red Head Betty Springer, 1964-65

Late nights were spent getting ready for the next day and the next game. We washed our uniforms, ironed clothes, colored and fixed our hair. As I was a professional hairdresser, I was volunteered to do everyone's hair. We also packed our luggage at night so we would be ready to go early the next morning.

More often than not, there were lots of miles between games. On occasion we had to travel most of the night, after a game, in order to get close enough to make it on time to the next game.

For instance, one night we left a packed gym, traveled all night and all the next day, heading to Cloudcroft, New Mexico. We stopped only to eat a couple of times and to refuel. This is a prime example of why we had learned to order dessert first. If we didn't, we didn't get dessert.

In Cloudcroft, we walked into a packed gym and a standing ovation, this from a gym full of people who were awaiting our arrival. This demonstrates how, as we traveled this great country, we received warm welcomes from packed houses. Also, how our fans felt about our skills, and the entertainment that we brought them.

Becky Harp (Pritchett)

CAREER 1965-69

ALL AMERICAN RED HEADS

As told by Becky Harp Pritchett

I'll try to make this short, but we gotta go back a long time ago — March 25, 1965 to be exact. That is the day I received a letter from Coach Orwell Moore introducing me to the All American Red Heads. I had never heard of them before, and I certainly couldn't understand why he would be looking at me. I had made the All-State team (and was told by officials that I would have been chosen MVP if we had not lost in the state championships by two points). But still … professional? I was about to pursue a career in commercial art in a college near my hometown, but I wasn't about to let this opportunity pass me by.

I had full support from my parents. My mom gave up a career with the Sports Arena Blues basketball team (later called the Atlanta Tomboys) to follow my dad in his career as a minor league baseball player. My brother was playing in a semipro league in the Navy, and my sister was just beginning her freshman year in basketball. Well, here this little Georgia girl takes off to Caraway, Arkansas for an experience she would cherish for the rest of her life.

The very first night we reported to training we dyed each other's hair. Oh well, I guess I just let the secret out. There were a few natural Red Heads, but I wasn't one of them. I cried like a baby and thought to myself, I wish I had gone back to Georgia with my parents. But I got over it and blended right in. The next few weeks were grueling. I can still feel the pain from the workouts and sprints. I remember one girl who had to go home for a while to get over shin splints.

Then came the travel. We played somewhere different every day. I can still hardly believe they paid me to play ball, travel all over the U.S. meet and play against some of the greatest professionals ever. Heck, I would have paid them to let me play. I still consider myself very fortunate to have been associated with some of the most talented female athletes this country has ever known.

There was Jolene Ammons, who could dribble rings around any player I know and who had a trick up her sleeve while at the same time was keeping her eye on the basket. She was truly an entertainer whom I always looked up to.

Then there was Charlotte Adams. You name it, she could do it. When she shot from outside, you knew it was headed for the net. She was a team player who encouraged each girl to always give that little extra. Pat Overman was a great ball handler and comedian. She loved her Pepsi-Colas too. I can still see her pulling up the ref's pants leg or giving him a stiff kick in the backside as he bends over to pick up a ball she had cleverly put near her foot on purpose.

We had to prove ourselves many times. You could tell a men's team would not know what to expect at the beginning of a game, but it wouldn't take long before they realized they were up against some very talented and very competitive ballplayers. Before long they would realize they were going to have to put out some effort to stay in the game. We won their respect many, many times.

Music on the road was our eighth player on the team. It was the '60s. We listened to the Beatles, the Beach Boys and many other artists. However, there was a song on the radio that all of the players would tease me about — Dusty Springfield's big hit "Son of a Preacher Man." Well, I had a boyfriend, and it so happened he was the son of a preacher man. He would even follow us to some of the games. I was to be on the show "The Dating Game," but instead became the wife of that preacher's son and have been ever married since.

Red Head Becky Harp shooting from knees in front of a packed gymnasium, 1965-66

Aaronette Eiffling (Housley)

Career 1965-66
All American Red Heads

As told by Aaronette Eiffling Housley

Our high school team won the Louisiana State Class A Championship in May of 1965 and shortly thereafter I received a letter from Mr. Orwell Moore on All American Red Head stationery, congratulating me on our accomplishment and asking if I would be interested in playing for the Red Heads. Of course, at that point in girls' basketball, going to college and playing was not an option. So, needless to say, I was blown away by the thought that the All American Red Heads would even know who I was, much less offer to discuss me playing as a Red Head.

Aaronette Eiffling of the Red Heads, 1966

In less than a week he was sitting down at a table at a local restaurant in Vidalia, Louisiana, with me, my parents and my high school coach (Katherine Tucker). He offered me a one-year contract to play with the Red Heads. My parents were thrilled, but they didn't even get a chance to ask many questions, as anyone that knew Mr. Moore knew they could not get a word in edgewise.

And then it all began. I reported to training camp on October 1, 1965 in Caraway, Arkansas. And my, my — after two days, I realized I had never been in shape — I just thought I had. We had to load up in a Mercury station wagon and go to the local high school gym for our practices. I hated it when I had to crawl into the car and go all the way to the back seat. Sore, was not a strong enough word to describe the pain. Every muscle in my body hurt. Even smiling was painful. But I made it through training camp and then we "hit the road."

What a year! We visited amazing places and met amazing people along this journey. I will never forget my teammates and the fun times we had on the road each and every day. Nor will I forget the beautiful country we had the privilege of seeing along the way to each stop. Never in my wildest dreams did I think I would ever have the opportunity to travel *and* get to continue to play basketball. I even got to go up in the Empire State Building and had my picture made with my "red hair."

I remember playing — I think it was Indianapolis — and one of the men playing was a former NBA player, Clyde Lovellette. It was an honor playing against a professional. He was the first player to ever be on a team that won the NCAA Championship, NBA World Championship and Olympic Gold medal and then be inducted into the Basketball Hall of Fame. Big, big guy, but so nice!

At halftime we had a special circle routine, where we each had our little specialty. We would all form a circle about 15 feet in diameter. Around the back, through the legs, a high step and pass the ball under the knee and then high step with the other leg. And if I remember correctly, someone would turn their back to another teammate, stick out their butt, and the other player would bounce the ball off her butt. And of course the spin the ball in the finger and go under her arm and come back to starting position still spinning on her finger.

One of my most special memories was, of course, playing in my hometown to a packed gym — pretty darn special. In fact, to this day, that game still holds the record for the largest crowd ever at my high school.

Brenda Moon (Davis)

Career 1965-68
All American Red Heads

As told by Brenda Moon Davis

In order to truly share the impact the four seasons that I played basketball with the All American Red Heads had on my life, I have to start my story with how I became acquainted with this amazing game of basketball.

I was born in 1947 in middle Tennessee, between Nashville and the Kentucky border. This is where Destiny and Fate began to shape my life journey. This part of the country began girls' basketball in many of the elementary schools, but my exposure to basketball didn't really happen until I was almost through elementary school.

My dad was a tenant farmer and I was the oldest child by five years. My dad and mom were both fairly tall for their generation — 6-foot-4 and 5-foot-10. So my destiny was to be taller than most everyone else my age throughout my entire childhood. And my fate was to grow up helping my dad on the tenant farms, working side by side with the farmhands.

Red Head Brenda Moon, 1965-66

A tenant farmer lived on and worked the land belonging to someone else and was paid from the profits of the land. We raised most of our own food and lived in the farmhouse on the property. It was a working version of a "room and board" relationship. Every day began and ended with milking and feeding the cows and calves. We also raised hogs and chickens. And there was at least one pair of working horses or mules. In the fields our main money crop was tobacco, but we also grew corn and oats for the livestock and wheat to make flour for our bread and other baking. The days were long, dawn to dust, and working in the fields during the summers was hot and sticky. This is significant because I was raised without even the slightest hint that gender could or should play a role in what I could or could not do.

Fate continued to influence my life when it was time for me to start school. The tenant farm we lived on at that time meant I would be attending one of those elementary schools that had both girls' and boys' seventh grade basketball, but at the time I had no idea how significant that would be. My non-school life was helping on the farm. I don't even remember having a basketball or outdoor goal as a young child.

The coach at that elementary school was also the principal. What that meant to me was that he was someone to fear and to stay away from — kids that misbehaved or didn't follow school rules were sent to the principal to be disciplined. And among my various personality traits, which are probably also a gift from Destiny, is that I am a rules-based person. So once again Fate came into the picture. When I was in the fifth grade, we were making replicas of forts from wooden sticks. My mom had let me bring a little metal hammer to school to work on the fort I was making. Another kid took the hammer and I grabbed for it, hitting a nearby aquarium and causing it to crack. Needless to say, I got sent to the hall to wait for the dreaded principal. I was in tears when he came down the hall. After asking me why I was in the hall and me struggling to explain what happened, he looked at me, smiled, and asked if I was interested in playing basketball with the seventh grade girls' team? Really? He even said I could pick any friend I wanted to also join me.

To this day I am not sure how I survived the next year. I was a very shy and somewhat insecure child, especially in comparison to those older, more mature seventh graders! And of all things, I wore an undershirt and they wore bras. I was so self-conscious I changed clothes in the very back of the locker room between two open locker doors and waited until I got home to shower. As far as those first few games of basketball — it was a good thing we played half court rules back then, because all I did was stand at the foul line pulling up my socks when the ball was on the other end.

Despite this somewhat awkward start, I soon grew to love the game of basketball and was pretty good at it. Soon after I started the eighth grade, we moved closer to Nashville and a more suburban neighborhood. My new school had an eighth grade team, a ninth grade team AND a varsity team! I was already 6-foot-2 tall by the time I was in the eighth grade and basketball was the center of my life. When not on a basketball court, I was still very shy and insecure, but on the court I felt a lot more in control.

Now fast forward to the end of my high school senior season. I was honored with numerous awards and recognitions, resulting in quite a bit of publicity in the major Nashville papers. That is how Mr. Orwell Moore, owner of the All American Red Heads, learned about me. But if Fate hadn't stepped in once again, our introduction would not have happened. I had never heard of the Red Heads; I didn't even know there was such a thing as a barnstorming, women's basketball team. There wasn't even women's college basketball — just a few AAU teams. So how could there be such a thing as getting paid to play basketball and of all things, against men and full court? Someone must be playing a prank on me.

When I answered the phone that day and a man I didn't know (Coach Orwell Moore) started telling me all these unbelievable things, what was I to do or think? That was pretty easy for me — I hung up on him and wouldn't answer the phone when he tried to call back! Fortunately, Coach Moore called later and talked to my dad. Even though the thought of living with strangers and being away from home eight to nine months was so out of my comfort zone, Dad convinced me playing for the Red Heads would be a wonderful opportunity and great adventure. Besides, I would be able to continue playing the game of basketball that I loved so much when there were few options in 1965 for that to happen for a girl.

I was nowhere near ready for that first training camp my rookie year — two intense weeks of basketball, ball handling, trick shots and getting in shape — real shape that would allow a body to play six or seven games a week, every week. There were three-a-days and two-a-days and an occasional scrimmage against some local Caraway, Arkansas men that I think got a kick out of testing out the skills of the new crop of Red Heads every fall. I was so sore and used so much Absorbine Jr. that it ate holes in my undergarments.

Speaking of getting in shape, what about those miles of "roadwork?" You would think that playing a game every night and practicing shooting and ball handling after many of the games would be enough exercise. Wrong. When we traveled a particularly long distance between games and the road conditions were safe, we would all pile out of the car and Coach would drive a couple of miles ahead. Then all seven of us would proceed to run — frontwards, backwards, sideways, and even jumping. I often wondered what passing motorists thought when they saw seven redheaded girls running down the median of an Interstate.

Everything was not just about basketball. I have so many memories of wonderful places that we drove through or visited when we had one of those rare days and nights off. Until my time as an All American Red Head, I hadn't been outside the borders of Tennessee and Kentucky. As I learned first-hand crisscrossing the highways and back roads of the USA, there are so many amazing things to see and people to meet. Those experiences lit an ever-burning fire in my soul and I have loved traveling ever since. Because of my Red Head travels, plus a little from my post-basketball career and leisure travels, I feel fortunate to have truly "visited" every one of the states, not just passed through them. We are truly blessed to live in such a beautiful part of the world.

Being from the Nashville area, folks "assumed" I was a country western music fan, so when it was my turn to control the radio, I ALWAYS selected a country music station. Things that were popular were "Six Days on the Road" by Dave Dudley, "King of the Road" by Roger Miller, and various songs by artists such as Johnny Cash, Tammy Wynette, and Pasty Cline. Since these were usually easy sing-a-long songs, we would often use our pretend microphones and join in. Now for full confession — when I joined the Red Heads I did not like country music at all! I would start shaking my red hair all over anytime I heard "These Boots Are Made for Walking," "Good Vibrations," "I Heard It Through the Grapevine" or anything by Elvis or the Beatles when they came blasting (as much as it could) out of our little AM radio speaker.

I especially remember my first exposure to New York City. That was one of our day/night off opportunities. For safety reasons, we were never allowed to do anything alone so there were usually three or more of us together at any one time. That in itself was an interesting sight I'm sure — bright red hair, taller than the norm, young girls in black jackets with a big Red Head circle emblem on our backs! In any case, a group of us took off walking the streets of New York without a clue as to the differences in the communities or that some areas might not be so safe. We were all so innocent in those days. Such fun looking at all the storefronts, smelling the delightful aromas coming from the little restaurants and street vendors, and of course with dark came the thousands of lights. I think we pretty much walked the streets until well after midnight. Definitely something to write home about, especially for those of us like me that had hardly ever been but a few miles away from home.

Another special travel memory is of Washington, DC, Arlington Cemetery and the Tomb of the Unknown Soldier. This visit was not many years after President Kennedy had been assassinated, so this opportunity was very humbling and will forever be etched in my memory.

Many of us girls were from rural areas and were pretty naive. One year we stayed in downtown Chicago and had some time to explore. From our hotel we could see an X-rated movie theater right on the main street and since none of us had never seen an X-rated movie we decided to be adventurous and check it out. A group of us walked to the theater, bought our tickets and went inside. Almost immediately we knew something was different about this theater so we all sat on the back row and tried to look inconspicuous. To our surprise it really wasn't a movie theater like we were accustomed to, but rather more like a peep show. We exited as quickly and quietly as possible, laughing all the way back to the hotel. At least our black jackets sort of blended in with the guys wearing the black topcoats!

One of the years I was with the Red Heads we had the opportunity to play basketball in Alaska. Late in our season that year we played our way across the northwestern part of the USA to end up in Seattle. Then we got a rare opportunity to fly as we headed to Alaska. We did our normal barnstorming across the southern and central parts of the state, using various modes of transportation and playing in all the larger towns, such as Ketchikan, Sitka, Juneau, Fairbanks and Anchorage. But when it was time to fly to Point Barrow, the most northern point of the United States, we flew in a small seaplane. In fact it was so small that there were just enough seats for the players and Coach had to sit in the co-pilot chair! And if that wasn't scary enough for someone that had flown just a handful of times (all due to Red Head travels), as we were flying over the mountains heading north to Barrow, the pilot said something like, "over there is where Will Rogers was killed when his plane, similar to this one we are in, crashed." Boy did my ears perk up and my heart was nearly pounding out of my chest.

Red Heads Charlotte "Sweetie" Adams, Brenda Moon, Carolyn Linzay, Brenda Hubbard and Mary Parsons enjoy the flight to Alaska during the 1967-68 season.

The whole Point Barrow experience was full of more memories. We played several games there and mostly against the same guys. We were told that we would have good crowds unless whales were spotted and then everyone would be whale hunting. Whales provided much needed heating and lighting oil, as well as food. The little gym was packed every night as no whales were spotted during our trip. After one of our evening games, we were guests at the nearby military base. I remember that night because we were served Champagne in plastic cups with pizza — my first exposure to Champagne and plastic seemed perfectly fine to me. And yes indeed, it stayed light there pretty much 24 hours a day, at least that was the case when we were there. We all went out in the snow around midnight to take pictures and I still have many of those pictures. In retrospective, the funniest thing I remember about this trip was the fact we negotiated and bought white arctic fox pelts, which we planned to pack in our suitcases to bring home. Before this offends anyone, all this was legal and not considered politically incorrect during that time. Ladies actually wore fur and it was considered a prestigious thing to do, which was the source of our excitement at owning real fur! Did I mention these pelts were not tanned; they were just air and salt cured. Good thing our season was ending shortly after our Alaska tour. Oh, I failed to mention another funny thing about this whole experience. When we all started comparing what we paid for our prized pelts, Pat Overman realized that she had paid almost double what some had paid later in the day. So Pat went back to the trading store and explained the situation. To her surprise, they GAVE her extra pelts to make things more consistent!

One of the hardest things about being on the road was missing family and old traditions during the holidays. Christmas was probably the hardest of the holidays. First off, most restaurants were closed from early evening Christmas Eve until the day after Christmas, making it a necessity to plan ahead for food. And we seldom played on Christmas Day, meaning we often had some spare time on our hands. My rookie year I told some of the girls it would be the first Christmas that Santa would not leave me a sock filled with goodies. To my surprise, Christmas morning I found one of dirty basketball socks hanging from the head of my bed filled with the everyone's leftover food from the prior night — partially-eaten hamburgers, cold onion rings, greasy french-fries, and the like. Not sure which smelled the worse — my sock or the food?

Our hotel setup was normally two rooms with two beds each for the players, and a third room for the Coach and his wife. Coach assigned us to the rooms. Room assignments changed every night because having your own bed was highly coveted.

When there was spare time someone start a quest to begin a penny poker game by declaring a time and a designated room. If there was enough interested in playing we might have two games going at once. We would use the middle of a bed as our table and either sit or lie along the sides. Coach was almost always up for a penny poker game as was many of the girls. Everyone kept their little stash of pennies from game to game. The dealer would declare the game for each hand such as five-card stud or seven-card draw and what was to be declared as wild, so we were often making up silly versions of poker. There was always lots of, laughter and joking around. And it was always fun breaking in the rookies to our unorthodox penny poker games.

Back in those days it was considered a very special occasion for most families to eat out in a restaurant, but in the barnstorming life we ate in restaurants every day, three times a day and sometimes four. We each received a daily eating allowance, but to make it cover all our meals we often ate breakfast at the hotel where we were staying and lunch at a truck stop or diner en route to that night's game. These were our best bets for reasonable prices and good, close-to-home cooked food.

After a while eating in restaurants got very old and boring, even though each one was different. There were three things that helped break up the monotony. One was due to Coach Moore's scheduling. He always tried to play at least one game close to every girl's hometown at some point during the season. And when time allowed, that girl's family would have all of us over for a real home cooked meal.

Then there were the occasional "care packages" that moms would send to the post office of one of the towns where we would be playing on a weekday. These care packages, as was any personal mail we received, was marked "hold for pickup by the All American Red Heads" and the post office would always be our first stop when we arrived at a new game town. No such thing as emails, cell phones, texting, just old-fashioned letters. Moms would send enough goodies to share and most of the time the girls did share.

The third thing we would do is occasionally go grocery shopping. This was a bit of a challenge because this was before hotels had microwaves and mini-refrigerators. My favorite grocery store meal was a can of tuna, a can of pork and beans, and a piece of fruit. We would buy one of the small, manual can openers during our first grocery store trip of the season and someone would pack it for group use the next time we needed it. We would buy a small package of plastic ware and often ate right out of the cans. There was no way to really heat or cook anything, but sometimes in the winter we could keep something cold by setting it outside our motel door or by using the motel ice bucket and ice from their ice machine.

Some of the girls would get cheese and crackers and various other things but my favorite was the tuna and beans! So, here we were, queens of the court during the night in small town America, eating pork and beans out of a can back in the hotel — and loving it. How could life be any better?

You might wonder how seven girls could live out of suitcases for eight months. First off, it was more like one large suitcase and one small cosmetic case. And we had a special case for our uniform and other basketball gear — long socks, leather kneepads, belt, shoes and warm-ups. We wore wool slacks most of the time until spring, with loafers and white socks. We also had one dress or skirt and blouse for "special events." Sometimes those care packages from home would include a new pair of slacks or shoes or sweater. If that was the case, we either shipped something back or tossed it in the trash because everything had to fit in that one big suitcase. And for the first couple of years that I played we had to put those big suitcase on top of a station wagon under a tarp cover, so it was not a good idea to have too big of a suitcase or one that weighed too much.

I mentioned earlier spring and that was always a significant time in regard to our clothes. In the spring we would start shopping for lighter weight slacks, often in cheery plaids, and short sleeve or sleeveless tops, shipping the winter weight items home. I am still not sure how we managed with one suitcase for all those months, but we did.

Mickey Gay

Career 1963-65, 1967-68
All American Red Heads and Southern Belles

As told by Mickey Gay

My name is Mickey "Sis" Gay. I played two seasons of professional basketball with the All American Red Heads from 1963 through 1965, and then the 1967–68 season with the Southern Belles.

I grew up and attended school in Floral, a town in north central Arkansas. Floral was a small school, but it had a gym that was known for having a great floor and backboards, a shooter's dream. Basketball was my life during my high school years.

My high school coach, Wesley Stewart, contacted Orwell Moore, owner of the All American Red Heads, and invited him to one of our games. Coach Moore had me go out on the court after the game was over and ran me through some drills. He was impressed with my set shot and my hustle. He later signed me to tour with the Red Heads.

There were two teams my first year, and my team played on the east coast. We played every night and twice on Sunday. We only played against men's teams and played men's rules. The teams that we played usually consisted of coaches and former high school players. However, each year we played a game against a semi-pro team that was based in Winston-Salem, North Carolina. They were great guys and we always enjoyed playing them.

I played "rough and tumble" basketball and was often accused, by my teammates, of "mopping the floor." I played like I was playing football,

Red Head Mickey Gay, 1963-64 season

with a "hustle plus" — literally diving for a ball. Anywhere the ball went, I was there as well. They also teasingly claimed that I could trip over the center or free throw line, always falling down (thus the "mopping the floor"), and getting to the free throw line. However, we played men only, by men's rules, so these qualities were actually appreciated by my teammates.

Often the distance between games would be great, making it difficult for us to be on time, but we were determined that we would not disappoint our fans. We were up very late at night, getting our clothes and uniforms ready for the next day and the next game. Then we caught up on our sleep, in the car, as we traveled.

Carolyn Grantham (Booth)

CAREER 1966-67
ALL AMERICAN RED HEADS

As told by Carolyn Grantham Booth

Carolyn Grantham of the Red Heads, 1966-67

Up North I was known as "Goober," but to the people in my town I was "Go Granny Go." I had received a letter in the mail in 11th grade wanting me to join the Red Heads but I wanted to finish high school first so I didn't accept at that time. My senior year I got a phone call from Mr. Moore and he wanted to know if he could come visit me and my family. My coach from high school set up a time for me to go to the gym with Mr. Moore so he could see me work out and in a few weeks I signed a contract to play. It broke my mama's heart because she already paid for my first year of college.

The day after I was told I had to dye my hair red, and I mean l flame red! I'll never forget that. It took two years to get that red color out of my hair after I stopped playing.

While traveling, we rotated seats in the limo. When I sat up front with the coach we played country music on the radio and drove the other girls crazy, since they did not like country music.

I remember nights when we had to travel all night to get to the next game. We were all so tired and so cramped we could not get much sleep. I crawled in the back on top of all the suitcases and rested for a while until the coach got on me and said if he slammed on the brakes that it would kill me. So I got down.

The day after Christmas we went to Norman Park, Georgia to play an outstanding group of guys. The big limo pulled up to the gym. The kids were so amazed as I stepped out of the limo. Made me feel like a queen or movie star, signing autographs, taking pictures and more. You see, we were back in my hometown.

We won the game and showed those guys who were the real basketball players.

After the game my mother had prepared a meal for the team. We ate in the cafeteria of the school. She invited some close friends and we had a delicious meal. Mama really worked hard on that meal. Good ole southern cooking for us for southern Georgia girls. The girls who weren't from Georgia enjoyed it also.

After the meal all of us girls gathered around the piano. My favorite song is "How Great Thou Art." All of the girls knew the song because we had sung it in the car plenty of times "a cappella." This time we had music, and the people there could not believe what they heard — it was like seven red headed angels had descended from the heavens.

Debbie Smith (Loftice)

CAREER 1967-68
ALL AMERICAN RED HEADS

As told by Debbie Smith Loftice

Debbie Smith of the Red Heads, 1967-68

I loved basketball. However, being a girl I had no future playing beyond high school. It was August 1967 and I was just getting ready to pack it up and leave home for the first time. I was 17-year-old and enrolled at the University of Tennessee for the fall. I wasn't looking forward to it either.

Then, I got a call from Mr. Orwell Moore, the owner of the All American Red Heads, about playing basketball, and even getting paid! Huh? I had never heard of them. Who was this man, and why was he pulling my leg? I didn't find this joke to be funny.

He had heard about me from another coach in Jefferson County, Tennessee. I was so excited about him coming to my house to talk basketball. I still remember the excitement. But my parents were skeptical about it. My dad was a school photographer and even contacted the Jefferson County coach to find out if it was legitimate.

No father is going to just let his 17-year-old daughter hit the road and travel around the country. This was the mid '60s and there was enough going on with the "Flower Power" generation as it was.

Mr. Moore came to my house and made an offer. I signed the contract, kissed college goodbye for a bit, and that's how my adventure began.

I showed up in Caraway, Arkansas in October 1967. What a great feeling to be able to continue playing basketball! I met some really talented girls. There were only two rookies on the east coast team — me and a girl named Cathy. We were in awe of the other players. They took us in, helped us get settled, and explained what was to come.

The first thing we did was get acquainted with Miss Clairol! I had long, thick, black hair. It took several bottles to get to the auburn color. After that, we just had to touch up every few weeks. (After I finished playing, it took many trips to the salon to get the red out. At one point, I had spotted hair.)

We practiced three times a day and ran lots and lots of laps as well as going up and down stairs. I hated that, but after we started the games, I understood why!

Back then, we didn't have fancy weights to work out by. Our leg weights were bags filled with sand and tied together by a rope. I had shin splints and didn't have time to rest my legs so I played in leg pain most of the time. We just played through it. My back hurt too. That came from sleeping in so many different beds and riding in the limo for long hours each day. I learned how to crack my back using a rolling pin.

Becky was the comedian and made everyone an "RH" pillow out of washcloths and yarn to use while we traveled in our 31-foot limo and needed a bit of rest during the middle of the day or late at night.

I remember playing in a coal-mining town in Kentucky. It was eye opening for a 17-year-old. The gym was wooden and echoed. When you bounced the ball you could literally feel it vibrate through your body. And the backboard shook every time the ball hit it. What an experience.

Men don't like to get beat by women at anything. But it seemed to have more of a significance in this little town more than any other I had experienced. They were very physical and we had to physically (if you know what I mean) defend ourselves. Each ball game in each new town brought new experiences, new friends, and continued love for the game.

In all of my short 17 years, I never had a destination vacation. My family and I always went home to Mississippi to visit family. My time with the Red Heads gave me many first time experiences.

I saw six feet of snow and learned how to make snow angels in the snow banks in Delaware. I saw the Atlantic Ocean for the first time as we picnicked on the beach in Florida. Seven Red Heads on the beach, all together eating lunch — sounds like a scene from a Frankie Avalon and Annette Funicello beach blanket movie, doesn't it?

I ate oatmeal in New York, which was great. However, they didn't have grits or sweet tea in the north! I sure missed my grits and sweet tea. In the north, people were fascinated with my very southern speech. The slang I used really amused them. In one diner in NY, they asked me to talk. I remember asking what did they want me to say. The response was "we don't care, just say something." This happened often. These are the most important memories to me.

Charlotte "Sweetie" Adams

Career 1967-77

All American Red Heads

As told by Charlotte Adams

Approximately 70 miles south of Jackson, Mississippi is the very small community of Bogue Chitto.

My senior year of high school, my team won district and overall state, becoming the only Bogue Chitto girls' team to win the state title. I made All District, South Mississippi All-star selection and First Annual Mississippi Girls' North-South All-Star team.

After graduation, I enrolled in Copiah Lincoln Junior College. At that time, college basketball had not been organized for girls, but I realized I wanted to continue playing. I got a tryout with the All American Red Heads and made the team in 1966. Dreams do come true, so I left college and began my career as an All American Red Head, under the direction of Coach "Little Jack" Moore, who was a strict disciplinarian.

Red Heads Charlotte "Sweetie" Adams, 1973

Over the next few years, my friendship with Coach Jack and his wife, Betty, grew and they became like another father and mother. I was honored when they named their daughter after me.

Coach Jack taught me the Four D's of Life: Dedication, Desire, Discipline and Determination. I have used them in all areas of my life and passed them to my players when I coached.

During the 10 years I was a Red Head I traveled extensively. I went to Canada, Mexico, and every state in the union except Hawaii. I toured Alaska three times. In 1986, after retiring, I traveled to Hawaii to complete my visit to every state in the union.

During my career I scored 26,746 points. Once we had a doubleheader and in the two games I scored a total of 101 points in a single day. I became a player/coach during my seventh season. I would then go on to be coach/driver and business manager the last three years of my career.

For a small town girl, traveling with the Red Heads was an opportunity of a lifetime. I was able to see many beautiful and interesting places and meet many influential people. We played professional teams like the Kansas City Chiefs in the year they won the Super Bowl, the Washington Redskins and Boston Patriots (New England Patriots).

In 1977, I left the Red Heads and coached basketball at Tallulah Academy for one year. I was also assistant coach of the Mississippi All Stars.

I was interviewed and later offered the job coaching the WBL. Milwaukee Does. I was the first woman to be offered a coaching job in that league. I declined to be near Mother. Also I wasn't sure the league would survive — it didn't.

Mary Alice "Carp" Carpenter

CAREER 1966-67
ALL AMERICAN RED HEADS

As told by Mary Alice Carpenter

The basketball season was in progress of the fall 1966 season when I decided to try and take my basketball career to the professional level. I found out some information on the famous All American Red Heads and called their home office and inquired about playing. About two weeks after my call they had a girl that had just dropped off the team and were needing someone to finish out the season, so I got a call and they asked me to come play. I didn't try out but realized Mr. Moore must have checked with my coach and others to ask about my playing ability. Sight unseen, I was going to become a professional basketball player. I packed my bags immediately and jumped on the bus downtown and headed off to the town I was told to meet them at.

It was a bit difficult at first as I didn't know all of the plays and tricks the team knew, but one of the players, Jolene Ammons, took me under her wing and worked with me day after day until I was up to speed.

Mary Carpenter of the Red Heads, 1966-67

Along with playing against many local towns, we also would play against some major league baseball players like All-Star third baseman Max Alvis of the Cleveland Indians when we were in Jasper, Texas.

We had quite a large number of games in the southwest before heading into California. In late February we were on Art Linkletter's "House Party" TV show. Right after being on that show we went over to another stage and watched the taping of "The Red Skelton Show" as well. During this time The Brown Derby was a popular restaurant for the movie stars. We had lunch there and during our meal we saw none other than Andy Griffith's deputy Barney Fife (Don Knotts) and other Hollywood stars.

When we got to Nevada we really enjoyed going into Las Vegas. We even played a bit at the slot machines and caught a couple of shows afterwards. Even in the casinos we were celebrities. Any time seven tall, red-haired girls were out, we drew attention. Some had never heard of us, yet many knew who we were — often people who had played us or attended a games. Even in Las Vegas some would ask for an autograph, or inquire about how to book a game.

I remember when we would all walk into a restaurant. We virtually lived in them for seven months, so one of the players would usually go right up and grab the coffee pot and started filling all the others cups up so the waitresses wouldn't have to worry about it. Sometimes we would even help start another pot. The waitresses really liked that.

One time in Arizona a retired couple from Missouri found out that I was from there. They went to the store brought me a big bag of shelled almonds. We were always the queens wherever we went.

Once we played against some teachers of Northwestern School. I knew all of them and they were very gracious when we beat them on their court. My career highlight came on April 4, 1967 when we played in my hometown of Mendon, Missouri, winning 70-62.

Sue Dawson (Gomez)

CAREER 1965-66
ALL AMERICAN RED HEADS

As told by Jolene Ammons

The 1965-66 season we reported to Caraway, Arkansas for training and meeting the new team, which included Sue from Tulsa, Oklahoma. Training was always very hard. We were all very sore, used muscles that we had forgotten that we had.

But rookies like Sue had it much harder. Not only did they have to learn to do ball handling, trick shots, the magic circle and our comedy routines, they had to dye their hair RED with Miss Clairol Flame 33. That was always a big shock for the new players, sometimes even bringing tears to the eyes of the youngest players, fresh out of high school.

Orwell Moore selected Sue to be the team comedian. Sue also had to learn the comedian routines. Well, needless to say she had to be a top-notch basketball player as well. The comedian always had a pleasing personality, was very energetic and had to learn to be outgoing, if she didn't join the Red Heads with that personality trait. She had to make the best of a situation to get the audience in her hands.

Sue could make even her teammates laugh at the drop of a hat. We visited a state hospital for kids in Newberry, Michigan. These children had emotional as well as physical challenges. Sue was great with the kids. They followed her around like the pied piper.

Along the way we did lots of sightseeing and horseback riding, and we went to Disneyland. While in southern California we crossed the border into Mexico. While in Idaho, former Red Head

Red Heads at Christmas time, 1965. Patty Eubank, Sue Dawson, Sharon Glenn, Delphia Allen, Coach Jack Moore as Santa, Alice Washington, Jolene "Jo Jo" Ammons, December 1965.

Lee Kacshmitter, a former Red Head, came to our game. We had sisters Georgia and Alice Washington on my team.

Sue had a real passion and love for basketball. Most of all she was a great player and loved people. She had a special something that would not let you forget her. I can see her now with the top hat and cane, doing the referee act. I laughed as much as the audience.

Our coach that season was Jack Moore, who also has passed on. You guys would have been proud of Sue Dawson, as she would have been proud of you. It was an honor to play on the same team with her.

Alice Washington (Dockins)

Career 1965-66
All American Red Heads

As told by Alice Washington Dockins

We reported to training in Caraway, Arkansas. My sister Georgia was a veteran and I was a rookie. Slowly the players started to arrive. Training was always rough and I was fortunate that I had an edge on some of the players since my sister was a seasoned veteran. Over the past few years she had taught me a lot of the ball handling and fancy passes. Yet, as much as I knew, that did not make the drills and conditioning any easier when I got to camp. I ended up on the same team as Georgia, playing guard.

Red Heads Alice Washington, Georgia Washington and Jolene "Jo Jo" Ammons, early 1966

We all made it through training, all of us dyeing our hair red together. Next was training games. Even back before the days of professional leagues, we realized the importance of a few "practice games" to work out some of our kinks and identify what we needed further work on. Our first game was in Sickle, Oklahoma. We lost by score of 51-36 and we knew we had a long ways to go. We ended up playing most of the training games in Oklahoma and, by the end, we were on our way to being a fine-tuned machine.

Our schedule sent us off to Missouri to start our season where we played several games. We then headed west to Wyoming where we had car trouble. This was one of the biggest inconveniences. We had to take our uniforms and a few days of clothes out of our limo and pack them into a station wagon — that's seven tall women in a station wagon, not much different than stuffing people into a telephone booth back then. The coach stayed with the limo and the rest of us moved on to play the games.

While in Michigan we visited a state hospital for kids. While seeing the kids was heart breaking, it was at the same time very rewarding to see their smiles. We were able to put a smile in their face and some warmth in their hearts as we did our ball tricks, signed autographs and took pictures with them.

We then headed to the southern states and a grueling schedule. In eight days we played three doubleheaders. Then it was down in Louisiana and Mississippi where we still did very well, winning eight and losing only three.

When we headed west we did a lot of sightseeing before ending up in California. We then headed up the Pacific coast and played a game I will never forget. We were in Corbett, Oregon. Jolene was guarding a 6-foot-8 guy and she is about 5-foot-6. That meant her nose was his elbow height. She caught an elbow and it broke her nose. The opposing player was very upset that he hit her. Jolene had to leave the game for X-rays. Yet she missed only one game before returning wearing a face guard. Nothing kept a Red Head off the court. We had a successful season of 130 wins and 61 losses.

Donna "Spanky" Losier

CAREER 1967-78
ALL AMERICAN RED HEADS

As told by Donna Losier

In the fall of 1967, Ted Walker, the Director of the Recreation Department in my hometown, wanted me to try out for the All American Red Heads. He wrote to a sports writer with one of the Boston newspapers, asking if he knew how to get in contact with them. Fortunately for me, he received the information he requested. Ted contacted coach and owner Orwell Moore about me, and the Red Heads happened to be playing in New Hampshire in November. Ted and my mother took me to Lebanon, New Hampshire, where I had a try out after the game.

Jack Moore was the coach of the team. Some of the players were Jolene Ammons, Charlotte Adams, Brenda Moon, Mary Parsons, and Becky Harp. I was asked to shoot around from all over the court, as well as free throws and right and left handed lay ups. Moore also asked me to do some ball handling. Coach Jack told me that I was good shooter, but at 5-foot-5 I was kind of short.

I wasn't offered a contract on the spot, as Coach Orwell Moore took care of that aspect of the business. Coach Jack reported to Coach Orwell. A couple of weeks later Ted informed me that he had heard from Coach Moore and he wanted me to join the team in Charlotte, North Carolina in 10 days. I accepted the contract offer and got busy preparing to leave home for the first time on my new adventure, which ended up being an 11-year wonderful and educational experience.

The first week on the road was great. I loved basketball and I was honored to have the opportunity to play with the Red Heads. I was able to bring my guitar, so I did a lot of singing during our trips from town to town. We all had fun laughing and singing and it certainly helped pass the time in the limo. All the girls were from the south at the time and they had a great time making fun of my New Hampshire accent. I would give it right back, telling them "I didn't know a 'winder' was a window."

At the beginning of the 1968 season, Coach Orwell Moore was traveling with us in the limo to Little Rock. I was playing my guitar and we were all singing, laughing, and having a great time. Coach Moore was sitting in the front seat enjoying himself, too. He turned around and said to me, "You remind me of Spanky on the Little Rascals. 'Spanky' — that's a good name for you." I have had that nickname ever since. It has been 49 years now. Coach Moore also played the guitar and sang. He often did so when he came to visit our team.

Red Head Donna "Spanky" Losier with sister of Red Heads teammate Jana Giles after a game, circa 1971

When Title IX started getting in full swing, women's basketball became very popular. The Red Heads had three teams on the road for a couple of years, but always two teams. Unfortunately, Title IX meant less open gym time, so my last couple of years we only had one team on the road.

This is one of my favorite Red Head experiences and I am very proud to share it with you. In 1977 we played in Farmingdale, New York. This particular year we only had three veteran players — me, Barb Hostert, and Sheryl "Woody" Wood. During pre-game warm up Woody severely sprained her ankle. This was at the beginning of the season and the new players were still learning the Red Head style of basketball. Our coach, Cheryl Clark, told the new players to set screens and give the ball to Barb and I as much as possible. Barb and I were on fire. I don't think we missed five shots between us the whole game. At the end of the game, we were down by three points with seconds left and I was on the free throw line. I made the first shot then told Barb to come up by me so she wasn't under the basket. I deliberately missed my second shot. The ball came off the rim

Red Heads Donna "Spanky" Losier (with ball) and Teresa Bergeron during a 1970-71 game

right to Barb. She jumped in the air, rebounding the ball and putting it back up before her Converse sneakers touched the floor, tying the game. We ended up winning in overtime. Barb scored 45 points and I scored 39. Between us we had all the points but six. It just goes to show how determination and pride in your team can motivate you to the next level. Coach Clark and Woody said they wish that the game was on video because it certainly was amazing.

Many players had the opportunity of playing back in their hometowns. It was a big honor and the town and school would pull out all the stops. Sometime they would dedicate the day to the player or give them a key to the city. Other times the player would receive a plaque in recognition of their accomplishments with the Red Heads. In the fall of 1970, I played in my hometown of Gorham to a packed house. At halftime I received an engraved watch and a citation from the Governor of New Hampshire. My mom also received roses. It was a proud night for my parents and a very special night for me.

On September 19, 2003 I had the honor to be inducted into the New England Basketball Hall of Fame. This never would have happened without the hard work and dedication of John Molina and my dear friend and teammate Barb Hostert. Heartfelt thanks to you both. God bless you Barb. You are surely missed but forever in our hearts.

I feel very fortunate to have traveled all around the country, seeing many beautiful sites and meeting so many wonderful people. I had 11 years of wonderful experiences too many mention. If I had to sum it up, I would say I cherish the lifetime relationships I made with my teammates. We are and always will be family.

Cheryl Clark

Career 1967-82
Texas Cowgirls and All American Red Heads

As told by Cheryl Clark

I was the daughter of a welder and elementary school teacher in the Upper Peninsula of Michigan. Enjoying every team sport I encountered and always up for a physical challenge and travel, I was always on the move.

While still a teen I had purchased a 10-speed bike in Marquette and rode it home to Wetmore in just about four hours.

After graduating from high school in 1967, basketball quite literally became my life for the next 14 years, playing first for the Texas Cowgirls for two and a half years.

While with the Cowgirls, one of my teammates had gone to an All American Red Heads game and had saved a program from the game. She gave it to me.

Red Head Cheryl Clark directing the team in Memphis, Tennessee, May '73.

I had stopped playing for the Cowgirls and was back in Michigan in the winter of 1969. I had written to the owner of the Red Heads at the address listed on the program I had saved, inquiring about the possibility to play for the team. Within a week Mr. Moore had written me back, informing me that the team would be in northern Indiana and that I would be their guest.

This was no little drive to just go to a basketball game back in the 1960s. It was over 10 hours away, one way. My brother and I jumped in the car and headed south.

My brother and I sat and watched the game. The talent that this team displayed was something I had never witnessed before. The coach, Jack Moore, came up and introduced himself to me and I got to meet some of the players as well.

After the game, I went out onto the court, all by myself, with Coach Moore and the players watching from the sidelines. It was pressure time. Basically, win or go home.

I went through some dribbling routines, shooting and ball handling, much of which I learned while traveling with the Cowgirls. When I was done, the Red Heads applauded my display of talent. Coach Moore came over to me, quite impressed. He offered me a position, right on the spot.

I was so excited, I had to excuse myself for a few minutes. I went over and hugged my brother, told him the good news and then left to go outside. I returned, a few short minutes later to everyone's delight.

There, in my hands, was my suitcase. I jumped in the car with my new teammates and began a career that would last until the early 1980s.

I eventually coached the Red Heads. During my basketball career, I played in 1,600 games and score over 26,400 points, which is a very respectable 16.5 points per game, but just a small statistic of who I was as a Red Head. I strived to get better at everything I did. Coach Orwell Moore and his brother, Jack, always emphasized the importance of being a good free throw shooter and being disciplined at the line. Over those many years, I averaged better than 91% at the line, a number very few professional men even attain in today's game.

Shorty after leaving training camp the team played in a town where one of the players had mentioned that he considered himself an exceptional free throw shooter. One of the girls told him that the coach (me) was too. After the game he challenged me to a free throw contest. I removed the jacket of my three-piece suit and rolled up my sleeves. Fortunately, I was wearing flat shoes. After we each took a couple of warm up shots, we began to shoot one at a time. The man was an excellent free throw shooter, missing only three out of 100 shots. But I, in my business suit, bested him by making 99-100.

As one of the coaches for the Red Heads in five seasons my teams' won-loss record was 677 wins and 91 losses, for an 88% winning percentage.

Janet Cox

Career 1968-69
All American Red Heads

As told by Janet Cox

Timing is everything! In 1968 it was my time to become a member of the All American Red Heads, and what a time it was in my life. I was enrolled as a sophomore in college but decided to take a "gap year" which most students do after high school before entering college. My dilemma was to decide what I would do during this year. I had heard of the All American Red Heads and decided to reach out to my high school basketball coach for his assistance in making contact with the team's owner, Orwell Moore. The news came back that the team had a vacancy and wanted me to join them for tryouts in Gainesville, Georgia.

I had been an outstanding player in high school, making the varsity team in the ninth grade. My basketball skills came naturally, so to speak, since both of my parents were outstanding players when they were in high school. I had been coached by my father from the time I could dribble a basketball and practiced at an early age on an outdoor goal attached to the side of our garage. I was the only female for counties around in Western North Carolina that could shoot a jump shot, and people drove long distances to see this anomaly. Basketball was my passion. It was in my genes. There was nothing I would rather do than play basketball.

I joined the All American Red Heads team in Gainesville, Georgia with natural blonde hair and having not played basketball for two years. When I graduated from high school there were no women's college teams that I knew of for a student like myself to combine her academic goals with playing collegiate basketball. Mr. Moore happened to be at the game. My "tryout" was to put on a uniform and play in the game that night. It was a dismal performance and very humiliating. I did not have red hair, was quickly out of breath and knew none of the twenty-something plays that were used every night. Again, timing was on my side because Mr. Moore needed a player. I left Gainesville that night with Coach Jack Moore and teammates (Charlotte Adams, Brenda Moon, Mary Parsons, Betty Everett, Pauline Barbo and Lois Glover) and headed south to the next town.

Janet Cox executes a difficult trick shot — bouncing the ball through the hoop with her back to the basket — with Red Heads temmates Brenda Ragan, Donna "Spanky" Losier and Judith Coghlan looking on during a 1968-69 halftime show.

I was immediately initiated by the other players when we got to the hotel room by having henna applied to my long blonde hair. The results were very shocking and another dose of humility, but dyeing each other's hair at the hotel with bottles of henna became a team ritual. Several other rituals became important those first few weeks of being on the team. Since I had joined the team after training was over at Camp Courage and the teams were already on the road, I had to quickly get in shape and learn all the team plays. My worst physical complaint, that I remember, was the blood blisters on the soles of my feet. We wore Converse tennis shoes with minimal cushioning and could not even imagine something like Nike Air. I wore two pairs of socks and would need to soak my feet in a bathtub in order to remove them. For several weeks to condition my feet, my teammates would forcefully hold my feet in buckets of ice water. I rolled Coke bottles on the floor to strengthen my arches and picked up coins with my toes. We were each other's athletic trainer and support system. Playing seven to eight games weekly, my physical conditioning program moved along quickly.

My other urgent need was to learn the numerous plays everyone already knew. Since we would often travel after a game in order to get to the next town, I would spend time in our stretch limousine, while others often slept, sitting in the back and studying the plays using a flashlight. I was determined to be respected by my teammates and not be the rookie who just joined the team. Since we played only men with men's rules, each Red Head needed to know how to execute each play from all five positions on the court. This was soon accomplished and I settled in to being a real Red Head.

Within my first few weeks I was transferred to a second team. I left Gainesville, Florida and flew to meet another team in Gainesville, Texas. This was my first plane travel, and it was very exciting. Again, the timing was perfect because the team was just the right fit. I was not the only rookie and there were a couple of veterans on the team that became my mentors. They became my family. We played basketball together, ate together, laughed together and sang together. Some of my best memories are singing in the stretch limousine as Donna "Spanky" Losier played her guitar. It helped to pass the time since many miles were travelled each day and many nights, sometimes all night long. Our coach, Chuck Plummer, was also our driver. It was an honor to play that season with veteran Jolene Ammons. She inspired me to not just be a good ball player but to be a great ball player. The accuracy of her half-court shot was mind-blowing. My other teammates were Judith "Miss Personality" Coghlan, Brenda Ragan, Carolyn Gooch and Pam McAnally.

Our game schedule was planned for at least one month in advance. The schedule dictated our movement as we zigzagged across the country. The players could send their schedule home, which allowed love ones to write to us in advance. We would go to the post office in each town to collect our mail and also send out our letters and post cards. At the post office, I would purchase a money order with my salary to send back home. We were paid in cash each month. Since all necessities were provided, there was no reason to spend our salaries. This money later helped pay my college tuition. We also received a daily allowance for food, which was quite generous and allowed us to eat very well.

We partied with The Monkees, played against the San Francisco 49ers, saw the Grand Canyon, gambled at casinos in Las Vegas, visited American Indian reservations for charity exhibitions games, and entertained in small town America night after night. We were a novelty, a sensation and often times treated like celebrities. After a game, the younger audience would ask for our signatures in their Red Head program. We would frequently be at the local radio station or television station being interviewed and promoting the game to be played that evening. It was customary to drop by the high school to entice students to come back that evening with their parents for the game against some local men's team. This ingenious marketing strategy worked beautifully since we typically played in packed gymnasiums.

Playing against men was fun but challenging. During the first half of the game, the men would typically be having fun, acting nonchalant and not taking us seriously. The majority of the time, the Red Heads would be leading at halftime. While the men went to their locker room, we would perform a half-time show for the audience that featured trick shots, ball handling maneuvers, and antics with the referees and members of the audience. We never had a rest period. During the second half, the men were more solemn, serious, and aggressive in their physical play. The pats and pinches on the derrières were replaced with swinging elbows and body shoving. During my tenure, I received a broken nose from an elbow and a broken index finger. These injuries did not stop us from continuing to play. In fact, due to two members contracting hepatitis while in Tijuana, Mexico and having to return home, our team continued for the remainder of the season with only five members. As such, there were no substitutions if someone had an injury, was sick or fouled out. Every team member needed to play every minute of every game. It was a special time with only five teammates and we pulled off a winning streak of 39 consecutive games. The season record for the team was 159 wins and 28 losses. It was a special team and a special time to be a Red Head.

I am blessed to have been given the opportunity to be a Red Head and a member of the greatest women's basketball team to ever walk onto a basketball court. I was in the right place at the right time. It is a time in my life that gave me so much – friendships and memories that are priceless.

Carolyn "Gooch" Gooch (Hix)

Career 1968-70
All American Red Heads

As told by Carolyn Gooch Hix

A friend of mine knew Mr. Orwell Moore, owner of the All American Red Heads, and had asked me to come to one of their games as his guest when they visited my town. I had watched the Red Heads since I was a little girl. A friend of mine had a sister who played for the Red Heads.

After the game he gave me a try out in the gym. I had my shoes on, took them off and walked across the basketball floor. I took three free throws. I missed them all. All three came close, but they just didn't go in.

Coach Moore laughed. He thought it was so funny and said, "At least you have the nerve to come out here in pantyhose and slide across the floor to try out for the team."

Later that night we drove over to his house and I signed a contract to go on the road as an All American Red Head.

Most of the guys we played against were really great, but some of them could get pretty rough. I had my tailbone broken, had my nose broken and broken fingers too. Most of it, I'm sure, it was accidental. They were just determined that we would not beat them.

A lot of people thought we were a band. We would pull up in our 31-foot stretch limo. Seven redheaded women got out of the car. Someone would ask, "Ya'll a band?" We would reply, "No, we're a basketball team."

We were always in the spotlight — doing interviews, being on TV and making personal appearances — if you were shy, this team brought it out of you.

The All American Red Heads posed with unidentified referees before a 1967-68 game. L-R: Donna "Spanky" Losier, Mary Emmison, Jolene "Jo Jo" Ammons, Wilda Kelly, Pauline Barbo, Betty Everett and Carolyn Gooch.

Brenda Ragan (Nalepa)

CAREER 1968-69
ALL AMERICAN RED HEADS

As told by Brenda Ragan Nalepa

My story begins before my playing. Coach Orwell Moore called me at home and told me who he was and that he wanted me to play for his team.

Red Head Brenda Ragan, 1968-69

I thought it was a practical joke and hung up on him. Never in my life did I imagine that I would have a chance to play for the Red Heads. But it was true, and I signed the contract.

We traveled in the limo, which was before the days of the famous limos you see now. After the season was over he flew me home. That was my first time on an airplane.

Coach Moore told us when we were not playing basketball to see America. He loved our country. He was a true All American!

We had Donna "Spanky" Losier on our team. She played the guitar. We spent many hours on the road, especially when we could not get a radio station, singing along with Spanky. My best memory was of her playing Linda Ronstadt's "Different Drum."

We had to be in shape to play 100% at a matinee, then travel 50 miles or so and play that night, again at 100%. We played hard every game to please the crowd that paid to see us, and they loved it. I think the men sometimes were quite embarrassed that we could run circles around them, but it was all in fun. I don't know which we enjoyed more, the winning or the fun.

Jolene Ammons was the captain of our team. She had the best skills of any ball handler I have ever seen. She could dribble like no other. No one could keep up with her or take the ball away from her unless she allowed them to do so, again for show.

One night we were playing in Flagstaff, Arizona and the ball went into the corner where you would go down into the locker room. I went for the ball and one of the men followed me. He pinched my butt and scared the day lights out of me. All he did was laugh. He knew he scared me. I was a naive 19-year-old.

Judith Coghlan (Lewis)

CAREER 1968-69
ALL AMERICAN RED HEADS

As told by Judith Coghlan Lewis

Coach Orwell Moore had heard of me through his brother, Jack, who was also a coach for the Red Heads. He was friends with my dad and knew I had made all district in basketball 1968 for playing in my small hometown of Benoit, Mississippi. I was on the state championship track team for four years in a row. Coach Moore was getting a dedicated athlete. I quickly became known as "Miss Personality."

I have wonderful memories of my season as an All American Red Head, but I also remember the work and discipline it took to get ready and stay in shape for the games. Jolene Ammons was our leader as most of us were "rookies." Even though I was a track athlete, running up and down stairs and other drills in training camp made me realize I needed more work on my endurance.

Judith Coughlan (second from left) with her Red Head teammates during the 1968-69 season. L-R: Brenda Ragen, Coughlan, Jolene "Jo Jo" Ammons, Pam McNally, Charlotte "Sweetie" Adams and Janet Cox.

We won 129 games and played before huge crowds. In Brevard, North Carolina, we played before a standing room only crowd. They had to turn fans away as they could not fit anymore into the building.

For a time, when we were out west and in the midst of a 29-game winning streak, two of our players got so sick and they had to be sent back to their hometowns. The remaining five of us all played every minute of every game and kept the streak alive until they returned.

Who would have known we would have been so popular that we would even have our warmups stolen while in Arcata, California? Luckily they were recovered and returned to us later in the season.

Dianne Kirkland (Warren)

Career 1969-71
Southern Belles

As told by Dianne Kirkland Warren

For a young farm girl who worked in chicken houses, corn fields and tobacco patches growing up and who walked in plowed dirt many times, playing basketball for the Southern Belles, a professional girls' travel exhibition team, was a dream come true.

Having been a South Georgia, Jeff Davis County High School basketball star of Hazlehurst, Georgia during the late 1960s, a sports writer asked me a simple question: "What created your interest in basketball and when did you become interested in the competitive sport of basketball?" My answer was not what you might think. My interest was not kindled by a professional superstar or any other individual. I can recall when I was 9 or 10 years of age flipping channels on the television looking for a basketball game. I could never identify a single reason for my interest – it was always just in me.

I grew up in the country, and we had a basketball goal with a wooden backboard attached to a pine tree in the yard. My brothers, Reggie and Dale Kirkland, and I would play twenty-one, horse, or just shoot hoops. Dale remembers that, after I made a shot, the ball would hit a pine root at the bottom of the tree and bounce off to the side. After dark, I would continue to shoot hoops by my daddy's truck lights. *That* is having a desire to play basketball.

Later, I began playing during recesses at my community country school on a rocky, dirt court. We assembled a team and began to compete with other county schools. As a sixth grader, I was named an All-County player. In 1964, my ninth grade year, I knew I had a deep love for the game. My innate talent garnered me a starting position midway my freshman year. My high school coach recognized my love for the game and my talent. He worked diligently teaching me the art of shooting a jump shot, shooting hook shots left and right, and the many fundamentals of playing the sport. As a high school senior, I averaged 35 points a game and had a four-year career total of 2,166 points. In a rare and sentimental move, for the first time, at our senior Athletic Banquet, Jeff Davis High School retired my #14 jersey and placed it in the trophy case.

A college in Iowa and professional scouts began taking notice my senior year in high school. A scholarship to play basketball in Iowa was offered; however, I declined the offer to remain closer to home and attend South Georgia College. I turned down an offer to play for the All American Red Heads because I did not want to dye my hair red. After having completed one year at South Georgia College, a local sportswriter approached me about playing for the Southern Belles from Caraway, Arkansas. Within a few weeks, a contract was signed — basketball was still in my blood. Newspapers such as *The Atlanta Journal Constitution*, *The Macon Telegraph*, *The Savannah Morning News*, as well as local newspapers wrote about my signing a professional contract.

In October 1969, I left home to board my first airplane flight ever. I was scared. Prior to joining the Southern Belles, I only had traveled in two states and I was nervous and emotional because I would be so far away from my family and friends. Soon after I arrived and met my teammates, I was chosen as the team comedienne. Every night, I would lead the show and entertain our fans, a task I initially was not too certain about. As time passed, I became experienced and comfortable with that role, and I served as team comedienne both years and learned to really enjoy it.

My two-year tour with the team routed us through some 38 states and into Canada. Not only did we have fun playing the sport we loved, but the tour allowed the team to take advantage of many educational experiences. When time permitted, we visited historical sites such as the Mount Rushmore National Memorial, Little Bighorn Battlefield and the Custer National Cemetery, Boot Hill Museum in Dodge City, Kansas, President Kennedy's Assassination and Memorial Site in Dallas, Texas, the Country Music Hall of Fame, and many others. I recall we were scheduled to perform in Port Edwards, Wisconsin, on December 1, 1969. I remember that day very well as we got lost and were an hour and a half late for the ballgame. We notified the organizing sponsor, and they still wanted us to perform, even with the late arrival. We played that night and to help make up for being late, the owner and the team donated all proceeds to the organization that sponsored the game.

A favorite memory occurred in February of 1971. Our schedule carried us to Medicine Lodge, Kansas. A severe blizzard had been predicted and after the ballgame, the coach decided we needed to depart the area. We quickly checked out of the motel and began to head toward our next destination. The snow had begun to fall heavily and rapidly. Within the first few miles, snow had covered the highway and cars were sliding. Our coach immediately made a decision that we should return to the motel until we learned more about the weather. We returned and there we stayed for the next three or four days. Power was lost, and phones lines were down. We took turns walking to a nearby restaurant for food. The winter storm conditions and frequent 40 mph wind gusts caused major blowing and drifting of snow. The wind chill factor was 60 degrees below zero. The blizzard paralyzed the area, and the federal government declared it a disaster area. The cattle industry in the area was one of the largest in the state, and the American Humane Association arranged for a gigantic hay lift to feed stranded cattle in the surrounding counties. It was the coldest and most bitter weather ever witnessed by this group of Southern gals. We learned quickly that we were not equipped with appropriate clothing for a blizzard.

To pass time, we played card games and simply had fun bonding with each other. After being shut in for several days and canceling three ballgames, we were ready to hit the road again and perform for our great fans, something we all loved doing. One amazing thing about this group of girls was that we learned the art of pacing ourselves and then going full steam when the need arose. The grueling pace was tough at times, but playing with a group of girls in tip-top condition who loved the sport made it seem easier. Another unique factor was that our team of young women really liked and respected each other. That is quite a compliment, since we traveled together in close quarters for seven months straight.

Southern Belles comedian Dianne Kirkland, 1969-71

Something else that stands out in my mind is how much the fans loved and appreciated us. We never got tired of the standing ovations after the games or signing autographs for the fans and young ball players. Sometimes, we would have an escort of police cars and fans waiting to escort us into their town. That made us feel very special.

In addition, I have memories of the coach giving us seating instructions for the car. In order for each player to have an opportunity to ride in the front seat, the players would rotate daily. That usually meant that each player would have at least one day a week in the front seat. We averaged traveling about 300 miles a day, and it was a common occurrence for the girls to sleep in the car. We would either lean against the window/door or on each other's shoulder.

When we weren't sleeping, we enjoyed the scenic beauty of the USA. Of particular amazement to me was traveling in the western states and seeing native animals such as deer, elk, antelope, bison, and other animals graze in the fields, something that was very uncommon and never seen in south Georgia.

Our team received quite a complement after we toured *The Nevada Evening Journal* offices in December 1970. Recalling the article from that day's visit, the writer wrote: "Seven Southern Belles alighted Tuesday noon from their specially built limousine and promptly proved that rough and tumble basketball playing misses can be both poised and polite. Dripping 'yes ma'ams' and 'no ma'ams' all over the place in their varying degrees of soft Southern accents, they charmed all with whom they came in contact. Why is it that we all don't bring up our children on 'yes ma'ams' and 'no ma'ams?'"

Another great memory and a favorite game was the night we played in my hometown of Hazlehurst, Georgia. The gymnasium was packed with an estimated 1,200 people that night. The crowd was excited and greeted us with enthusiasm as they rose to their feet with a warm welcome when we took the floor. I remember, though, how difficult it was to perform that night because the expectation was so great. The opponent team consisted of talented high school and college players, most of them I knew. We beat them 62–55. After the game, Lurner Williams, the sportswriter who was instrumental in recruiting me, treated us to a meal at his home. The next day, my parents had the whole team over for a classic southern home-cooked meal.

Travel basketball was not all glamour. I remember vividly the task of hand-washing our uniforms late at night. After getting hot and sweaty, it was a necessary job to get done. We washed our uniforms in the sink or the bathtub. Many times, the next morning, the uniforms would not be dry. Of course, we could not pack them in a suitcase damp or wet, so after packing the eight-door limo with the luggage, we would layer our uniforms on top of the luggage, hoping the sunshine would finish the drying process by the time we reached our next destination. The next task after arrival was to iron the darn things, which was absolutely necessary to have a nice and crisp look. We placed a towel over a suitcase or on the bed to iron the uniforms.

With no modern technology such as cell phones and computers, our basic communication was writing letters. We received our mail by either having it mailed to the home base in Arkansas or sending our next month's schedule out in advance to our family and friends. We always checked with the post office when we arrived in a new town. Often times, there would be a stash of letters addressed to the players with a special notation on the envelopes to hold them for the arrival of the team. It was very exciting to receive mail from friends and loved ones.

Ft. Pierre, South Dakota gave the Southern Belles a warm welcome and a nice farewell. Upon arrival to the town, it seemed it was like any other small place but before our team departed, we had a different opinion. I do not remember much about the game that night other than the gym was packed and the fans were so very warm in welcoming us there. The Belles had a knack for reading a gym full of people. It was evident when we entered their facility, what a night it would be. The fans were happy to see us — they clapped, they yelled, they were exceptional. The children were remarkable that night with their rounds of applause. The Southern Belles could do no wrong. We signed autographs and hung around to meet the fans. They deserved it!

After the game, the Belles had dinner and returned to the motel only to find several children from the area waiting for us. They wanted to talk and share and get a close-up glimpse of the Southern Belles. We stood outside with them for the longest time and did some basketball spinning and ball handling. I showed them I could do a special spin that our fans always loved, by twisting my arm and hand under while the basketball continued to spin and bring the basketball back up while still spinning. This tric takes a lot of practice. It was one of my half-time show antics. Everyone loved it.

The next morning, as always, we were up and running. We packed the car and headed out the door when we noticed notes from the children that were stuck to our specially-built limousine. A note was left for each Southern Belle and I have all of those notes until this day. The children were entertained by us, but we went away from that small town with a true blessing from those children.

The coach tuned in to the local radio station. The disc jockey was ever so complimentary as he spoke of the Southern Belles performance the evening before. He talked about the ballplayers with great enthusiasm and admiration. He even talked about #9 – Dianne Kirkland, team comedienne — being a great basketball player and how she performed as team comedienne. We listened to the disc jockey intently as we drove out of range from the radio station. The Southern Belles all felt a bit nostalgic about leaving Ft. Pierre.

Through the great sport of basketball, I learned that dedication and hard work pay off. The sport taught me self-discipline, responsibility, loyalty, devotion and determination. Being an athlete and playing basketball created in me a burning desire to win and always to strive for the best. It taught me that life at times is about loss, but when we stumble and fall, we must pick ourselves up and move forward. If we do this, success will come.

Sue Petzold (Dudek)

Career 1969-70
Southern Belles
As told by Sue Petzold Dudek

I started school at a small country school, City View, from first grade through third. My dad was a school board member so we went to all the basketball games. Back then, the coaches didn't care if we went out on the court after the games. I would run out there almost immediately and grab a basketball and try and make baskets along with other children. Of course at such a young age, I'd be fairly close to the basket and out to the free throw line, but I was determined and didn't give up. My dad had to yell at me several times that it was time to go home before I'd leave.

We moved to town, Mangum, Oklahoma, where I started fourth grade. In the fifth grade the high school coach and the junior and senior basketball team started a basketball league for the fifth and sixth grade girls. There were 18 teams each coached by two of the junior or senior girls. Games were scheduled versus the other teams. We played every Saturday morning on the junior high school basketball court. I was immediately in love with the game and was very competitive at an early age.

In junior high, the seventh grade did not play with the junior high team that consisted of eighth and ninth grade. The junior high principal decided he would coach the seventh grade girls. He scheduled games with surrounding towns playing on weekends. Eighth grade was a big step up —

getting to play on the junior high team. I worked hard in practice and when game time came I was the only eighth grader that got to play in the games. It didn't take long until I became a starter on the team.

I'm left-handed and had a pretty mean fake and could drive in for lay-ups that were hard to be guarded. My dad knew how strong my love for ball was and put up a goal for me at our home where we had cement drive. I spent many, many hours shooting, working on making baskets.

My sophomore year, high school, I was determined to make the team. There were only 15 suits to be handed out, with 24 girls going out for ball. The day coach handed out suits, two days before our first game, I was a nervous wreck. Being a sophomore with so many upper classmen I wasn't sure how that would come out. I made the team and was a starter from the first game as a sophomore all the way through my senior year.

Most of the games I was high point scorer, averaging 24 points a game for the three years. All those years I played my mother sat in the same place, right next to the center line, and kept all my scores in a little writing tablet. My dad worked for the school for many years after selling the farm I grew up on and was a maintenance man for all the school buses and the gymnasium.

I remember a game that was on our home court against the Sayre Eagles from Sayre, OK. It was a tight game and I'd been fouled. There was a stage on the east end of the court and that's where I was shooting free shots. I'll never forget seeing my dad, standing just to the right of the goal with a broom handle leaned up against himself and holding his hands like he was praying. When I hit those shots he jumped up with the biggest smile on his face. With only a few seconds on the clock, the game was basically over, and the Sayre guards never got the ball across the half court line.

A week after senior graduation my coach called and said I'd made the East-West All Star Team for the West. Everyone chosen for the teams went to Lindsay, Oklahoma for a week of practice and getting to know the players and the plays. Saturday night was the big game, East vs. West. All players on both teams got the same amount of playing time for the first three quarters. The fourth quarter, coaches could play whomever they wanted. I got to play the entire fourth quarter and was on top of the world, especially since the West won!

In September there was a telephone call and my mother said it was for me. It was Ben Overman, owner of the Southern Belles, who asked if I'd be interested in playing professional ball with a traveling team. Of course I said yes, not even thinking I needed to visit with my parents about such a big decision. Mr. Overman had been at the East-West All Star Game and he saw talent in me. I was on top of the world again, even though I didn't even know at the time that we would not be playing the regular six-on-six against girl teams, but would be playing five-on-five against men. It was definitely a big change, and I loved the idea and challenge ahead.

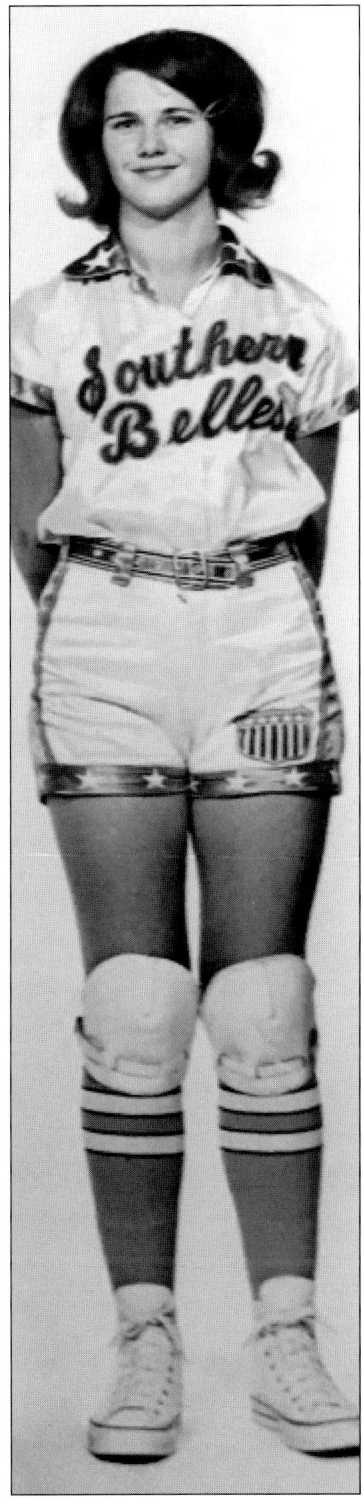

Southern Belle Sue Petzold, 1969-70

My parents and sister took me to Caraway, Arkansas were we met Coach Overman. After saying goodbyes to my family, Mr. Overman took me to the motel where the team and coach were staying.

I'd gotten the call from Coach late about joining the team so I missed the week of training with the other girls. I was behind on learning the five-on-five plays, but I worked hard and learned the game.

We traveled in a limousine and had to take turns riding in the front seat with coach. I was so excited, not just for being able to be on the team, but for the chance of a lifetime to be able to travel the United States.

I don't know what I was thinking would happen about getting our suits washed for each game, but after the first game, we all had to wash our suits either in a lavatory or bathtub. Then, we had to hang them up on hangers in order to get them dry by the next morning. When we arrived at the motel for the game that night, we had to iron our suits. Within the week we quickly learned about washing and ironing our suits.

Another thing I never thought about was meals and how they would be paid for. We were given our meal money every three days for breakfast, lunch and dinner. We had to manage with that amount until the next three days came around. It didn't take long that first week to figure that out.

One of our games in Missouri was against a men's team that had not been beaten in three years. That was definitely our goal to bring them down. It was a tough, hard fought game with the men treating us just like any other men's team they played. We were up for the challenge. After regulation time expired, we were tied up at 80-80 and went in to "sudden death" — not the normal overtime period, but the first point scored wins. I'm not sure how long it was without anyone scoring — it seemed like another whole quarter — but we persevered. It was tough and rough under the goal and out at the circle. Every player was holding his or her ground on both teams. Finally, there was a shooting foul against the men that was so obvious it had to be called. We needed to make only one of the two free throws to win the game, but we sealed the deal with the first shot and won 81-80. That game had to be my favorite. To win was great, and to do it against that particular team was like icing on the cake.

We got lost on our way to one of the games and arrived a little over an hour late for the game. I was good at reading a map, so after that I was designated as "co-pilot." I had the front seat most of the time. No one wanted to ride in front but I thought it was great and was a better view of the scenery. We saw a lot of beautiful country and even drove by Mount Rushmore. That was awesome for a small town country girl.

I enjoyed every game we played in all the various states and towns. However, I was fortunate to have had a few games scheduled in Oklahoma. The first game in Oklahoma was at Davis on February. My parents and sister came to that game along with my aunt, uncle and four cousins. We won 73-51 and it was really special that my family was there to see us play a great game. March 4 we had a game scheduled in my hometown, Mangum. The team stayed at the Duffer Motel there in Mangum. We live only about 14-15 miles from Lake Lugert, Quartz Mountain State Park and Quartz Mountain Lodge. I decided I wanted to take the team to the lake and see what a beautiful place it is. All the girls — Dianne Mitchell, Nita Sherrod, Phyllis Brown, Dianne Kirkland, Sandra Duran, Linda Shanks and I — packed ourselves in my mother's station wagon and we were off. We drove around the park across the low water bridge, down by the golf park and the amusement park. We enjoyed the afternoon adventure and were ready for the game that night.

The gym was packed and we won 71-64! It was so much fun, knowing all the guys that had made up the men's team. After the game, my parents hosted a dinner for the team and any of the guys that wanted to come. That night I slept in my own bed. It was a great feeling to be home with my parents. After breakfast at home, I met the team back at the motel and we were "back on the road," headed for Muenster, TX for the next game.

We had played in Bottineau, North Dakota and stayed at a lodge nearby that was really neat. We were close to Canada with no game scheduled that night. We were able to go across the border with some of the guys around the Lodge who were nice enough to take us snowmobiling on Lake Metigoshe. We saw men ice fishing — something I didn't think I'd ever see. It was definitely another wonderful experience as an 18-year-old traveling the United States.

Our final game was May 2, 1970 at Flagler, Colorado. We finished in style, with the Belles ruling the court and coming away with a win. My parents and sister made the trip for that game. After the game I said goodbye to the team and we headed for home. I was so proud for getting to play with the Southern Belles and make friends for a lifetime. But I was anxious to be heading home and seeing all my friends in Oklahoma. I had planned on playing the next season with the Belles, but the boyfriend I'd left behind was still waiting for me. We were married on August 7, 1970 and are still happily married, living just 15 miles from my hometown of Mangum.

Teresa Bergeron

Career 1970-72
All American Red Heads and Kansas City Royal Maids

As told by Teresa Bergeron

Grass never grew under the basketball goal in my backyard as I was growing up. When I was knee high to a basketball, I was shooting with my brothers and attempting to dribble. Basketball became my passion at a very early age.

My Mom also played in her school days in the 1930s. Dressed in her bloomers, she played center court passer, back in the days when a girls' basketball court was divided into three sections. Basketball was the thread that bonded us, and she became my biggest fan throughout my career.

My first memories of playing competitively against other females were with the recreation department in St. Charles Parish at the age of 11. It was an addiction that took over my mind and thoughts. From then on I dreamed and strived to be the best and lived to play. The competitive drive I felt from basketball stirred my adrenalin every time I picked up a ball.

Other than the skills on the court, I learned so many life lessons from playing sports. I learned how to play with others and how to develop a team that would work and think together. It was teamwork and took a team to win – there was no "I" in team. Loyalty was also built into my character through basketball and all sports. There were so many friendships born on the court. I learned respect for my fellow players, my opponents, and for my coaches.

Discipline and perseverance were the greatest attributes. One had to have discipline to practice daily, to study hard to maintain the grade to play sports, to listen, to stay focused and to maintain self-control. My motto has and always will be "I can, and if I can't I'll die trying."

Loyalty was also built into my character through basketball and all sports.

Throughout my high school years I played varsity basketball. My true inspiration and idol was the monarch of men's basketball, "Pistol Pete" Maravich. I spent hours mimicking his moves and ball handling abilities. When I played we had offense on one side and defense on the other. But it wasn't until my senior year that girls were at least allowed to have a court rover; that was me. Finally, I was able to run full court and to chase that orange ball. My goal was to steal the ball — I was obsessed with having the most steals.

I thought those were the best days of my life until one night in December 1968, the night a friend asked me to join her and her aunt to see the All American Red Heads perform at Nicholls University.

My eyes were glued to the court – mesmerized by the basketball skills displayed by the Red Heads, and against men at that. Talk about visions of sugar cookies dancing through my head… The dribbling, the halftime stunts, and the antics throughout the game

Red Head Teresa Bergeron, 1970-71

were phenomenal. My motto popped into my head — "I can." After the game, I met Jolene Ammons and Donna "Spanky" Losier. You would've thought I met the president, I was so thrilled. I had so many questions — how, why, when and what does it take to be a Red Head? Sleep escaped me that night as I dreamed with my eyes opened.

Orwell Moore was impressed by my enthusiasm and stats and before I knew it Chuck Plummer was coming to Destrehan to see me play and to talk to me. It was decision time — go to college as I had planned or realize my dream and make it a reality. College lost out to the realization of my childhood dream. Needless to say, my mother was also beside herself with my signing with the All American Red Heads. It was hard to fathom that I would get to continue to play basketball, to get paid for it, to travel the country, to meet new friends. What more could a basketball-playing fanatic ask for?

After graduation, I hit the road as an All American Red Head. There was that team-building thing again. Here was a group of strangers that had two weeks to learn how to play as a team. To this Cajun all the other girls all talked funny, dressed differently, and ate weird stuff except for two. On my team were two opponents from my archrivals in high school — Pat Deroche from Lutcher High School and Margaret O'Neal from Walker High School. These two enemies became my friends in no time — more friendships born on the court.

We had a game scheduled to play at my high school alma mater, Destrehan High. The feelings I had were beyond description as I stepped onto the court where the formation of my basketball career all began. The welcome — a standing ovation — and the support from all my family, neighbors, classmates, and past coaches was unbelievable as I was introduced that night. My ultimate goal was accomplished – there was nothing that would ever surpass the high I had. It was evident as my knees trembled and the tears of joy flowed down my cheeks.

I played only one season with the All American Red Heads. The death of my biggest fan, my Mother, kept me home to be close to my dad and the rest of my family.

It was at the end of 1971 when I was approached by Chuck Plummer to play ball again, this time with the Kansas City Royal Maids, a team formed by two steel mill owners. The team was named after, of course, the Kansas City Royals baseball team. The uniforms were of the same color and the logo was a crown.

Chuck Plummer, my former Red Heads coach, was the coach and the one that signed me. His wife, Kathy also played on the team. A few other names I remember were June Taylor, Barbara Toler, Brenda Weems and Pam McAnally, also a former Red Head.

We had training in Kansas City, Missouri at a high school gym. There was a seamstress in the town that made our uniforms. We traveled in a converted Checker cab. It was forever breaking down.

Chuck tried his best not to mimic all our plays and antics from the Red Heads, but it was hard not to. We still drew a crowd when we played. It was pretty much the same as playing with the All American Red Heads, but without the red hair. That was irrelevant because I was content in my comfort zone, the basketball court. But there wasn't a close connection between the team and the owners; we very seldom saw them. The team only lasted one season.

After that season I opted to begin a career in my hometown and hung up my Converse high tops.

My heartfelt gratitude goes to my mother who believed in me and afforded me the opportunity to grow up an athlete.

Pat "Watusie" Deroche (Hymel)

Career 1969-71
All American Red Heads

As told by Pat Deroche Hymel

One of my most memorable moments playing with the Red Heads was when we played against the Kansas City Chiefs football team in 1971.

It was my first time to be the team comedian, and there was a packed house at the coliseum. You can only imagine the feelings I had, playing and clowning in front of all those people. While we were used to a packed house everywhere we went, I felt a lot of added pressure. Will I do the comedian act right? Will they like me? Will the show be a success? Can I make them laugh?

It went very well, and so did my act. I had the crowd laughing. The Chiefs were laughing and even Coach Moore was laughing. It was such a success that for the rest of the year I was the team comedian. What a great sense of achievement. Not only could I play basketball, but I could entertain hundreds of people every night.

One time when we were traveling to a game we had a mishap with our car. We were traveling on the road and all the sudden we hear a big thunderous, noise. It had us all jumping in our seats wondering what happened. Coach was trying to steer the car on to the shoulder so we won't get in a wreck and get hurt.

As we are pulling over to the side of the road, we look out our window and what do we see but a tire passing our limo and continuing up on the road. It was initially a bit amusing, until we realized the tire we saw going by was our own. We had lost the back tire. Needless to say, we had to stay out on the side of the road until a wrecker came and we were able to make the game that night.

Red Heads Brenda "Brooksie" O'Bryan and Pat "Watusie" Deroche outside motel room, 1971-72 season

Brenda "Brooksie" O'Bryan (Koester)

Career 1970-73
All American Red Heads

As told by Brenda O'Bryan Koester

I scored 10,017 points in three seasons, playing on a team that won 96 games in a row in 96 days. I was also the same team that won 199 games and only lost six. In the three seasons I played a total of 644 games and won 585.

I was playing some softball down in Louisiana when an ex Red Head (Pauline Barbo) on the opposing team came up to me after the game. I was tall and a pretty good athlete. She asked if I played basketball. I told her "That's my favorite sport!"

She got me in contact with Coach Orwell Moore. I was married at the time and he told me he didn't like taking married girls, since he didn't think they would stay. He then told me if I still wanted to play that he would give me a tryout at Camp Courage. Of course I wanted to play. After two days of tryouts Coach Moore called me into his office and had a contract ready for me to sign, but he said if I had to call and check with my husband to not bother signing. I replied, "Give me the pen!"

When my team went to Alaska in 1971, I remember driving up to Washington to catch the jet. Coach Orwell Moore had told us to be in shape when we arrived in Caraway, Arkansas for training. It was a good thing I took his advice.

Coach Wilbur Coggins would stop the limo two or three times a day and drive up two miles up the road and park it. We not only had to run to catch up with the limo, but also pass a basketball back and forth while running! This is what we called "road work." Talk about getting looks from all the cars and trucks passing us. Just imagine seven bright redheaded girls running alongside the

Red Heads Brenda "Brooksie" O'Bryan sells programs

highway, passing basketballs back and forth! I always said that we ran half-way to Alaska but we were in shape when we got to there! It was a good thing too, as we played 44 games in 30 days!

First week on the road as a Red Head was kinda scary. I came from the very small town of Cairo, Missouri (population about 199) and I was very shy. I hadn't been away from home on my own before. I probably didn't speak more than 10 words that first week.

It didn't take long, though, until the girls couldn't shut me up! I just loved playing the game that I loved!

Teammate Lynn Holst Thomas and I became friends my second year on the road, even though we were on different squads as there were three traveling the country that season. We thought that it would be cool to play on the same team the next year but you never knew what team Coach Orwell Moore would put you on. We thought and thought on how we could make sure to be on the same team and decided to invent a new halftime act. Lynn decided to come up for the summer so we could work on one. We finally decided on trying a double dribbling act. We worked all that summer in the heat, sweating our buns off, to get it perfected. We would both dribble the same exact routine, and then she would go between my legs while dribbling and I would be dribbling at the same time. It paid off, since the next time we went down to Caraway, Arkansas and saw Coach Moore, we showed him our new act. He really liked it and said that we had to be on the same team and perform our new double dribbling act. This was the season of 1970-71. After that, the Red Heads always had a double dribbling act in their halftime show.

I also remember the time Coach Jack Moore was driving and I was half asleep when all of a sudden I heard this terrible loud grinding noise. The front tire had come completely off the limo and we were running on just the axle (sparks flying everywhere), I still don't know how Coach kept the car on the road. Anyway, I looked out my window and saw the tire bouncing down the hill. There was a house there and that tire bounced right up on the roof and into the back yard. Some of us girls went to retrieve the tire and when we got around back, we found the tire had landed right beside their dog! That dog was barking his head off and kinda scared us, but we got the tire and took it back to the limo. Of course we had to get a tow to next town.

Lenna Carey (Tucker)

CAREER 1970-71

SOUTHERN BELLES

As told by Lenna Carey Tucker

I was a basketball player. This was my identity. As a Berrien High School, Nashville, Georgia, senior in 1970, my career was about to end. One afternoon during practice Coach Benny Wayne Overman stopped by the gym. He hoped to recruit players for The Southern Belles, a women's professional basketball team, for the 1970-71 season. My high school coach, Stanley "Ramrod" Simpson, thought some of his players, without college plans, may be interested.

Being familiar with the reputation of the All American Red Heads as outstanding players and skilled ball handlers, I was definitely interested. The opportunity to continue to play and travel the country, with a professional team, would be a dream come true. My greatest obstacle was Mama. I knew her consent would be a miracle. It was only after several conversations with the parents of veteran Belle Dianne Kirkland that she gave her approval.

My adventure began the fall of 1970, as I boarded a very small plane in Albany, Georgia headed west toward Arkansas. Coach Overman met me at the Jonesboro, Arkansas airport driving the most awesome limousine with the beautiful Southern Belles logo down the sides. This vehicle was to be my home away from home for the next six months, October to May, and would be excellent advertising where ever we traveled. Our arrival always drew shouts, waves and excitement as soon as the limo appeared.

Other players arrived over the next day and a half. The hard work of getting in shape, learning ball handling skills and trick shots lasted one to two weeks. This team of seven young women would be together 24 hours a day. The amazing thing is that there were no personality conflicts and no drama between us. We began the season as friends and ended the season as friends.

The season on the road finally began. The schedule usually included a game almost every night in a different location. Our games were usually community fundraisers. Our opponents were teams made up of local male players, many of them hometown heroes.

We always played good, competitive basketball, and at halftime entertained the crowd with a display of ball handling and trick shots. Our team comedian, Dianne "Kirk" Kirkland kept the audience laughing as she interacted with the referees, opposing players and the audience.

"Kirk" always seemed to know when to slow things down and lighten the mood when a game became a little too physical. One team was particularly aggressive and I caught an elbow in the mouth that loosened my front tooth. I always thought their aggression was the result of being unprepared to face a group of tough women athletes.

Lenna Carey of the Southern Belles getting ready for a game, 1970-71

Children would line up after the games for autographs from each of us. We were truly honored.

Many nights we returned to the motel late, depending on the distance from the game location. Our uniforms had to be hand washed and hung to dry on any available ledge or hook. We would iron them early the next morning or at the next motel before the game. Our bright white uniforms were very attractive and had to be durable to stand up to all we put it through.

We spent motel time writing home, sometimes calling home collect, snacking, laughing, playing cards and sharing our family life back home. We enjoyed shopping for family members whenever possible. Veteran Sandy Mann kept a watchful eye on the rookie players. There were many times I shared problems going on at home, feelings of homesickness and my faith with her. She was always a good listener and counselor, our surrogate mother and guardian angel.

We used our limo time to share highlights of the previous game, play Uno, nap or enjoy the beautiful countryside as we passed by. Traveling with the "Belles" took me places I would have never traveled and introduced me to communities of wonderful families all over this country. The memories of roadside cafés offering home cooking, the jukeboxes filled with Neil Diamond and John Denver come to life when I hear "Cracklin' Rosie" and "Country Roads."

Coach Overman expected us to maintain our appearance and our attitudes were to reflect respect for ourselves and others. The only time I remember him becoming angry with me, we were in a small town restaurant that prepared homemade cream pies daily for their patrons. As the team finished lunch, I offered to purchase a whole cream pie to share after the night's game. The waitress refused to sell a whole pie. This made no sense to me and I began to argue with her. Coach Overman called my name and I could see the fire in his eyes. I quickly apologized. He later explained that her regular customers looked forward to their daily treat. She didn't want to run short of pie. Disrespect reflects on the team. Lesson learned, thank you Coach.

Coach Plummer joined us about midway the schedule. He was always smiling, chewing his gum and fun to travel with. One afternoon as we traveled a winding mountain highway, Coach Plummer pulled over, pointed out a highway far below and offered a ten-dollar bill to any player that could beat the limo to that point. Linda Shanks, our team center, immediately jumped from the limo and down the steep side. After driving several minutes, Coach realized this was not the same road. We returned to the starting point and called Shanks back up the mountainside. She finally returned, scratched and scraped, but in good humor. I don't know if she was paid or not.

There was the time in Louisiana we had rare day off. The locals invited us to a genuine Cajun boucherie (a communal hog butchering), complete with a band and dancing. We were allowed to experience every aspect of cooking authentic Cajun, from crawfish to barbecue. Nothing was wasted. Even the blood was made into pudding (no thank you). Most remaining parts of the hog were tossed into a great boiling pot and stirred with a long wooden paddle. As I began to stir the pot the hog head came to the surface and I was done. The crawfish and barbecue was amazing and the time spent with these families was unforgettable.

I thank you Coach Overman for the opportunity and my mother for letting me go. The six awesome women I shared this experience with will forever be a part of me. Lucille Thomason, a.k.a. "Little 'Un," was my best buddy. We bonded as soon as we met and did everything together. Dianne Kirkland, our team comedian and best record keeper on the team, documented every town, every game. Linda Shanks, our fearless center, never backed up from any opponent. Madeline Hoing was one of the most thoughtful and kind people I have ever known. Kathy Gaither, the pretty one, had an awesome outside shot. Sandy Mann, the veteran, super ball handler, became a lifelong friend. She still calls me "Kid."

Lucille "Lucy" Thomason (Whetsel)

CAREER 1970-72
SOUTHERN BELLES, ROYAL MAIDS

As told by Lucille Thomason Whetsel

Southern Belle Lucille "Lucy" Thomason, 1970-71

My family always told me that I chased basketballs when I was a little girl, and I never lost my love for the game. I began to learn how to dribble when I was about 8 years old. In fifth grade, I was on the main string at my school. I was the only girl in my class through eighth grade so I always played with the boys.

There are five children in my family. I am the only girl. I was a tomboy. I liked hanging with my four brothers, which meant I rodeoed with them. We ribbon roped, calf roped, and barrel raced. We would earn money to purchase school supplies and basketballs. I remember fondly that daddy would buy me dolls, but I did not want them – all I wanted to do was play basketball, rope, and ride horses.

We had a smoke house. Our basketball goal was a rim from a barrel and the smoke house was our backboard. After we ate, my brothers and I would head outside and shoot basketball at the smoke house goal. My brothers loved basketball almost as much as I did. We would play until dark and, after dark, we would play by the porch light.

By the time I reached ninth grade, I was a ballplayer to be watched. I earned a first string slot all four years of high school, earning All-Conference and All-Star honors each year. When I was a senior, I made All State. All of this was truly an honor to me. The long hours of playing basketball with my brothers, including my rodeo experiences, shaped me into the ballplayer that I finally had become.

My brothers taught me how to shoot a jump shot. Fans and family described my jump shot as "graceful and very deadly." I could hit long shots too — I learned how to focus on the basket, concentrate, and arch the ball in the air so it would fall just over the rim. Opponent coaches would say, "Get that girl!" Driving to the basket was a favorite skill of mine, too.

When I was a senior and played in the All-State Game in Lindsay, Oklahoma, Owner/Coach Ben Overman and Coach Chuck Plummer of the Southern Belles professional basketball team were there and approached my coach, Bennie Neal, to ask if they could talk with me about playing with the Belles. As soon as the game was over, they talked with me about coming on board with the team and playing professionally. On Sunday, they came to my house and I packed and went with them before sundown.

My daddy was very sad and did not want me to go. He cried for a week. My mama consented. What I did not know was that my daddy previously had received a letter addressed to me from the Southern Belles, but he never shared it with me. I found the letter after my daddy died about five years ago. After pondering over the letter, I have realized how proud of me Daddy was. If he had not been, he would have destroyed the letter but he kept it. He just didn't want his little girl to leave home.

When I arrived in Arkansas at training, the coach gave me three basketballs and said, "Lucy learn how to juggle." I did — it took practice, practice, practice. For the Southern Belles halftime show of entertainment, I juggled; I shot a "behind the back" shot; and from the foul line, with my back to the goal, I would step backwards toward the goal and bounce the ball over my head and into the goal. All of this took hours and hours to perfect and be consistent.

One of the most memorable times I recall was when the Southern Belles went snowmobiling. It was so much fun. I had never been around snow. I also remember being in a blizzard in Kansas. It was almost impossible to walk to a nearby restaurant because of the strong winds. Snowdrifts had blown against the motel door to our rooms making it very difficult to open the door. It was a ghost town — no one was around. As much fun as it was, I had rather been doing what I loved the most — playing basketball.

I also remember visiting historical sites while we were touring. One of my favorites was Mount Rushmore National Memorial in the Black Hills region of South Dakota. The sculpture's roughly 60-foot high, granite faces depict U.S. Presidents George Washington, Thomas Jefferson, Theodore Roosevelt and Abraham Lincoln. It was interesting to marvel at the majestic beauty of the Black Hills and learn about the birth, growth, development and preservation of the country.

Christmas time with the Belles was quite an experience. We were in Charleston, West Virginia, and we stayed at the Daniel Boone Hotel. The hotel was built in 1929 by a group of Charleston citizens to provide an elegant center for hosting politicians and visiting dignitaries in the bustling capital city. The hotel was beautiful. We were a bit nostalgic because our busy touring schedule did not allow time for the Belles to make it home to their families for Christmas. So we decided to make the best of it. Sandy Mann, referred to as our protector, came to our rescue and was instrumental in finding the Belles a Christmas tree. I believe she talked an employee at the hotel out of it. Having a tree did seem to make the holiday season a bit easier. This was my first Christmas ever away from home and it made me sad, but now that I think of it, we really did make the best of it and had a good first Christmas away from our families.

After playing the night before, we would often be tired the next morning. Sleeping in the car was a given. The girls would lay against the doors and lay on each other's shoulders. I was the smallest Belle on the team and I would even sleep on top of the luggage. When we arrived at our next destination, we would begin to do our hair and makeup, dress for the game, go to the game and perform;

eat after the game, hurry back to the motel and shower; wash our uniforms, hang them up to dry and pray they would get dry by the next morning. If not, we would try to iron them dry. Sometimes, we had to wear them with the seams a bit damp.

I fondly remember our team being invited by our sponsor to a Cajun boucherie in Louisiana. We were served corn, potatoes, onions, shrimp, and crawfish from a barrel. It was delicious! There was an older gentleman who tried to teach Sandy Mann how to crack the crawfish and he also was trying to feed her. He dripped some of the spiced juices on her shirt and Sandy quickly explained to him that she could do it herself. I also remember that these gentlemen were cooking a hog in a huge pot. They were stirring it with a wooden paddle. It was a fun, interesting, and very entertaining afternoon and evening. This group of Cajuns truly rolled out the red carpet for us.

My favorite game was when we played in my hometown of Pittsburg, Oklahoma. We had a great crowd. The coach entrusted me to put on part of the show and pull some stunts with my high school coach, Bennie Neal, and others that I knew. I cannot remember if we won or lost. During my tour with the Belles, we played against college greats and other very talented ballplayers. Other times, the ballplayers were not very skilled at the game. In my opinion, it was much easier to perform against skilled basketball players than against players who did not play well and who would not corporate with our show. After all, we were in their town to perform and entertain.

I hated to see the season end — it was bittersweet.

I played with the Royal Maids, another professional women's basketball team, the year after I left the Southern Belles. For the following year, I was asked to be the team comedienne for the Royal Maids, but I came home from the first tour and met my husband, John Eubank Whetsel, and we married October 18, 1972. That ended my professional basketball career.

I thank the Lord for the opportunity to play professional basketball and for keeping us safe during all the traveling, and for the success He has allowed my family. Without Him, I could not have made it.

To my Southern Belles teammates — thank you for all the memories. Lenna Tucker and I were the same age and the rookies during my tour with the Belles. We hit if off instantly and she was my best buddy. Lenna was a super ball handler and a very sweet and pretty girl. Linda Shanks was our 6-foot-1 center and hook shot artist. Dianne Kirkland was called "Miss Basketball" and was the team comedienne. I always enjoyed watching her clown with the referees and others. Sandy Mann was the famous dribbler and playmaker. She was also considered as our mother figure and protector. She kept us straight. Kathy Gaither was a real "cutie" and was a great set shot artist. Madeline Hoing was a very low-key but sweet person. She was the Belles' defensive ace.

The Southern Belles will always be a part of me.

Madeline Hoing

CAREER 1970-71
SOUTHERN BELLES
As told by Madeline Hoing

I grew up and went to school in Memphis, Tennessee. I lived and breathed basketball throughout my school years, both junior and high school.

During the summer of 1970, I was playing softball in a Memphis League. Ben Overman, owner of the Southern Belles, a women's professional basketball team, approached me. He asked me if I would be interested in playing professional basketball. Of course I said that I would, and later that fall, I joined and played the 1970-71 season with the "Belles."

That year was a very special time in my life. We played men's teams only and played by men's rules. We won most of our games. We added a lot of show, during the game, and performed a half-time show.

The halftime show consisted of fancy ball handling, trick shots, ball spinning, juggling, and passing and dribbling routines. We had a team clown, Dianne Kirkland, and she dealt the referees a lot

Madeline Hoing (second from right) with Southern Belles, 1971. L-R: Lenna Tucker, Sandy Mann, Kathy Gaither, Owner/Coach Ben Overman, Lucille "Lucy" Thomason, Hoing, and Linda Shanks.

of misery, as well as some of the guys. We all participated in the fun, calling the guys names such as Curly, Shorty and Skinny. If we had one that got a little "out of hand" we'd call him "showboat." When one of the Belles did something fancy we'd say to our man, "hey, can you do that?"

After the game, the crowd would come down on the court to visit with us, be close to us, and get our autographs. We always stayed, as long as it took, to talk to each and every one of them, even though it was usually going to be a lot of miles to our next game. We traveled about 60,000 miles that season in our four-door stretch limousine.

I am of the Catholic faith. Occasionally, we would be in a town on a Sunday, where a church was available to me. On those days, Sandy Mann, who was the "back-up driver," would get up early and take me to Mass — in that stretch limo. Imagine seeing someone arriving at the local Catholic Church in a stretch limo!

We were up late every night, getting ready for the next day — fixing our hair, washing our uniforms, and ironing our clothes. We made sure to pack our suitcases at night, so we didn't have that to do the next morning. We caught up on our sleep in the limo as we traveled.

One night we played in Tiptonville, Tennessee, which was close to my hometown of Memphis. Sylvia Viglietti, my high school coach, arranged for several carloads of kids from my high school to be brought to that game.

We had a great group on that team. We all got along well and had a great time doing what we loved best — playing basketball.

Sue Whitten

Career 1971-74
All American Red Heads

As told by Sue Whitten

I was born June 10, 1951, the daughter of Opal Whitten, in Memphis, TN. As a child, our family relocated to Horn Lake, Mississippi. As insignificant as that might have seemed, it would become the paramount fate that shaped an opportunity that ultimately led toward me becoming an All American Red Head.

That was long ago.

What started as a seventh grade extra-curricular activity became a twist of fortune for me. This story is not to make me more or less captivating, because, as everyone knew, basketball was not just enjoyable but a tremendous shot in the arm as I became skilled at a sport that would dominate my early life.

As a 5-foot-7 junior and senior player, I helped Horn Lake's girls' team to a 26-6 record and was a two-time All-North Mississippi pick. My coach Van Chancellor (yes, the same Van Chancellor that coached LSU, the WNBA Houston Comets and is inducted into the Naismith Memorial Basketball Hall of Fame) said, "Sue is one of the hardest-working players I have ever coached. She is a defensive specialist and takes great pride in her play." That same year Chancellor invited the Horn Lake High School girls' team to an event at the Memphis Mid-South Coliseum to see the All American Red Heads. The idea was seeded but not thought through. After all, there was college and more basketball.

In 1969, I was the first Horn Lake High School girl's team player to be named to the North State All-Star Team. Summer camp counseling, the All-Star game and other appearances came and went.

Red Heads comedian Sue Whitten takes a bow at the 1973 reunion at Memphis, TN

In September 1969, I entered Mississippi State College for Women, with a major in Physical Education. In my first two years I visited nearby games of the Red Heads as often as possible. Then a knee injury during basketball practice placed me in the school infirmary, which sidelined me for the remainder of the season. That, I thought, would be the end. Not so. What would it take to turn a desire into reality? It was a red, white and blue uniform with stars and stripes and a change of hair color.

In the summer of 1971, Orwell Moore, owner of the Red Heads, made contact with me and inquired as to whether my interest in basketball would include playing for the All American Red Heads.

It was my junior year. Although it would mean leaving college, it was the RED HEADS! Did I leave? Absolutely. The All American Red Heads were queens of women's basketball. And I, Sue "Rosie Red" Whitten, from a little town in Mississippi, by instinct provided antics, skill and laughter as the Red Heads comedienne, 'Prima Donna' and the 'Clown Princess of Basketball' for the next few years of my life. Few ever could play the sport and entertain the way I did on and off the court, scoring over 10,000 points at the same time.

One of my favorite routines also included Brenda "Brooksie" Brooks. A screen would be set for me. I would drive to the hoop, step one foot on Brooksie's leg, then up to her shoulders, where I DUNKED IT! Who said women couldn't dunk in the '70s? To add humor to the routine, she left too early for the other end of the court with me hanging on the basketball rim.

Yet, all wasn't fun and smiles. Once when we stopped to eat, Brooksie closed the limo door on my right four fingers before I could get out and locked the door with her key, leaving me sitting in front driver's seat. All I said was, "Brooksie, can I see you for a minute?" I think everyone freaked but me.

Despite being a bit more from the South than a Connecticut Yankee, I was naive about the value of Stetson cowboy hats. So after a time-out, I ran up the bleachers to the top row, asked this cowboy if I could borrow his hat. I didn't wait for an answer and ran back down and inbounded the ball wearing a white Stetson hat, about ten-gallon size. The crowd couldn't see a thing but sneakers and red and white striped socks. The ball went through the guy's legs and my teammate NAILED IT!

I then pulled the infamous "dust off the hat routine," where I put it on the floor, jump up, bend my knees with my feet together like I was going to stomp on it, then at the last moment spread my feet and come down straddling the hat. I don't think I've ever seen a cowboy move that fast without a horse.

Coach Jack didn't know I was going to do that one. I think it scared the Texas "cow dung" clear out of his pants, since that hat cost more than I was paid each month.

Cindy "Pecos" Roybal

CAREER 1971-72
ALL AMERICAN RED HEADS

As told by Cindy Roybal

It was my senior year of '71. Members of our yearbook staff were in Las Vegas, New Mexico. I noticed a flyer that this group of girls — the All American Red Heads — were going to be playing. We never had a high school girls' basketball team. Yet, I was pretty good. The boys Coach tried to get me in the boys team, but to no avail. It was the year before Title IX came into effect.

I convinced our sponsor to let us attend. At the game I spoke to the coach and we arranged a tryout for me at Clayton, New Mexico. Because we got a huge snowstorm I was unable to attend and very disappointed that I missed my chance to play professional basketball. Ironically, I later spent 17 years at New Mexico Highlands University in Las Vegas and left as the winningest coach ever!

Cindy "Pecos" Roybal of the Red Heads, 1971-72

I was later invited to attend the Red Heads tryout camp in Caraway, Arkansas.

I got a letter from Mr. Orwell Moore, owner and coach of the Red Heads, just before my birthday in September. I received it as Dad and I were butchering a deer he had shot! I was going to be a Red Head. Dad finished butchering the deer as I packed up my bags once again headed for Arkansas.

Mr. Moore found out I was fluent in Spanish and teammate Denise Mauris was fluent in French. We worked out a little routine together, usually having something to do with the officials. For example, we would pretend we didn't like a call and started rattling off in our different languages.

Once time we were going to be playing in Roanoke, Virginia for Christmas. My folks had never flown before, although my sister was a stewardess. They flew out there to watch me play. It was special for me, since our family of eight had always spent Christmas together. Everyone sacrificed so my parents could be with me.

Once when I was coaching we were traveling late at night after a game that we had just lost in Gunnison, Colorado. I was upset cause I felt the girls didn't play up to their potential. We also were driving very slow and cautiously because it was snowing, when all of a sudden we hear a THUD.

We got out of the van and removed a six-point buck from the road. I then had my male assistant take the wheel. Shortly afterwards another THUD, here we go move another buck out of our way! By this time I was upset (it was a wonder the van was okay) so I took over the driving duties. About 15 minutes later — you guessed it — another THUD! Now we remove a 10-point buck! As we got back in the van a voice from the back says "Coach can I say something?" I answered reluctantly, "Go ahead." She said "if we could have used all the points you coaches got, we would have WON the game!" We all just laughed and enjoyed the rest of the trip.

Lynn Holst (Thomas)

CAREER 1971-73

ALL AMERICAN RED HEADS

As told by Lynn Holst Thomas

I found out about the Red Heads through my high school coach Shirley "Trooper" Howard, who had played for the Red Heads in the 1950s and even went to Alaska. A friend of mine and I went to Holly Springs, Mississippi in the summer to their basketball camp my senior year and ended up trying out. Luck was on my side as this was the year Mr. Moore started a third team. I got the call and off to camp I went for training.

I laugh about my first game. I was so excited that after I got to the gym to get into my uniform to get dressed and warm up, but I realized I forgot my shoes. That meant I sat on the bench the first game.

Being the smallest player on our team, I did a lot of sleeping on top of the luggage in the back on occasion and would use a sweater or a jacket for a pillow. Most of the sleep was short naps and the taller players could get a bit jealous at times, but sleeping in the back did come with its own issues. Coach Ben happened to be colorblind and didn't always see stop light changes. The brakes would get a hard and quick stomp of the foot and everything would come to a quick stop — except for me.

Yet, because I was the shortest I was also relied on to help with tasks that others could not do easily. We were traveling to a town called Happy Camp, California way up on a mountain. On our way up the muffler fell down. I had to crawl under and wire it up with a coat hanger, but we made it. We were very thankful as the next morning had to take a different route due to landslide on the very same mountain.

I played and went to Hazelwood High School in St. Louis. Pam Rowlett and I did the "piggyback play," a Red Head tradition and fan favorite. I was only 5-foot-4, but was the only one on the team that could dunk as Pam would crouch down as I put my left foot on her knee grabbed her hand and swung my leg over her shoulder. Then I would get a pass from half court and dunk the ball.

We had little time for entertaining ourselves and Christmas away from home was the worst, but we found some special Christmas pajamas one Christmas and got ourselves all ready for Santa to visit.

We also had our own little traveling band. I had my guitar. Jeanne Oehlman did some mean picking on her banjo and Kathy Tipton could clog and make the ground rumble. We'd start playing that old Cajun "Crawdad" Song ("You get a line, I'll get a pole, we'll go fishin' in the crawfish hole"). We would go on and

Lynn Holst (right) with Red Heads teammates Mary Leasure and Brenda O'Bryan pose with a fan on the way to Mexico, 1972-73.

play that a long time. We couldn't play in the car, but did in the rooms or outside the motels. We really had fun with it in Camp Courage as those old wooden floors would just rattle when Kathy would dance. Being on the road for 7 1/2 months we always hated to hear Simon and Garfunkel's "Homeward Bound."

Jeanne Oehlman

CAREER 1971-73
TEXAS COWGIRLS, ALL AMERICAN RED HEADS

As told by "Spanky" Losier

Jeanne began her professional basketball career while she was still in high school. Going to school and studying during the week, she would exchange her schoolbooks for a basketball and meet up with the Texas Cowgirls on the weekends and play for them.

Jeanne joined the All American Red Heads in 1971. She was an outstanding outside shooter who had a soft accurate shot. She also was a great ball handler. Jeanne prided herself on her ability to make free throws. She used the same form as Oscar Robertson. One hand on the ball then the other just before she released the ball to shoot.

Jeanne was a woman of many talents. She was an accomplished tenor banjo player. Her second year with the Red Heads she and teammate Spanky Losier — who played guitar and sang — would entertain the audience before the game. The crowd loved it as much as Jeanne loved playing the banjo. It became a regular part of the show.

In 1973 Jeanne hung up her basketball shoes. She moved to moved to Casper, Wyoming where she was offered a job to play her banjo at Shakee's Pizza Parlor.

Jeanne Oehlman at Red Heads reunion in Memphis, Tennessee, May 1973

Kay O'Bryan (Burk)

CAREER 1972-76
ALL AMERICAN RED HEADS

As told by Kay O'Bryan Burk

My sister Brenda O'Bryan played on the All American Red Heads for two years while I was still in high school. Anytime her team played close to our home, Mom, Dad, my grandparents and I went to her game. So I got to shoot around before the games and got to know what playing on the Red Heads would be like. I also got to go to their basketball camp (Brenda took me and some of my high school teammates) before my senior year. Mr. Moore talked to me and asked if I would be interested and I said, "yes sir." After I graduated in May and turned 18 in August, Mr. Moore sent me a contract. I had the advantage of already knowing somewhat it would be like. I played my first game in New Augusta, Mississippi.

We would rotate who would sit in front as Coach Charlotte Adams was doing all the driving. Whoever sat there had to stay awake and help read the road map. Mr. Moore sent a man to do the driving after our first nine days on the road. (I'm sure it was really tiring for Coach to do what all she had to do). I know that first day the driver got lost and we went about an hour's drive out of the way and had to back track. Coach Adams was a little upset, to say the least, and told him to take the map in at the motel each night and study it and know how to get to our next night's game place. The driver did well after that.

In January 1975 we played in Acuna, Mexico. I always called it our bullfighting gym since we were told they held bullfights there. The floor was just concrete with dull painted lines for the free throw lane. It was a really dusty, dirty floor, and we would slip and slide whenever we tried to stop or change directions. I think we could have written our names on the floor and have read it from

Red Head Kay O'Bryan, 1972-73

the stands. The walls in front of the stands were concrete and about six to seven feet high. They showed us the door through which the bulls entered (no, they didn't release any bulls that night). The gym had small, wooden backboards to shoot on.

Before the game we knew it would probably be a fast-paced game. Hardly any of the Mexican guys we were playing spoke English, and all I remember hearing from the guys was "Andale, andale!" We soon figured out that meant "Go, go!" They were really fast and just wanted to get the ball and dribble as fast as they could go to score a layup. I normally did a dribbling routine during our halftime show that had me dribbling while lying on the floor, but coach told me to stay off the floor. He figured our uniforms would be dirty enough, he was afraid mine would never come clean if I got on the floor. We ended up losing the game in probably one of the lowest, if not the lowest-scoring game every played by a Red Head team, 44-38. I can remember them laughing and clapping, so guess they enjoyed the game!

Now picture this: Four redheads in one small bathroom trying to get ready in the morning in sometimes as little as 30 minutes after playing a game the night before and washing our uniforms out in the sink. Yes, we washed our uniforms after most games in the sink (cold water only, so they wouldn't fade) after taking our showers. We would then roll the uniform up in our used towels, stomp on them to get out the excess water and then hang them to dry, hopefully by the next morning. One night Coach said to dye my hair again, since we were expecting Mr. Moore to visit soon. So I put Miss Clairol Flame 33S on, waited the allotted time, jumped in the shower and — NO HOT WATER! The water was FREEZING COLD. I was hollering and screaming, but Coach Adams said I had to stay in there till I got the dye out of my hair.

We always had to be well dressed in nice slacks and tops with makeup on and hair teased and styled whenever we were out in public. At least we didn't have to wear our bright red lipstick till game time. I got pretty good using my small night case with a small mirror in it to put my makeup on sitting on the bed.

On Sunday April 29, 1973 we played a doubleheader. The first game in the afternoon was in Belcourt, North Dakota, where we won winning 86-65. As usual, we stayed long enough after the game to sign autographs and for Coach to settle up the money, then we traveled 190 miles to Napoleon, North Dakota for that night's game, winning 85-74. After the postgame routine, we loaded up and headed on the road once again, this for an all night and day trip to Dexter, Kansas, about 820 miles away.

That year there were three Red Head teams on the road, and we had the oldest, smallest limo, which we called "Lit'l Whitey." We were saying, "Lit'l Whitey, don't fail us now." Lit'l Whitey got us to the game barely on time We changed into our uniforms in the dressing room, put our bright red lipstick on and out on the gym floor we went. You would have thought we would barely be able to move, but we won that night 102-87 — over a hundred points in just 32 minutes, mind you.

But that's not the end of the story. We had to be in Jonesboro, Arkansas by around noon the next day on May 1. So we loaded up again and traveled all night, our driver Bill, Coach Adams and Wanda England taking turns driving. We played in Jonesboro on the 1st, winning 65-59, then traveled to Grenada, Mississippi for a night game on May 2, winning 89-55. Exhausted, we then went to Memphis so we could meet up with the other teams and a reunion of retired Red Heads.

Ruth Hart

Career 1972-75
Arkansas Lassies
As told by Ruth Hart

I was growing up in a very small town in Southern Illinois when I got to watch the Arkansas Lassies play at my school. I just went up and started talking to them after the game and shot around with them after the game as well. They had me do a bit of ball handling as well. They were quite impressed.

However, I was only a junior in high school.

I went on to graduate from high school in 1972 and in October of '72 the Lassies contacted me. They wanted me to play for them. I went to the store and I bought a huge suitcase. They swung by my house in a huge station wagon and off we went. I was a professional basketball player, just like that. They gave me a uniform and I played in my first game that night!

I was very nervous, but the love of basketball settled me into it. I was one of the best ball players around in my day. We had no organized basketball for girls at any level in my town. All we had were the courts after school where I developed a real decent outside shot.

Arkansas Lassie Ruth Hart, 1974-75

Barb Hostert

Career 1974-80
All American Red Heads
As told by Barb Hostert

When I was 14, I saw some posters all around my high school, Lincoln Way Central in Mokena, IL, about the All American Red Heads coming to play our coaches. These coaches did not want to get beat by women.

I went to the game and watched these women play. They were awesome. I thought, that's what I want to do. I already played a lot with the boys. I had boys my age in my neighborhood. We always played in my driveway. I had a basketball hoop and the guys would come over. We also played flag football and baseball. They would come get me and say, "Hey, would you play with us? We need a quarterback. Hey, we need a pitcher."

I could not wait get home from the game to tell my mother and father. Wow, these women were great. I want to be an All American Red Head! On the back of the program that I bought at the game, there was an application about Camp Courage, a basketball camp, and the Red Heads were going to be there as counselors.

I went to Camp Courage for several years. It was so special. When you got there, you went up this hill to the top and there was the camp. There was Adams Hall, Ammons Hall, Clark Hall, and Moore Hall. They were named after the players and the Moores. We had three 2 ½ hour sessions each day, and boy was it hot! On Friday, the last day of camp, we would go down to the cookout place and have watermelon and homemade ice cream. It was a good ole time.

One of my favorite Red Heads and my idol was Jolene Ammons. I was 15 and she was probably 30. There was a track and I remember running against Jolene. She was really quick, so I raced her. Can you imagine competing in anything against your sports idol? It was the coolest.

Barb "Gabby" Hostert, with Lynnette Sjoquist loading up "Whitey," as the Red Heads depart Camp Courage and get ready to hit the road, 1976.

By the time I was 18 and all my school sports were over with, I signed a contract. Right after I signed the contract, I graduated high school with dyed red hair.

I was very quiet and shy my first year on the road. I hardly said anything. I was in awe of it all. Because I was so quiet, my teammates gave me the nickname "Gabby," which stayed with me all these years.

I could do everything in the Red Heads halftime show before starting my first year. Juggling, ball spinning, fancy dribbling, and all the trick shots. I prided myself on being in shape. I could walk down the court on my hands. Because I could do that, Coach Moore had me work on standing on my head and kicking the ball in with my feet. When my parents would come to the game, my dad would give me 20 dollars if I could make that shot the first time during the halftime show. I did a good job cashing in on that challenge.

My second year started off being very exciting. My unit went to Alaska to play for several weeks. We had to fly everywhere. We rode in a dog sled and had so many wonderful experiences. The people were great and welcomed us into their homes, since there weren't any motels or hotels in any of the towns. The audiences were great and they loved our red hair.

I also had the opportunity my second year to play back at my high school, Lincoln Way Central. It was quite a battle. As I mentioned before, these coaches certainly didn't want to get beat by a women. It was an honor to be able to play in front of all my friends and family.

Lincoln Way Central has a Wall of Fame in the lobby of the gym. All the players who went to school there who made it to the professional level have their uniform jersey displayed there. I am very proud that my Red Head jersey is hanging there too.

One of my favorite memories was one season we were to play at Gallaudet National College for the Deaf in Washington, D.C. Coach Moore had informed us many weeks in advance. I picked up a book on how to learn sign language and we practiced as we were traveling around the country. All of us started teaching ourselves how to sign during the many long miles we traveled. When we got better, we even decided to try to order at a restaurant in sign. When we finally got to play the game, we all walked out one at a time and used signed language to introduce ourselves and to communicate with the players.

Another great memory is when we played at Western Ontario University against their alumni. Fergie Jenkins, who pitched for the Chicago Cubs, was there. I am big Cubs fan, so I was really excited. We had a luncheon before the game and I got to sit across the table from him. We talked a lot about baseball. Fergie was not only a great pitcher but he was an awesome basketball player too. I had the assignment of guarding him. It was quite a challenge, but fun.

Cyndi Meserve (Bona)

Career 1974-75
Pratt Institute

As told by Cyndi Meserve Bona

Back in 1970, in a small town in rural Maine, there were no opportunities for girls or young women to participate in sports. The only organized sports team for females didn't begin until the high school level. There were baseball, basketball, and football teams for boys at the junior high level, but girls' only involvement was to be a cheerleader on the sidelines.

In the spring of my eighth grade year of junior high, the high school varsity girls' basketball coach decided to run a two-week intramural basketball program for the eighth grade girls to see if we had any talent coming up for next year's team. It was a very informal program where we were taught some skills and played some games. Coach Bean pulled me aside to show me how to do a layup, as he saw some potential in me, and I remember spending most of the practice perfecting the skill. Prior to this, my only experience with a basketball with shooting at a crooked basketball hoop at the primary school playground. The playground had dirt as a surface, so dribbling wasn't even an option.

I was already 5-foot-8 inches tall, which at that time was considered tall. He said he hoped that I would try out for the basketball team next year, and not to continue to be a cheerleader as I had done for my two years in junior high. I told him I would, since I was competitive by nature and liked the idea of playing a sport to help the team win, not just watching on the sidelines.

So sometime in October of my freshman year he had all of the girls interested in playing basketball start running the boys cross country trail every day after school to get in shape for tryouts. We had the tryouts, and I made the varsity team as a fifth or sixth player on the team. It was difficult being a freshman starter, since the upperclassmen resented having someone take playing time from one of their friends was on the bench. But I learned to love the game and put my heart into it, and that year went very well. We won the Mountain Valley Conference and couldn't wait for the next year as we were only losing one senior.

There were no state championship tournaments at that time, so we were satisfied with our small and basically unknown title. The next three years, the Livermore Falls varsity girls' basketball team went on to win the conference Championship. We also played other schools that weren't in our conference, as our coach liked the challenge, and it was rewarding for us to beat some Class A schools. We actually did get quite a bit of press at that time in the local paper because we were getting a reputation as being a great team, and our coach did a great job of promoting us and offering us new challenges.

We used to have more spectators at our games and the boys did. My senior year of high school I had to make a decision about where to attend college. There was no doubt in my mind that I would attend college, but the decision wasn't to be based on athletic scholarships. To my knowledge, there weren't even any offered to women at that time. My choices were the University of Maine to major in physical education, or Pratt Institute in Brooklyn, New York to major in fashion design. One of my high school English teachers noticed my artistic and creative talents and she talked me into applying attending Pratt. If I had attended University of Maine I'm sure I would have played basketball, and it was one of the reasons I hesitated about attending Pratt. Their catalog didn't mention a women's basketball team, so I chose to pursue my artistic interests, and forgo playing basketball.

Sometime around the beginning of October, my freshman year at Pratt, I went into the dorm after a day of classes and saw a sign posted in the elevator. It said basketball meeting tonight at 7 p.m. in Room 101, North Hall. It didn't say anything about men or women, so I decided to go to the meeting and see what it was all about. When I walked into Room 101, there were a lot of guys already sitting at desk, and a couple of coaches standing at the front of the room. The 6-foot-5 coach asked me if I was there for the cheerleading meeting, which he said was the next night. I replied, "No, I'm here to play basketball!"

His jaw dropped, he asked me to have a seat and immediately chuckles were heard all over the room. The coach proceeded with the meeting, then afterwards he came up to me and asked if I was serious about playing on the men's varsity basketball team. I told him that I really liked to play and would like to play on the team if at all possible. He said he would check it out with the athletic director and see if there any rules or regulations stipulating that a woman could or couldn't try out for the men's team.

The next day the coach Tony Missere came to see me. Because Pratt didn't offer a women's team, I was given the go ahead to try out. There were no rules in the NCAA stating that a woman couldn't play on a men's team. The coach asked me if I was going to try out and I said I thought I would. He said there might be some publicity surrounding this, especially since we were in New York City (and boy, that was an understatement). But he wanted to see me try out and he felt I had a good chance to make the team, since Pratt isn't a sports orientated school and there aren't huge amount of participants.

I was a little hesitant, especially seeing the size of some of my future teammates, but I wasn't the shortest person at the meeting either. Two weeks later tryouts began. During the conditioning period we had to run around the gated campus in Brooklyn. I was only allowed to run around half of the campus, as they didn't want me going into the dangerous section of the neighborhood.

Also, a few of the guys were posted around the area to make sure I was safe. At the end of the week, coach came to see to tell me I had made the team. He didn't have to cut anyone, but a couple of guys did drop out. Practice began the next week. My new teammates were very supportive of me joining the team. They were nervous about bumping into me, or following me, but soon realized that I could handle myself.

Cyndi Meserve from Pratt Institute shoots a layup during pre-game warmups, 1974-75.

The public relations department at Pratt sent a press release to the newspapers about having a woman on their team, and all hell broke loose! From then on there were cameras and reporters filming my every move. It was difficult trying to play basketball knowing every move and mistake you made was being filmed and documented for the next day's headlines. Pratt even gave me my own personal secretary from public relations to field all the calls, set up all interviews, appearances and appointments that were coming in every day.

I had no idea this was going to happen. After all, I just wanted to play basketball

The most publicity occurred before the first game, which was scheduled against Baruch College in Manhattan. All of the media was anxiously waiting to see me on the court, whether to succeed or fail, I wasn't sure. At this point I wasn't sure I wanted to go into the game. But eventually the coach did put me into the game. I only played a couple of minutes, since the game was quite close and the starters played most of the game. I didn't shoot, but I did drop the ball after a jump ball with a Baruch player, and of course the pictures of this were all over the newspapers the next day.

Every week presented a different challenge, and depending on which college we would be playing. All of the schools have to have separate changing rooms for me, and that was an issue when we played an all military school, Kings Point, on Long Island. They didn't have a women's locker room, so I just changed in the restroom. The mostly male audience at the game were really hoping for me to play, and I was begging my coach not to put me in. But eventually I did play and they were all cheering very loudly. I was glad when it was over.

The majority of my exposure was positive. I did upset some people involved in a women's liberation movement, as I was misquoted as saying I was against women's liberation. I never said this, I merely stated that I didn't consider myself a women's libber, and it was not the motivation behind me playing on the men's team at all. I received a lot of fan mail and flowers — even orchids from Rome, Italy. Walter Cronkite featured me on the six o'clock news. I even got to be on the TV show "To Tell the Truth," was honored by the Boston Celtics, and even asked out to dinner by Terry Bradshaw and Joe Namath. For a young woman from a small town in Maine this was quite an experience.

When the whirlwind season was over, I buckled down and concentrated on my design courses. I was able to attain better grades the second semester, not having basketball practice six days a week and traveling to out-of-town games. I decided not to play basketball the next year.

Thirty years later, I'm still playing basketball on a Maine senior women's basketball team and we have won gold and silver medals at the National Senior Games.

Marsha Tate

Career 1974-77
All American Red Heads

As told by Marsha Tate

At the age of 15, I was fortunate enough to play in a district softball tournament against a team from Caraway, Arkansas. At the end of that tournament, little did I know that the man who was congratulating me on being the most valuable player of the tournament was Orwell Moore, owner of the All American Red Heads!

Later on Mr. Moore contacted the basketball coach at my high school in Black Rock, inquiring about me and wanting to talk to me about playing with the Red Heads. When he found out I was only 15 he said he couldn't talk to me about playing but wanted me to come to his basketball camp, in Holly Springs, Mississippi, called Camp Courage.

Of course, when I found out about this, I was elated! For a girl who only had the opportunity to play basketball in the fifth and sixth grade and never had the opportunity to play basketball in high school, this was a dream come true.

I attended camp for the next three years, learning from Coach Moore, his brother Jack and so many of the Red Heads. Charlotte Adams taught me the art of hook shots and Jolene Ammons helped me learn to juggle. My goal changed from going to college and becoming an nurse to playing basketball for the All American Red Heads!

After my high school graduation, I went on the road with the Red Heads for the next three years, then later fulfilled my other dream of becoming an RN.

We learned about respect, dignity, dedication, determination and hard work. There were a couple of times I can remember that we were an hour late for the game and we walked into a packed gym to a standing ovation. We were tired but hurried and changed into our uniforms and put on the show for our fans.

Red Heads Marsha Tate at Camp Courage, 1975

One of these times was in Bethel, Alaska. Our flight was delayed and we landed to a minus-30 wind chill factor. We ended up spending the night in the gym! The other occasion occurred due to a number of incidents. First of all, our car had broken down and was in the shop in St. Louis, Missouri and we had a game in the southern part of the state. Our coach could not find a vehicle large enough to carry the team, our duffle bags, uniforms and our four bags of basketballs, so he rented a U-Haul and we rode in the back of it. Well, down the road the tie rod fell out of the U-Haul and we had to be towed into the next town, Peculiar, Missouri. As we hung out at a gas station trying to figure out how we were going to make it to our game in Dora, Missouri, a very nice man offered to take us in his Bronco. We piled into that Bronco and some of us laid across the ball bags in the back. Oh but that was not the end of our adventures. We then had a flat on the Bronco. An hour after the game was to start we entered the gym to a packed crowd still waiting on us! Whatever we had to endure to make a game, we played hard and put on the show for the fans.

One of the funniest things that we did was tie shoestrings to our windshield wipers and used them to work our nonfunctional wipers the last few miles to the next town.

Martha Carswell

Career 1974-75
Indianapolis Pink Panthers

As told by Martha Carswell

I was born in Homerville, Georgia in 1949 and acquired a basketball shortly after that. I remember having about a five-foot goal to shoot at before my Dad went all out and built me a full court with clay.

We used to meet every day after school and choose up teams. I was usually the only girl and we would play until we had to go in for homework and supper. We also played on Saturday mornings.

My coach happened to be Jolene Ammons, who was a great star for the All American Red Heads. She was my first coach and last coach, so I guess "the basketball does go around." I lived basketball. That's what you did in Homerville, Georgia in the 1950s-'60s. I played through junior high school and made the varsity my freshman year in high school.

Pink Panthers Martha Carswell, 1974

Basketball was very competitive in Georgia and we had some great teams. I never knew I had a chance to play in college, so my dream was to come back to "Clinch County" and coach girls' basketball. I said, "A girl will never have to ask me to practice," or "We will never be denied gym time." We had a green sign up in our gym called the "Old Barn" that was hung up right behind the backboard. The sign said "CONSTANT PRACTICE OFTEN EXCELS TALENT" until the day it was torn down.

I went to Georgia Southern University and majored in health and physical education. I played on intramural basketball teams because Title IX had not gone into effect yet. I graduated college and here came Title IX, the greatest thing to ever happen to women's sports, thanks to people like Billie Jean King. I got my BS degree at Georgia Southern and started coaching basketball.

I was home in Georgia for the summer of 1974 and Jolene Ammons was also home. We were friends and always enjoyed talking about basketball. She mentioned me about this new women's league that was forming and she was going to be a part of it and coach. She asked me if I would like to come out to Phoenix and try out. I almost fainted. I went to Phoenix and worked harder than I had at anything to be able to play with that team.

I made the team, and we played our first games in Phoenix. We also went to see a Virginia Slims Tennis Tournament. I had been determined to meet Billie Jean King. I saw her walking and ran after her and introduced myself and told her I was with the Pink Panthers. She said she wanted to meet us and to do an article for her *Women's Sports* magazine. We all got to go in her trailer after the match and talk to her.

While in Phoenix, we trained for several months in the same gym with the Phoenix Suns. We played in the west for a while and then moved our headquarters to Indiana. We played mostly at small towns versus men's teams in the area. We played most every night, traveling through New York and Canada. We were having a lot of financial problems, and our owner said he could not support us anymore.

We all decided to take off on our own and make a go of it. We hung in there, a team of five players for several months but were just unable to meet the financial needs of staying on the road. We weren't even getting paid at the time, we just wanted to play basketball. We just hoped to make expenses.

I got to play basketball with Billie-Jean King!

The players of that historic team (alphabetically):

Jolene Ammons, Georgia
Gwen Bachman, Colorado
Martha Carswell, Georgia
Lois Glover, Tennessee
Mary Hounsell, Wisconsin
Jackie Junkman, Iowa
Karen Logan, California
Connie Vance, Tennessee
Linda White, Texas

Patty Bruce

Career 1975-76
All American Red Heads

As told by Patty Bruce

I attended a small country school known as "Garrett U" outside the town of Beaver (Cow Chip Capital of the World), Oklahoma that had a total population of 50.

I played on the first All American Red Heads team whose players all attended college previously.

As far as I know I was the only Red Head that could not only dribble with my knees, I could dribble with my feet! That's right, I was able to go down the court during our halftime show dribbling the basketball with the bottoms of my Converse All Stars. One time I had twisted my ankle and still did this routine. Lots of kids would come up to me and want me to show them how. I would tell them to practice a lot, but that it could be pretty dangerous if you got caught off balance.

We played almost every night during my season and during that time we had a record of 128-18. I scored 1,819 points for the season. Yet it wasn't just the points. We saw America during its Bicentennial. We traveled over 45,000 miles in a red limousine, known as "Big Red." We passed the Bicentennial Wagon several times throughout the states we were traveling. This was a wagon train that started in the west and headed east towards Pennsylvania to celebrate the start of the American Revolution.

During this season we played on an Indian Reservation, learned sign language to communicate at a college for the deaf and more. We played through 35 states, as well as Canada and Mexico. We

Red Heads Patty Bruce and Carolyn "Californa Girl" Wooldridge with some Native American fans, 1974-75

went to the Painted Dessert in Arizona. When we played on the reservation, none of the students had ever seen red hair and wanted to touch us.

We got to touch the one and only Secretariat at Claiborne Farms in Kentucky! We met Bill Russell as he coached the Seattle Supersonics and Sally Ride, who later became the first woman astronaut.

When we were in Memphis we went by Elvis' house. He was still alive, but already sick. The team wanted me to jump the fence and run, because he had bunch of big dogs running the place, and they wanted to go in to see Elvis. Needless to say, we didn't see Elvis!

Once we had to rent car in California and drive to Arizona for a game. The muffler on the limo fell off and had to be towed. The car we rented was a small car and we all were cramped in it. We got there just in time. Even though we were still stiff from the ride, we played very well that night as we scored 101 points in just 32 minutes.

We played on big ship in North Carolina, which turned out to be one of our few losses. The team we played were servicemen — including some former pro players and Harlem Globetrotters — and they were not going to lose, no matter what! That was a very tough game.

Linda Jones

Career 1975-76
All American Red Heads

As told by Linda Jones

There is one big difference playing as a Red Head as opposed to a college or pro team. After the men play a game they go home to their families with home cooking and their own bed. If they have an injury they have a team doctor and athletic trainer to help them heal and return to the game. They fly to games or sometimes have a short bus ride, which includes a driver and, of course, multiple assistant coaches and those to keep stats and scoring. Their uniforms are cleaned and maintained for the players.

We had no traveling team doctor or athletic trainer, no assistant coaches, no driver for our only mode of transportation, no scorekeeper or stats personnel. We didn't even have laundry service — we did our own.

Many times we played eight games a week. On occasion we would play a doubleheader with travel in between. If there was a day without a game scheduled it was used to wash and wax our car, do our laundry and practice.

All holidays were spent on the road, usually on the court for a scheduled game. Our coaches were everything — they drove, coached, got us into our rooms and to scheduled games. Our coach literally did everything and never, ever complained.

I can tell you we slept a lot in the car, too much at times because on day while traveling in Nowhere, Kansas, Coach Charlotte Adams slammed on the brakes and said, "Get out." We all looked around and saw nothing but nothing just a long straight road.

Coach Adams said, "We are traveling places you have never seen and all you do is sleep. I'm going up the road, so you better start running." She drove off and kept going until we couldn't see her anymore. I make this point because, like I said, we were in "Nowhere," Kansas. We all looked at each other and started running, even though we were in our dress clothes and street shoes. Needless to say, by the time we got to the car we were wiped out, but we learned a great lesson and enjoyed our travels much more after that.

Coach was everything rolled into one, highly respected. I remember going to her just to talk because I missed my family and was home sick. She was always in total control, but would also be caring and very understanding.

1975-76 Red Heads. Clockwise from left: Linda Jones, Marilyn Nelson, Lynnette Sjoquist, Carolyn Wooldridge, Deb Parashak, Connie Howe, Kay O'Bryan.

Debra "Shak" Parashak

Career 1975-1977
All American Red Heads

As told by Debra Parashak

I began my sports career at Meramec Junior College in St. Louis and then Southern Illinois University–Edwardsville, where I played a multitude of sports, including basketball. I contemplated participating in track and field, but knew that what I really loved about sports could only be found as part of team.

At that time, I played for a short time on the men's ice hockey team and played semipro volleyball. Upon graduation, I found — similar to other women that played sports before Title IX — that I was at the end of my sports career at 21 years of age.

Even though sports seemed done with me, I wasn't done with sports, so I sent a letter of interest to a professional women's basketball league that was trying to get off the ground. When I was contacted for a "tryout" I thought it was for the women's basketball league being started by Orwell Moore. So, I set up a tryout location at the local junior college. When Coach Moore arrived, a couple of my teammates from college and I were shooting warmups. After several minutes of shooting, Coach Moore asked that we scrimmage against the guys shooting at the other end of the court. I asked the guys if they would play us and they accepted the invite. So we played three-on-three.

After about 15 minutes or so he just said "thank you" and left. He left no info or anything, so I blew it off. Then a couple of months later, I received a contract in the mail to join the All American Red Heads. I accepted, assuming that it was a team in the new women's league. I had no idea what I was in for — I was going to be an All American Red Head. In 1975 a woman playing sports for a living was considered, at best, impractical, the opportunity to continue playing a sport I loved was simply too tempting to pass up. So, ignoring the raised eyebrows of my friends and family, I left my part-time job at the Army Corps of Engineers and hit the road.

Not until I reported for training camp did I learn of what was expected of me. WOW! Was I shocked!

Well, the first two weeks were crazy. Having never dreamt of this type of basketball, I was afraid of the unknown. I played in school and on club teams, but this? I began to wonder what I had gotten myself in to. I had to learn all these trick shots and how to play effective defense against men. I had to learn get someone on my shoulders during a game. Really?! Then there was the whole dyeing your hair "RED?" Not just red, but as bright as you can get it. And to Coach and Mrs. Moore, it was never red enough, so back again for another bottle!

Deb Parashak (left) with Red Head teammates (L-R) Carolyn Wooldridge, Linda Jones, Patty Bruce and Connie Howe, 1975-76

Plus, I was basically a shy person at 20, but after countless basketball games, halftime shows, interviews and autographs I overcame the shyness.

Due to our hectic schedule (drive all day and play a game a night), we seldom had time for a slow meal. Therefore, one lesson I learned was to order dessert first so you could eat that while you were waiting for your meal.

The camaraderie of a team that travels in a station wagon and is on the road almost every day is amazing. For those two years my teammates were my best friends. Although we have grown apart over the years, we often see each other at the Red Head reunions, which always a pleasant time for reminiscing and for recapturing that feeling of "shared experience" and the comfort of knowing that you will always belong to something larger than yourself. A reunion is like living in the movie "A League of Their Own."

Playing with the Red Heads not only provided me with two more years of playing basketball but also with a multitude of additional memories and experiences. Without the Red Heads I probably would never have seen Graceland, petted Secretariat, met the Seattle Supersonics and the San Francisco 49ers, been interviewed on TV, gotten caught in a blizzard, seen the Bicentennial Wagon Train, traveled through 35 states (plus Mexico and Canada) in eight months (a total of 45,758 miles by car) or played basketball both in a barn and on a battleship. These experiences were a favorite part of the Red Head experience. While the professional women's teams may get better pay now, I doubt that these women get to have these kinds of travel experiences, nor do I think they have the opportunity for the same kind of camaraderie that I and my Red Head teammates shared. After all, dyeing each other's hair red is certainly a bonding experience.

The influence of the Red Heads in my life has evidenced itself in my career and in my personality. In addition, playing against men in the '70s wasn't always fun and games and the experience taught me how to get along with men in my chosen career field, which at the time I began was a "man's world." I learned the simple value of making people happy. Later, I learned that although some of what we did for entertainment seemed "quirky" at the time, it has paved the way for other women's professional basketball leagues that are taken at face value for the entertainment value of the women's basketball game alone. Knowing that I played some small role in a special part of the history of women's basketball makes me proud.

Interestingly, 95% of the staff I managed after leaving the Red Heads were men, so I guess I went from playing against them to "bossing" them around. But seriously, playing against men at a time when women weren't "supposed" to play basketball taught me important lessons and helped me put together a career as an engineer, beginning at a time when women weren't "supposed" to be engineers either.

Sue Branham (Kohler)

CAREER 1975-76

ALL AMERICAN RED HEADS

As told by Sue Branham Kohler

Red Head Sue Branham, 1975-76

I started dreaming about playing for the Red Heads when one of my guy friends that I played basketball with all the time told me about them. I only knew of them what he had told me, but just listening to him speak of the famous women with the flaming red hair set a fire in my heart. I knew I just had to play for them. Finally, in my sophomore year I got to see them play at a junior college near me. After the game, nothing was going to stop me from meeting them in person. I worked my way through the crowd and got down to talk to one of the players. I got goose bumps as I spoke to her and she told me how to contact Mr. Orwell Moore. I wrote him and told him my dream of playing for them.

He personally contacted me and he had me go to Camp Courage at the end of my junior year. He watched me at camp and said, "You look pretty good. Why don't you come to try out when you graduate?"

Of course I did, and I did very well. He didn't let me know at camp. Then one afternoon, the mailman came and in the stack of three-cent letters was one that said "All American Red Heads" on the return portion of the envelope. It was a contract to play professional basketball. I was so happy I began to cry. My dream had come true.

But my dream coming true didn't mean that it was easy. Learning to do all the tricks and plays in just two weeks of training camp was the biggest challenge I had faced to that point in my young life. I was trying to remember everything and it was overwhelming. I was worried I would not be able to get it. But the veterans pulled me aside and worked with me until I figured it out. These women were my heroes, and now they were teaching me one-on-one.

It was the time of my life. Life on the road was an adventure every day, sightseeing, even fixing flats on that ol' limo. We would even get pulled over by the police. They were curious. An officer would pull the limo over at night. They would then walk up along the 31-foot limo to the driver, shining his light through the car, his jaw dropping as he saw who was in it and say to the driver, "Wow, all red heads. Hi there. Was just curious about this big ol' car driving through town and wanted to find out a bit more."

Susan "Spike" Callahan (Brady)

CAREER 1976-82

ALL AMERICAN RED HEADS

As told by "Spanky" Losier

When Susan was 18, she attended the Red Heads basketball camp in Holly Springs, Mississippi, where I was a counselor. She was 6-foot-10 at the time. She never played basketball or any sports at all in school, so learning to play was a big challenge for her. Coach Moore had her jumping rope and shadow boxing to improve her coordination.

At camp after supper, the campers would play volleyball. When Susan got to the front of the net, she towered over it by at least three feet. When the ball came to her she was so tall she didn't have to jump. She just flicked her wrist and the ball went flying to the other side. I started calling her "Big Spike." The nickname stuck and was eventually shortened to just "Spike."

When Spike was ready to go on the road and play she became a drawing card. The kids wanted to see her and talk to her. Spike was a kind and gentle person who was proud of her height. During a game Spike and teammate, Barb Hostert, went up for a rebound at the same time. Barb's face ended up hitting Spike's elbow. Barb ended up with a big black eye. Barb and Spike certainly had fun explaining how Barb got the shiner. It was enjoyable having someone so tall on the team.

When we would wash our 36-foot long limo, "Big Whitey," Spike was in charge of washing the roof. None of us got even close to reaching up there. Spike's career came to an end when she fractured her foot.

Red Heads 6-foot-10 Susan "Spike" Callahan (left) and Marilyn "Ralph" Nelson at Camp Courage, summer 1974

Carolyn "California Girl" Wooldridge (Williams)

Career 1975-76
All American Red Heads

As told by Carolyn Wooldridge Williams

I had played basketball since I was in fourth grade and wanted to attend a summer basketball camp to help me with my skills, but in the '70s there were no camps for girls. I found a camp in Holly Springs, Mississippi that I wanted to attend because it was coached by women. I had no idea who the All American Red Heads were and signed up to go for two weeks to learn some more basketball skills.

When I arrived it was quite a shock to see the courts were all outside, the rooms looked like my old Girl Scout camp cabins and I had a hard time understanding what people were saying with the southern drawl. Ha!

There were girls from all ages attending and the some of the "Red Heads" were the coaches. I had a fantastic time at camp and met many new friends. I had no idea that after two weeks in the camp I was asked to sign a contract with the "Red Heads." I was shocked. I had no idea I was even auditioning for a place on one of the three teams that Mr. Orwell Moore, owner of the Red Heads, was sending out on the road that year.

It was 1975. He was wanting me to play on the "collegiate" team that he was putting together. I told him I would have to go back home and think about it and would let him know in a few days. I decided I could put my life on hold for at least a year to experience playing basketball full time and get the opportunity to travel the country. I spent the rest of the summer at home, working on my basketball shooting and my ball handling skills I would perform at halftime.

I met the team for the first time when we all reported to camp in Holly Springs, Mississippi on October 10, 1975. If you think reporting for training camp was just about practicing basketball, you would only be partially right. Yeah, we did that, but in the first few days we also had to sew buttons on our uniforms that had fallen off during the previous season. We then had to head up to Arkansas to take pictures for programs, billboards and even Christmas cards. Coach Moore would promote us every way he could dream about.

One of the biggest ways he promoted us was through our traveling. If we were going to travel over 40,000 miles in a season, what better way than to do it than right on the car we traveled in — our "Big Red" limo, which basically was a traveling billboard.

Yet, this season it needed some cosmetic work, so along with practicing shots at the free throw line, we got to paint "Red." First, we had to sand it down — it was so huge (close to 30 feet long) it took us two full days. Yet, as we built up some muscles from all that hand sanding, we were also building up a sense of team without even being totally aware of it at the time.

We then got a heavy day of rain and could not paint it, so we stayed in our cabins and practiced ball handling. Then, we lost power. You might think that might have been it for the day. Not for the Red Heads. We lit candles and continued our practicing by candlelight as we would soon hit the road.

Red Head Carolyn "California Girl" Wooldridge displays her ball spinning skills, 1975-76.

We were able to start painting Big Red the next day but didn't finish. By the 18th we went on the road, played our first game and then came back to camp to sleep. We were awakened at 6 a.m. the next morning to start painting the lettering on both sides of Big Red, which took until 6 p.m.

The other team on the road was just as fortunate as we were. They were busy with the other limo, "Whitey."

By the 22nd we finished up painting Big Red and were breaking camp to hit the road for the next seven months. I was so excited. I was already building memories of a lifetime, even though I had only played one game so far.

The first day we hit the road, you would never guess what happened. Big Red broke down, and we had to hitch a ride with two Winnebagos to the game.

It was a great start to an interesting year on the road, and we never looked back. Although there were some tough times, I have to say it was a "once in a lifetime opportunity" and I am so grateful that I took the risk and played.

We once played in a barn in Freetown, Indiana that was made of tin, painted blue. The barn was very small, with bleachers only on one side and the top of each free throw line, which is now the three-point line, was in the middle of the gym. The floor was tile of some sort. It was very different. We were shooting from half court most of the night and taking free shots from half court. The crowd was very small, as was the town. We played a 2:30 game, which was most unusual, but the crowd was very excited to see us play. We found this particular gym to be the most unusual we played at all season. It was the true definition of "Barnstorming."

In late February we had to drive for 5½ hours up a mountain pass to get to our game in Othello, Washington. It was snowing all the way. It was really pretty but it was snowing so hard that we needed to put on chains. But Coach didn't want to chain "Big Red" up, and we ended up getting stuck. So we had to get out and push Red up the hill for about a mile. We were really tired and cold. A guy finally stopped and helped us put chains on the car. We made it over the pass, got our mail, and went to hotel before heading out to game. We didn't play very well as we were all pretty tired from the ordeal with Red earlier in the day. Yet, we never gave up and made it to the game to entertain the crowds, something to be very proud of.

Marcia Adams

CAREER 1975-77
ALL AMERICAN RED HEADS

As told by Marcia Adams

My journey to the All American Red Heads began during my senior year in high school in Augusta, Maine. The state was having its Girls' State Basketball Tournament (after Title IX) and our school qualified in our district. Our coach arranged to have us practice at the local Civic Center to prepare for the larger venue we had hoped to play in eventually. Upon arrival for the first practice, we were waiting anxiously as our coach found out where we were supposed to go. We had made the state tournament and were the local heroes. While we were waiting, my future could be overhead through the intercom that was playing music from a local radio station. I heard an advertisement come on and the only thing I remember hearing was "Professional Women's Basketball League."

When I got home, I called the station for the information and found out it was an advertisement from Mr. Orwell Moore. He was requesting girls and women to contact him to play basketball in a league he was forming. My good friend and high school competitor Sheryl Wood and I sent our information to Mr. Moore and continued with our lives.

Graduation came with college for Sheryl, but I was home with mononucleosis that fall of 1975. In late September Mr. Moore called me while my parents were away for the day in New Hampshire. He said the league was not going to happen just now, but he needed players for his current team, the All American Red Heads. He gave a quick synopsis of the team and what it was about, but I'm sure I don't really know all he said. But I do remember he also said he needed to know right now — today. I stuttered and blurted out "yes" without knowing what that really meant except that I would be playing basketball. My dad called Mr. Moore at his office the next day to get some questions answered, a contract was sent, and arrangements were made for me to go to training camp on October 15. My first plane ride was to Memphis, where I was picked up and taken to Camp Courage.

Red Heads Sherry Mattson, Marcia Adams, Gretchen Pinz, summer 1975 at Camp Courage

My first season there were three teams of All American Red Heads and our team was the "Southern Team." I was one of four rookies, with Sue Branham, Gretchen Pinz and Sherry Mattson, along with two veterans, Lynnea Sjoquist and Rhonda "Rosie" Waters. Tina Treat joined us later. Our team car was the old Pontiac that is now in the Women's Basketball Hall of Fame in Knoxville, Tennessee. I enjoyed showing the car to my daughter when the Red Heads were recognized as Legends of the Game.

We carried a spare axle — true story — with packed bearings, as we seemed to have an issue every few days. Lynnea became quite adept at removing the tire and changing the axle, which kept us on schedule for the better. Some of the mechanics we encountered along the way were a bit dumbstruck when we showed up at their garage requesting packed bearing service.

I think it was another axle issue that delayed our arrival for a game at the Gallaudet University for the Deaf in Washington, DC. By the time we arrived, the gym was filled to capacity but was very quiet for the size of the crowd. There was some clapping, but many of the spectators were "clapping" as deaf people do, with hands raised to eye level, fingers splayed, and twisting from the wrists simultaneously. We all had learned some sign language to communicate with the players and I remember asking/

signing my competitor to play man-to-man defense. He emphatically shook his head and signed back "man-to-*woman* defense" with a big smile! What a memory!

In mid-January, Mr. Moore asked me to go to the Northern Team, as they had been affected by injuries. This new team was comprised of Barb Hostert, Donna "Spanky" Losier, Marsha Tate, Wanda England, Cheryl Clark, Lynnette Sjoquist (Lynnea's twin sister), Susan Callahan and Coach Charlotte Adams. Because we had two Marcia's-Marsha's on the team, Spanky nicknamed me "C-I-A" for "MAR of the CIA."

We had some games near New York City and had time to see the Statue of Liberty. As we rode the ferry out to the island there was a TV crew following a group of people, including a young girl on her way to the statue too. They were from ABC Wide World of Sports and were filming background for this 14-year-old who would be better known after the Olympics in Montreal that next summer. They were right, as it was Nadia Comaneci from Romania, the first gymnast to score a perfect 10 in competition!

I also experienced a game in my hometown at my high school against teachers whose classrooms I had been in the year before. It seemed like the every person I knew was in the gym as I only saw familiar faces in the stands. The girls came to my house for a home cooked meal. You know what attention that long car attracts in a residential neighborhood, too!

My teammates for the second season included my high school friend, Sheryl Wood, Diane Martinson, Lynnea Sjoquist, Donna "Spanky" Losier, Cindy Lalliberti, Connie Howe, and Cheryl Clark as coach. I visited 45 states in my two years of traveling.

Sheryl "Woody" Wood (Borgman)

Career 1976-78
All American Red Heads

As told by Sheryl Wood Borgman

Marcia Adams, also a Red Head, and I played against each other in high school when I was living in Clinton, Maine. Over time, we got past the rivalry between two opposing schools to eventually become best friends. After high school graduation, I moved to her hometown of Augusta to live the summer with her family. She and I played softball on the same team, and we played basketball with the guys almost daily. That summer, the organizers of the Women's Pro League were trying to organize franchises throughout the country.

Marcia had heard an announcement asking women interested to send their basketball portfolio to be considered for a tryout with this new league. On a dare, she and I both sent our statistics, pictures, and information to the address given. We went through the rest of the summer without hearing anything so Marcia started calling the contact number for some information. Mr. Orwell Moore answered the phone and told her that because of a recent injury, they could immediately use Marcia on the All American Red Heads. Two weeks later, I also got a call from Coach Moore to play.

Because of some events going on in my life at the time, I did not join the team the fall of 1975, but after seeing the Red Heads play in Augusta, Maine, during the spring of 1976, I was eager to play with these amazingly talented group of women. Therefore, I called Mr. Moore asking for another chance to play during the next season. He said, "Alright, Hot Shot; now you need to come to training camp to try out." This shy Maine girl who had rarely been away from home, especially for birthdays and holidays, would soon have my eyes opened. I loved spending summers with my family at beautiful Moosehead Lake fishing, swimming, and boating, but following after a once-in-a-lifetime opportunity was more important than lobster feeds and clam bakes.

That July, Marcia and I drove all the way from Maine to Holly Springs, Mississippi, to attend Camp Courage. Wow! What a week that was, as we trained daily in the hot southern summer months outside in 90 degree weather with other All American Red Heads and Diane Martinson, one other rookie prospect. Not only was the heat a change for me, but eating Okra, black-eyed peas, fried foods, all vegetables diced with bacon, corn bread and drinking sweat tea tickled my taste buds. Coming from a state that dropped all the *R's* on our words, I loved hearing the deep southern drawl. We started training each morning by 8:00 a.m. completing ball handling, dribbling, halftime routines, shooting, game play, and conditioning until 9:00 p.m. At week's end, I had met some fantastic players along with being told by Mr. Moore that I would start traveling with the team in the fall of 1976. I was ecstatic, and I remember just how proud my parents were that I had the chance to play the game that I had loved for so long.

Red Head Sheryl "Woody" Wood, 1976-77

I only played with the Red Heads two years, but I treasure the memories and lifelong friends that I made. One such memory came when we played at my former high school, Lawrence High. We looked and looked for a hotel room but could find none. It was in November around Thanksgiving and two players' birthdays. My mom was bound and determined that we were going to be treated like royalty, so she housed the entire team over night and made a full Thanksgiving dinner for the team to enjoy. In addition, she and my sister-in-law made two birthday cakes for the birthday girls. After that, the players affectionately called my childhood home "The Wood Inn."

I traveled with some unbelievable players like Donna "Spanky" Losier, Barb "Gabby" Hostert, Susan "Spike" Callahan, Lynnea Sjoquist, my friend Marcia Adams and rookie cohort Diane Martinson. Never in all my life had I seen someone handle a basketball like Spanky or shoot and defend like Gabby. Spanky could move a basketball around her body faster than I had ever seen. Rarely did she lose control and often the men guarding her could not keep up, but rather be mesmerized by her skill while she passed them for a lay-up. Likewise, Gabby's defense was unmatched; she was only 5-foot-6, but rarely did any of the guys get by her, as she had perfect defensive stance and quick foot speed. In addition, she had one of the most fundamental shots that I have ever seen. These two ladies were an absolute thrill to watch play the game of basketball; they both taught me important principles about life, character, and the game.

All of us girls have specific game-time memories that we share, but to me the times of intense, competitive games of H-O-R-S-E with Gabby when we got to the gym early, Spanky playing her guitar on the side of the road when we broke down, meeting each other's families or former players, and the hours traveling across our country playing against men will forever stay with me. Spike and Gabby are now gone from us on this earth, but the lessons that I learned from them and the appreciation that I have for the Red Heads follow me wherever I go.

Gail Marks

CAREER 1978-79
ALL AMERICAN RED HEADS

As told by Gail Marks

Dear Gail Marks,

I received your signed contract and may I congratulate you and welcome you to the world's greatest female organization "the All American Red Heads."

Yours in Sports,

Coach Orwell Moore

And so my journey began as a Red Head. It started in Windsor Locks, Connecticut, where I went to see the all American Red Heads play. I knew that's what I wanted to do — the ball handling, spinning the ball on my fingers, dribbling with my knees, passing behind my back, and through my legs "from behind" and so I did.

A short time later a letter came which said that the All American Red Heads are very interested in me, and asked for information about me, the girl from Enfield, Connecticut who came to be known as "Miss Personality."

The five of us got to work right away. Yes, only five players all year — no substitutes. Our sneakers never dried out. The Women's Basketball League (WBL), with players like "Machine Gun" Molly Bolin, had just started and most of the players on the previous year's team had jumped from the Red Heads to give this new league a try.

Despite only five players, playing every game, every minute, we played seven to nine games a week, including doubleheaders on Sundays. We played against men with men's rules. Our record for the year was 127 wins and 16 losses — an outstanding winning percentage of 89%. The only thing that suffered a bit was documentation. There was no one to keep the scorebook with statistics for future reference, as in other seasons.

Gail Marks with Sandy Crist during a 1978-79 Red Heads game

While we drove in the limo listening to music all over the country, we found our "anthem" for our season. Jackson Browne was at the top of the chart and his cover of "Stay" is what we played on a little cassette player before every game.

"Oh, won't you stay
Just a little bit longer
We want to play
Just a little bit longer."

We would go over our plays — "Red Runner," "Big Red" (named for Spike Callahan) and "Shotgun," just to name a few. For example in the Red Runner, the comedian passes to each player. The other player passes back until eventually all players go through the routine, the last player gives a hand off and the comedian goes in for a layup.

We did strengthening exercises for our neck and upper bodies in the car. Susan Callahan, our center who was 6-foot-10, encouraged us to stay strong. She had started with the Red Heads just a couple of seasons prior with little knowledge and skill, but had grown into a dedicated leader. We loved her.

Susan love to dance, as did I, so that's what we did in our rooms at night — we danced. Picture this,

6-foot-10 Susan Callahan and 5-foot-2 Gail Marks, red hair and all, dancing to some of the greatest southern rock of the 1970s, along with the other players.

In order to stay sharp for the game, the parking lot of the hotel would become our basketball court to practice on until we could get to the gym. Ah, life on the road.

All of this for $75 a week and two dollars per meal. Life didn't get any better for me.

We played for the love of the game. Coach Moore would come to visit us and he always reminded us about his saying about what it was like to be an All American Red Head.

"Every day you wake up, it is Christmas."

Gwen Reed

Career 1978-80

All American Red Heads and New York Stars (WBL)

As told by Gwen Reed

I was first invited to play by Mr. Orwell Moore when I was a sophomore in college at Chadron State in Chadron, Nebraska after playing four years of high school ball in Gillette, Wyoming. My coach called me into her office and gave me the letter. I wanted to finish my degree program before I played, so I wrote to Mr. Moore and ask him if I could contact him after I graduated. He agreed and the week before I received my diploma, I received a contract from Mr. Moore.

Red Head Gwen Reed, 1978-79

My first week on the road was the adventure of my life. Playing for "Moore's All American Red Heads" was an experience that I will treasure forever. To be in the best shape of your life, to play the game you love five times a week or more, to be able to make crowds smile as we did in the comedy routines, and to also amaze them with our superior basketball handling and playing skills was an unforgettable experience. We lived and practiced high ideals. Life on the road was tough, but it is so rewarding to look back on all the memories we created there.

Once, we were playing a college team in Colorado. The team was young and undefeated and they were not going to allow a "bunch of girls" to beat them. The game started to get rough so Coach Moore called a timeout and told us to let them have the game because he did not want us to get hurt. By that time I was determined that they were not going to win, so when we went out and had another huddle on the court. All I said was, "I want this game!" It was like a miracle. The girls couldn't miss. We ended up winning the game and came out of it with just a few scrapes and bruises. I was so proud of each member of our team.

Another time we had just finished playing a doubleheader in Ohio and we had to be in Texas by 2 o'clock the following day for another doubleheader. I was driving and decided to stop for fuel. It was very late and all of the team was asleep. There was a median in the road that didn't have any signs on the end of it. I was tired and it was dark. I ran over it. I looked in the rearview mirror and their heads popping up all over the place. I had to laugh, it reminded me of the game where the groundhogs pop up and you have to hit them on the head to make them go back down. For some reason they didn't trust me to continue driving that night.

Traveling so much, we rarely were able to have holidays at home with family. One Thanksgiving we were playing close to one of the girl's hometowns (Martha Hix) in North Carolina. In honor of the day we all decided to attend church that Sunday. I was the player-coach for the team so I led the team into the church. While walking in, the team asked me if I was planning on singing (we had some very fine musical talent on our team, but I was not one of them) during the service. I joked, "I was planning on it. Why do you ask?" They said in unison, "Because if you are planning on singing, we don't want to sit with you so no one will know that you are with us." I told them that people would probably figure out that I was with them anyway as we all had bright red hair. We truly were a family. Our team spent many hours singing in the car, with Martha playing the guitar while we all sang (some of us croaked). Mostly we did John Denver songs, some hymns, and a little Neil Diamond.

It was always entertaining for us anytime we went shopping or to church because we moved in a group and we all had red hair. Many people would stop and ask us if we were sisters or part of some club. Everyone asked us if we were natural redheads or if we dyed our hair. Traveling together we became very close. Besides, we really did not know anyone else in the places we played, so it was only natural for us to do everything together.

Fame, skill, challenge, showmanship, pride, passion, a winning attitude — we experienced it all. We've built character in each other and ourselves. In the 1978-79 season we played 143 games. We won 127 and lost 16. I averaged 20 points per game.

I received an invitation to try out for the New York Stars basketball team, a part of the women's basketball league (WBL). I was not a very experienced flyer, so I checked my bags, complete with my contacts, glasses, and workout gear. Of course, the airline lost my bag. I went to the tryout crushed. I figured my one opportunity to play was shot. The people there scrambled to find me some shorts, a T-shirt, socks and shoes. I was very grateful. The bad part was I still had no contacts or glasses. I went through the tryout and then we all had a big meeting. The coach began to explain that they were only going to hire one of us. There were probably 40 girls trying out. He went on to explain that the chances for being chosen for a professional basketball team was something like one in three million. As you can imagine, I was devastated. The coach thanked us all for participating and let us know that if we made the team we would be notified within the week. I knew that there was no way I could have been chosen. I don't think I had sunk even one basket during the tryouts. I got close, but could not focus without my contacts or glasses. To my surprise, there was a contract waiting for me to sign when I got home from my return flight.

This was their second season and because of finances the league folded just five weeks into the season. We played our games in Madison Square Garden.

I don't think I had ever been so happy except for when I was invited to play for the All American Red Heads. God is good!

Cardte Hicks

CAREER 1979-81
SAN FRANCISCO PIONEERS (WBL)
As told by Cardte Hicks

I grew up in a family of eight in San Pedro, California. We only had two bedrooms, so my five brothers and two sisters all had to share the same small bedroom in four bunk beds.

We were an athletic family, and we never knew anything else. I would always play with my brothers and on boys teams. During my teen years I played with my brothers in parks and recreation leagues and summer leagues on boys teams, where I learned how to play the game better than most of boys. I had no idea of the talent I was blessed with.

By the time I was 16 I was playing AAU volleyball for a team owned by my godfather, the one and only Wilt Chamberlain. Wilt was a major inspiration to me and encouraged me to try basketball. I had a very high vertical leap. I also played with the USA women's volleyball team under Chuck Erby.

When I was in high school I was around 5-foot-7 and could dunk the basketball on the court. There was no girls' team, so I was doing this on the boys team. This was catching people's attention. I was then asked to play basketball in Holland on a men's team, and eventually a women's team as well. I even got paid for doing so.

Cardte Hicks of the WBL San Francisco Pioneers, 1980-81

When I came back I was recruited by the San Francisco Pioneers to play in the Women's Basketball League in the late '70s. The WBL was the first national professional women's basketball league to ever complete a full season. I played for three seasons until the league folded.

Coach Dean Meminger taught me a special pivot move with the basketball because of my speed. One time I pulled the move on an opposing player, the crowd cheering from the sidelines. I went up to dunk the basketball, but the ball slammed off the back of the rim and bounced out. Much to my surprise, you could hear a pin drop in that gymnasium. I think the crowd was stunned just by seeing a woman *attempt* to dunk a basketball, since in the '70s it had never happened.

There was also the time when we were playing the New York Stars and All-Star Althea Gwyn. We were down by one point at the end of the game and a teammate was at the foul line. If my teammate had missed, we would have had a couple of seconds for a last ditch shot, but we had to get the rebound. The coach on the Stars was yelling across the court for Althea to "block Hicks out!" My teammate took the foul shot and missed off the back of the rim. Althea stepped in to box me out, along with another Stars player. I jumped for all I had and jumped higher than the both of them, getting the rebound in the air as it came off the rim and tipped it back in for the win.

One thing I didn't care for traveling the country and world was flying. We often traveled by van in the WBL, but we also flew at times. My teammates would always tease me, but the last laugh was on them. I could snore, and let me tell you I could snore so loud that my teammates said I would move the furniture in the middle of the night. No one like to room with me because of it, and most of my time when I was playing professional basketball I would have my own room.

I even made it to the last day of cuts during the first season of the WNBA, but broke my knee and had to retire.

"Machine Gun" Molly Bolin (Kazmer)

CAREER 1978-81

IOWA CORNETS AND SAN FRANCISCO PIONEERS (WBL)

As told by Molly Bolin Kazmer

The birth of the Women's Pro Basketball League in the United States was such an exciting thing to be part of. In 1978, we had a tryout camp with players from different parts of the country that came to Iowa. Of course, I was thrilled to not only make the team, but found out that I would be officially the first women's pro basketball player signed to a contract. The signing took place in June at a press conference at the Iowa State Capitol building in then Governor Robert Ray's office.

My life dramatically changed from that moment on, starting with the filming of a movie that summer featuring our team, the Iowa Cornets. It seemed like a dream come true to get to continue playing basketball professionally AND be in a movie!

The best thing about that experience was getting to know "Pistol Pete" Maravich as I drove him to and from the movie set during the week or so he was in the film. We had a blast during the entire six weeks of the movie shoot that more than made up for the disappointment in the final result — a very silly and unrealistic movie.

We had a lot of challenges to overcome that very first season, including our coach being fired before the season started, and we did actually "barnstorm" throughout Iowa playing our home games in multiple cities across the state. I started as the 12th player of 12 to come off the bench, and was called a "designated shooter" and expected to score whenever I got on the court. It was a very difficult and frustrating role for me to play as the substitutions were all five starters, then the second five, then I would go in the last couple minutes at the end of the quarter. This continued until one game near mid-season, I got more time on the court because of injuries and set a team and league scoring record of 53 points.

"Machine Gun" Molly Bolin of the Iowa Cornets with WBL basketball (first time womens sized ball was ever used), 1978-79

Not long after that, an Associated Press writer saw me score a lot of points and I was called "Machine Gun Molly" in his article on the game, describing the rapid-fire way he saw me score points. Of course the Women's Basketball League office jumped all over this as a marketing opportunity and from then on it seemed as if every team in the league used this nickname.

I went to my team office and said, "Wait a minute, I don't want to be called 'Machine Gun'!" I was told not to worry, that it is all good to have a nickname. It took some time, but gradually I figured "if you can't beat 'em, join 'em" and ended up doing promotional photos as "Machine Gun Molly."

Another interesting thing that happened the first season is that I was selected to the first WBL All-Star game held in the Felt Forum at Madison Square Garden. Since I was a late addition to the squad, I didn't get much playing time, but I did have a lot of fun. My fellow Cornet All-Stars and I had to catch a 5 a.m. flight the next morning from La Guardia Airport to meet the team at our next game. However, once in the air it was determined the plane's hydraulic system may have gone out, so the plane flew over the ocean, dumped extra gas and made an emergency landing at JFK airport, with full foam on the run way and emergency vehicles trailing (so I was told later!). The funny thing was I missed this entire drama, because I was so exhausted from the travel and All-Star activities that I slept through it all. When we landed, our teammate Tanya Crevier entertained people on the plane, doing ball tricks for about an hour until we were allowed to exit the plane. Then they put us in a helicopter to fly through New York City (being from Iowa and first time there — this was VERY cool and VERY exciting!) and back to La Guardia to catch the next flight out. Of course we saw other All-Stars flying out who said, "what are you guys doing here — we thought you left early!"

That first season, we beat our biggest rivals, the Chicago Hustle, to go to the first WBL championship against the Houston Angels in a best-of-five series. The most interesting thing that happened during these

"Machine Gun" Molly during the second WBL All-Star game held in Chicago, 1980

playoffs is while we were staying at a hotel across the street from the Astrodome (where we were scheduled to play) the rain started coming down hard that afternoon. By game time, water was waist deep outside in a major flood of near biblical proportions! Needless to say, our championship playoff game was cancelled and had to be rescheduled because nobody could get to the arena.

We lost the championship to Houston the first year and to New York after making the finals our second year. At the end of the second year the Iowa Cornets lost our owner and the team folded after financing for new ownership collapsed. I was recruited to play for a new start-up women's league, the LPBA in Southern California, but it never made it off the ground after the first five or six days. By Christmas 1980, I was recruited to go back to the WBL and signed with the San Francisco Pioneers to finish the season. It was so much fun, as they also brought in several of my former Iowa Cornet teammates and hired former New York coach Dean Meminger. The rest is now history as I was involved in five different attempts to start a women's pro basketball league — prior to the WNBA's success 20 years ago!

I was fortunate to have come at a time to experience all this, as I had family issues that prevented me from being able to play in a pro league overseas. The hardest part, I would say, is being nearly forgotten in the progression of the sport we helped start. As far as I know, none of all the scoring records I set during the WBL have been "officially" recognized. It was an amazing experience to be the first, and took a great deal of self-sacrifice from all of us pioneers who wanted the opportunity to play basketball and pave the way for the future of the sport!

Althea Gwyn

CAREER 1978-81
NEW YORK STARS, NEW ENGLAND GULLS, CHICAGO HUSTLE (WBL)

As told by Althea Gwyn

I was born and raised, LOL. But seriously, when I was growing up I had a condition that doctors called Osgood-Schlatter Disease, something that they told my parents was the reason that I was growing so fast. I went from a normal child to a kid that had to have casts placed on me to slow my growth. I was placed in hip casts for periods of six months to, it seemed to me, forever.

Althea Gwyn

I can say that was the time that Basketball took a liking to my life. For some reason it seemed like basketball was the topic on the news. I can't say exactly when a round ball became such an integral part of my life, but, to be sure, this is where it started.

I played for Queens College, one of two powerhouses in women's basketball in the '70s. Well, in my senior year, word got around that some investors were looking to start a Women's Professional Basketball league here in the good ol' USA. Before that news, women who wished to make a living playing basketball had to go overseas to play.

Well, I heard the rumors, but wasn't really expecting anything to come out of it. I was wrong. To make a long story short, the WBL was born, and I ended up being the first draft choice for the New York Stars. In our first year, our home court was Iona College. We reached the playoffs, only to be ousted by the Houston Angels.

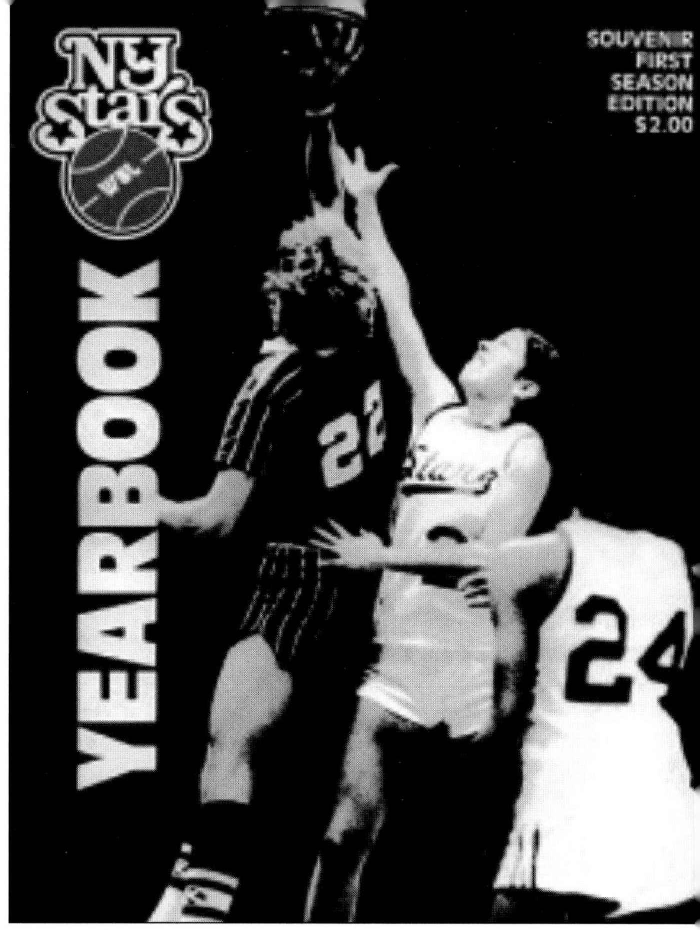

WBL Althea Gwyn of the New York Stars takes a jump shot against Chicago Hustle in 1978-79 season.

The second year our owners, Ed and Terry Riesdorf, decided to move us into Madison Square Garden. I felt right at home, since we were the first women's collegiate team to ever play there approximately three years before when I was at Queens.

I had a great group of players around me that year. Debbie Mason, Janice Thomas, Pearl Moore, the twins — Faye and Kaye Young — and a great bench! We won the 1980 WBL championship, headed by Dean "The Dream" Meminger.

It was great times, but then our team folded due to financial difficulties.

The WBL tried to make adjustments, but it was too little, too late. After playing for the New England Gulls and the Chicago Hustle, I finally accepted the fact that, if I wanted to continue to play professionally, I would have to go overseas. So, that was what I did. I ended up playing five years in Italy, five years in Spain and a year in Sweden (which was not my happiest time playing ball).

My funniest memory was when our owners were trying to drum up business for commercials for the team. Well, you, know that we had Kaye and Faye Young doing the Dannon yogurt and Wrigley's gum commercials, so, someone had decided if the rest of us wore make-up, we, too, would be offered commercials. I remember letting the 'make-up artist' try her skills on me, and the result was awful. She tried to use the same coloring and hair cut that she used on the twins! I told her, "Get this s*** off of my face!" Disaster!

My funniest off the court experience came with me spending the night at a teammate's house after a game because the roads were icy and I was afraid to drive home. A couple of us made a pallet on the floor to sleep on. About 2:30 in the morning, their dog began to bark and everyone got up to see what was bugging the dog. Somehow, a gigantic rat had made its way in out of the cold and the dog had it cornered. Not to fear, though, because my teammate's mother found a baseball bat and as the cornered rat leaped up, to either attack or get away, she swung! Took it out like she was aiming for the fence! Needless, to say, I got up, packed up, got in my car and drove home!

Patti Decker

Career 1978-79
Milwaukee Does (WBL)

As told by Patti Decker

In the spring of 1978 I was my final year of basketball at St. Cloud State. I was always a starter after coming out of Cold Spring, Minnesota as a 5-foot-6 guard. My basketball and softball coach Gladys Ziemer evidently put my name and that of teammate Noah Johnson in to try out for the 1978 Pan Am Games and 1980 Olympic team, tryouts to be held in St. Joseph, Missouri. During that first week of June 1978, 60-plus players nationwide were there to compete for team USA. Despite not making this team, it was a great honor to know we were chosen to compete for the USA team.

The exposure and timing and was very instrumental in how the next five months played out. About two weeks later I received a letter from the Iowa Cornets. I was asked to try out for their team in Cedar Rapids, Iowa. This was a team in a newly formed women's basketball league called the WBL. I called and said I would attend. This was the first time I had heard about a pro women's basketball league starting. Exciting!

Needless to say, I did not make the cut. However there were some general managers for the upcoming pro women's basketball league in attendance. Again, exposure and timing was everything.

Patti Decker of the WBL Milwaukee Does, 1978-79

About two weeks later I received a letter from the Minnesota Fillies who had just joined the WBL. They drafted me as a free agent.

Wow, this is real! Team workouts with the Minnesota Fillies began in October with 22 players. Cuts were made in mid-November. I was cut again, but three weeks later I received a phone call from the Milwaukee Does, and was flying out early the next morning to Milwaukee in pursuit of my dream. I was to be at practice by 1 p.m. in downtown Milwaukee. The Does were a perfect fit for me.

That night I lit the arena up. I was not a starter for the Milwaukee Does, but I was okay with it. I played wing guard and averaged between five to seven minutes a game. About 12 games into the season came my time to shine. The game was played at the Mecca in downtown Milwaukee, Minnesota Fillies versus the Milwaukee Does. Unfortunately, one of our starting guards twisted her knee during warm-ups and was out. I figured I possibly would start, but didn't. Within four minutes of the start of the game I was in. In the first couple of minutes I got a steal, hit a baseline jumper and grabbed down a defensive rebound.

This was me! This is how I play. I was in the zone. I began to drive, baseline dishing off to our post players. Fans loved it. I made a reverse layup that energized the 1,511 fans in the stands. We had great team play that night and won 84-77. I played 31 minutes, scratching out 11 points, five rebounds, three steals and three assists.

The next day in the *Milwaukee Journal* the coach was quoted as saying "we found an all-around team guard." It was a sweet compliment indeed, but I was disappointed that my playing time didn't increase in the games that followed.

But I got to live my dream!

Ruth Simmons

Career 1979-82
All American Red Heads

As told by Ruth Simmons

My love for the game of basketball began on the streets of Chicago. I was 10 on a high school playground with a chalked out strike zone on the school's red brick wall playing baseball with the neighborhood boys. It was then that I heard the coolest sound, nothing but net. Some older guys were shooting baskets and the nets were made out of steel. When the ball went through the hole, "swoosh" — music to my ears. I had found my passion. Since that moment, I have played basketball competitively for 35 years.

While living in Chicago, I went to a private Lutheran grade school and learned the six-player version of the game (look it up) — kind of boring. I was taught sportsmanship, basic fundamentals, and the rules of the game, not to mention faith, hope and love. I was fortunate to be raised in a very loving family filled with positive reinforcement.

Girls' sports in high school in the '70s was just unfolding. My freshman year was the first season ever for girls' basketball — eight games. My senior year, we were state runner-up with a 23-1 record. Not too shabby.

During my summers throughout high school, I went to an incredible fundamental basketball camp in Indiana — you know who you are. Honing my skills over the years, I turned out to be a bit of a dribbling and passing exhibitionist, with a pretty good shot. They always had guest speakers come to the camp, big names. And that's when I met my first All American Red Head, Jolene Ammons. She spun seven basketballs at one time. Amazing. I didn't think much of it at the time, but I liked the tricks and I taught myself how to spin a basketball.

After high school and racking up all kind of awards, I wanted to keep playing, so off to college I went. Title IX had really kicked in by now and scholarships gave female student athletes an opportunity to pursue their dreams. The competition was stiff and players came out of the woodwork. While coaching and also counseling at my favorite summer basketball camp, I received a call. The man said his name was Orwell Moore. What a funny name I thought. He spoke with a heavy southern accent and told me that he received a letter from a family friend of mine about my basketball abilities, and that he might be interested in recruiting me. Coach Moore gave me the "Cliff's Notes" version of the All American Red Heads story. He asked if I could come to Camp Courage in Mississippi for a week and tryout. I had to decline, but agreed for a weekend.

Red Head Ruth Simmons demonstrates her dribbling skills, circa 198

It was my first time on an airplane and on an emotional roller coaster ride at the same time, teetering that line between "I'm so excited" and "I want my mommy." After an hour of meeting with Coach Moore and trying out, he offered me a place on the team on the spot. He wanted me to commit before I left. I told him I needed to speak with my parents. My parents were very supportive. I signed the contract and reported for duty in September 1979.

The pickup at the Memphis airport was memorable. Coach Moore confirmed on the phone that two Red Heads would be there to pick me up and I would have no problem seeing them. He was right. Rookie Mary Benton from Georgia was over 6 feet tall, and Susan "Spike" Callahan from Nebraska, a two-year veteran, was 6-foot-10. I was a towering 5-foot-4 and looking forward to meeting the rest of the team.

Coach Cheryl Clark from Michigan and Donna "Spanky" Losier from New Hampshire were 10-year veterans. Barb Hostert was from Illinois, had been a Red Head for six years along. There was another rookie, Sandy Crist, from West Virginia.

Training was intense. We only had two weeks before the first training game. We ate, slept, lived, and breathed Red Head basketball. We worked on conditioning, learning plays, perfecting routines, and orchestrating the signature All American Red Head halftime show. There was nowhere else I'd rather be.

Coach Moore had bought a brand new full size extended van for travel. It was roomy and comfortable enough for us and all our gear — easy for me to say, since I was one of the smallest players. To be fair, we established a rotation for seating. "Shot gun" seat was the primary navigator, and co-pilot, in charge of the map. Being pre-GPS, the map was our "holy grail."

Like everything else on the road as an All American Red Head, if you didn't know it, you learned it. I played three-plus years with the All American Red Heads. My rookie year probably had the most impact on me. It was a great learning experience. We played in 40 states. I was able to play and be coached with players that had over 30 years experience with the Red Head organization. Barb Hostert was probably one of the best all around athletes I've ever known. We also played at my high school that year, against the faculty. I remember a very warm welcome from the community. They were proud, and I was thankful. I was the team comedian my second year. This was a big responsibility. Spanky was retiring and she nominated me as the primary candidate. She taught me everything I needed to know, from crowd-pleasing antics to referee ridicule. And, of course, the "passing of the torch" — the All American Red Head "Krazy Kit." The Krazy Kit is like Felix the Cat's bag of tricks. It was a hard shell case, red and blue, with white stars. Inside the kit, a sparkly white sequin top hat, a round satin red, white and blue powder puff, about the size of a tambourine, and a whistle. You see, the magic is not in the kit. The *MAGIC* is in the player using the *things* in the kit. What a privilege!

My third and final year, I was team comedian, player, and co-coach. Coach Moore always made sure his teams had the opportunity to see the sights across our great country, and appreciate its history. Come to think of it, we were creating history ourselves, and we didn't even know it.

I went back to school with the idea a college education and that piece of paper would prove my existence of growth, discipline, and knowledge. I had already gotten it. My life experiences on the road with the All American Red Heads were a degree in themselves. I had just finished my classes when I received a call from Coach Moore asking me if I could help the team finish out their season. I was available, packed my bag, and I was there lickety-split. I have been asked frequently, what was my favorite place while traveling with the team? "On top of the world," I said, because that's where we were. In every small town and every big city, we met all walks of life. People were kind. Each place had it's own uniqueness, but also a comforting similarity. If I had to pick a most unforgettable experience, as a competitive athlete, you are always striving for improvement, trying to be the best you can be, and reaching for that personal best. So with that in mind,

Culpeper, Virginia.
Red Heads 81,
Culpeper 80,
Ruth Simmons 41 points.
"Nothing but net."

Kathy Smith (O'Brien)

Career 1981-83
All American Red Heads

As told by Kathy Smith O'Brien

I had been on the road with the All American Red Heads during the 1981–82 season for several weeks when I had an experience that forever changed me. It was my rookie season, and our team of six had just finished a game somewhere in Missouri that, although we won, we did not play well. Coach Cheryl Clark called us all together courtside after the game and lit into each one of us, pretty much scaring us to death. When she was finished talking she had us run laps around the balcony of the gym for what seemed like hours but in reality was probably only 15 or 20 minutes.

The gym was an older one that had baskets on the sides of the court in addition to the main baskets at each end. After running laps until our legs shook, Coach broke us up into pairs, sent us to the goals on the side of the gym, and had us shoot free throws until we thought we'd never be able to lift our arms again. Of course, as we were shooting the free throws Coach Clark continued to make it clear to us that we did not play up to Red Heads' standards nor did we understand the responsibilities that came with being a Red Head.

The next day we thought we were in the clear until Coach Clark called a team meeting in her motel room. Coach Clark took great care to call each one of us by name and point out to us that the game was not about us as individuals. Coach Clark told us about the history of the Red Heads and made clear what was expected of each of us if we were to continue to have the honor of wearing a Red Heads' uniform. Coach Clark repeatedly told us how important it was for us to remember and respect those who, by paving the road before us, made it possible for us to have the opportunity to play a game we all loved. She stressed how important it was for us to play as a team and to leave our self-centered attitudes off the court. To use Coach Clark's words, "It's not about you, it's about the team. When the game is over the fans are not going to remember that Kathy played, they are going

All American Red Heads enjoy a snack, 1971-72. Front, L-R: Ruth Simmons, Kathy Smith, Pat Burgess, Marcia Schmidt. Back: Mary Benton, Orwell Moore, April Jensen.

to remember the All American Red Heads played." Coach moved down the line, naming each player in turn until she had spoken directly to each one of us.

When Coach Clark finished speaking, we just sat there in silence because there was nothing for us to say — she was 100 percent right.

It took some time before we were able to make jokes about our rough night in the gym and the lecture in the motel room. When we finally summoned the courage to openly make jokes, we told Coach Clark how hard it was to make free throws that night in the gym because we were seeing four baskets through our teary eyes. Although we were eventually able to joke about that night, it made a lasting impression on me and the rest of the team.

When I speak in front of groups I always tell that story because it had a lasting impact on how I look at my role in any organization in which I have ever been a part. My hope when I share the story is that it will have the same effect on others as it had on me.

When I reflect on those words spoken by Coach Clark in that long forgotten motel room in a long forgotten part of Missouri, I realize Coach Clark's one goal was not to break us down but to make us stronger. She taught me what it meant to be a part of something bigger than myself, and that with the opportunity to be a part of a team comes responsibility to that team. It made me a better teammate and, thereby, a better person. I am forever grateful for the lesson.

Pat Burgess

Career 1982-83
All American Red Heads

As told by Pat Burgess

I was recruited just out of Western Michigan University when I graduated. My very good friend at the time, Ruth Simmons (a.k.a. "Rosie Red") was playing for the All American Red Heads. She had called me and told me they had a player leave with an injury. Because we had played ball together in intramurals she asked me if I could fill in. Fill in? I was going to be playing some professional basketball! I left the next morning and flew to Wisconsin, cut my hair and dyed it red. My mom was not too happy about it.

The first week on the road was crazy, probably more so than anything from my college days. My hair was a different color, I had to practice the tricks almost non-stop to perfect them for the next game, and I had to have a uniform fit.

The biggest challenge was the tricks. I was a basic ballplayer, nothing fancy. I was fast and could jump. Orwell came up with some tricks he thought I would be able to do. Not many people could stand on their head and shoot the ball into a basket. I could. I could also stand at the free throw line, with my back to the basket and shoot and make the free throw.

The second challenge was my mom — convincing her that this was just something I wanted to do and this was my chance. She never gave up on wanting me at home again.

My favorite basketball story is when we went to my hometown, Byron Center Michigan. We were to play some alumni from my old high school and my brother Dave was going to be playing against me! That was a surprise for me, but a lot of fun too. All of my family was there and we won. The other part of that story was that my dad told the press that I was a deadeye dick from the outside. I was actually a forward loving the inside play. That game they wanted me to take more outside shots and it was not the most fun game I played because I was so nervous, but I made some key shots and we won the game.

I remember playing a team in Maine. The team we played was the meanest team we met all year. They were elbowing us, running into our screens and interrupting our tricks for entertainment. Basically, they just wanted to beat us and beat us bad, Orwell was on the bench and was a little frustrated with the way they were acting. I ended up with a bruised xyphoid process (the piece of cartilage attached to the sternum). It hurt like crazy when I took deep breaths, but we kept playing. Orwell told us to just play and play hard. No tricks, just raw talent. We ended up winning. It was actually fun seeing us come together as a team and just play for a change.

1982-83 Red heads. Unidentified, Ruth Simmons, Pat Burgess, Kathy Smith, Mary Benton, unidentified.

The next night we went back to business as usual and never lost a game the rest of the season. We learned to trust in teamwork that night. We knew we had each other and knew Orwell had our backs too.

I loved traveling with this team — the sights, the restaurants, shopping on free time and signing autographs. One night we drove through the entire night and then had to play the next afternoon. Not one of us got a good night's sleep and that night we just did not play well. One other situation that we had as a team was on an Indian reservation when we lined up to sing the national anthem. We were all ready to sing when their elders started to sing their own anthem. The whole game was crazy because the players in the reservation appeared to have something in what they were drinking and by the third quarter and were getting angry that we were ahead. We ended up winning this game by one point. It was very exciting, but we were escorted out of town.

Mechelle Pollard (Weyer)

Career 1985-86
All American Red Heads

As told by Mechelle Pollard Weyer

Red Head Mechelle Pollard with son, Michael, 1986

Hey y'all, my name is Mechelle Pollard. It all started when I was 17 years old, I had gotten a scholarship to play basketball at Mississippi County Community College in Blytheville, Arkansas, but gave it up to help with my family after my father became ill.

I was working in a grocery store in Caraway, Arkansas. Mr. Orwell Moore, owner of the All American Red Heads, had been after me to go play for his team. I wasn't so sure about it, but he came to my house one afternoon and talked with me and my parents. My mother encouraged me to go play, because it would be a once-in-a-lifetime thing. So after a contract signing and five bottles of hair color I was an All American Redhead, on a bus to Albuquerque, New Mexico, to meet up with the team.

You talk about a scared young girl, I rode in the front seat of the bus all the way there, and I can remember my dad telling the driver of the bus to make sure I got there with no problems, and the at each stop the next driver made sure no one sat next to me on that bus.

After what seem like an eternity I finally arrived in New Mexico. Coach Burnie Moore picked me and we headed to the gym where the team was so I could get dressed and start practicing. Talk about tough, it was tough. I had to learn all the plays and the tricks I would be doing, for the game that I was going to be playing in that night. Good thing I wasn't out of shape.

Some days we would practice three to four hours before going out to play to a large crowd that evening. Talk about stress — I had to adjust to all the traveling and get use to playing every day, sometimes twice a day. But through the hectic schedule I was having a good time.

We were playing in Wisconsin in early 1986. Oh man, talk about cold! Being from the south, I never knew how cold it could be, but it was cold there. We were in an old gym that didn't have any heat in the dressing room, and we tried to huddle close together while putting on our makeup, because being a Red Head you were never seen in public or on the court without proper makeup and lipstick. Here we were, trying our best to get dressed while freezing, and Burnie walks in and yells, "Hurry up, what's takin' y'all so long?" Well, Tammy Bledsoe yells back, "We weren't born this beautiful — it takes time!" Of course we hit the floor running, and it was there that Marla Carroll and I both ended up with black eyes. I also got a busted lip and a sprained ankle. We ended up winning that game, but let me say that in the mid '80s men didn't like to lose and they played us hard.

Y'all, while we were traveling we had convinced Burnie to stop at the White Sands of New Mexico. We all collected some of the white sand to bring home to our families as souvenirs. We made sure to put it all together in the back of the van and to keep it away from our laundry detergent. Later, while we were at the Grand Canyon, Burnie decided to wash our uniforms. He used the sand instead of detergent. That night while we were playing ball, we all started itching so badly that we had to take a time out. Burnie said, "What's y'all's problem tonight?" Rosie Red said, "We're itching to death! What did you wash our uniforms in?" He replied, "Those little bottles of detergent that were in the back of van." Lesson learned — never let Burnie wash uniforms again. Y'all should try to play basketball with sand in your uniforms. It's not fun.

When you're from the South you get used to having sweet tea year round, and you're used to having it with ice all the time. However, in Michigan during the lovely month of March, you don't always get that. We were eating and I had ordered sweet tea, and the waitress said, "Do you want peach or raspberry?" I told her neither, that I just wanted sweet tea. She brought me flavored tea, with no ice. I said, "Ma'am this is not sweet tea." She said, "Up here it is." When I asked for just regular tea she looked at me very funny.

I can vouch also that in Michigan they had really nice saunas in their hotels. It was there we decided to get back at Burnie for a few things, so we hid from him in the sauna. When he found us he was not a happy camper and we paid dearly for it.

I look back at the things we did and wonder to myself, "Would I be in charge of a group of young ladies traveling across the country?" We were taught to be very respectful while out in the community and we were taught to be dressed very appropriately and carry ourselves with dignity. We developed an unbreakable bond of friendship that still exists today.

Sandra Berry

Career 1992
All American Red Heads

As told by Sandra Berry

I was born and raised in Caraway, Arkansas, so I grew up hearing about the All American Red Heads and knew all about these local legends. I would get so excited when I'd hear about them being in town. If it was when school was in session, I would always find a way to get to the gym to watch them practice. I even skipped lunch and then missed half of my next class because I didn't want to stop watching them practice their plays. Fortunately, my teacher understood. If school was out, I would ride my bicycle the two miles to town just to see if I could catch them outside. I had always wanted to be a Red Head.

My junior and senior years in high school I went to basketball camp to learn from Coach Orwell Moore and his brother Coach Jack. In 1985, when I was a high school senior, Coach Moore asked me to play for the 1986 team. I had already signed to play ball in college so I wasn't able to. I was very disappointed. Yet, I could not give up my college education. It turned out that the 1985-86 season was going to be the last on the road for the Red Heads, an end of an era, a dream not realized.

Then, in 1992, out of the blue, my Mom told me that Coach Moore wanted to talk to me. I called him and he said that a book was in the works and there was some talk of a movie being made about the Red Heads. He wanted to promote the team and get people talking about the Red Heads. He said something about wanting me to be in the movie and then asked me if I would be interested in playing. I thought he was kidding as that boat sailed a few years ago, but he assured me he was serious. I said, "You bet I want to play!" A few days later we got our uniforms, had pictures made and started talking about practices and when we would play.

Our team never got to experience road travel like the other teams. The games we played were within a couple hours driving distance. In some ways a bit sad, as we didn't get to ride in those famous limos of earlier teams. We drove our own cars to the games. Sometimes a few of us would car pool.

Sandra Berry and the Red Heads during a time out. Clockwise from top: Berry, Karen Riggs, Coach Orwell Moore, Julie Boles, Kristi Pack, Jamie Pace, Angela Reed Dunigan, Sonia Schoolfield.

My favorite memory from the Red Heads isn't about playing ball, it is the first time I put the Red Heads uniform on. To me it was awe-inspiring, pondering what great players had worn it before, the places in the United States it had barnstormed, the games it played before the thousands of fans and stories that lived within its stitches sewn together by Butch Moore at Camp Courage. You couldn't wipe the smile off my face!

Sometimes after our games a few of us would meet somewhere to eat together. I remember one weekend a few got together and went camping. It was great getting to know the others better and talking about different things going on in our lives.

Some of us hadn't played ball for a few years but we made it happen. We played about 15 games and won all but one and only lost it by one point. The movie and book didn't happen at that point, but Coach Moore told us it didn't matter if we played in one game or 200 games, one season or three seasons. If we put on the Red Head uniform, we were Red Heads!

The players on our team also had other obligations — jobs to go to, school to attend and families to take care of, so it was even hard to get all of us together to practice. We didn't get paid much at all — $20 a game, just enough to cover gas and a bit of food or snacks. It didn't matter to me, I lived my dream of a lifetime.

The world had changed since the Red Heads and other teams first barnstormed across America almost 60 years earlier. So few opportunities existed for girls and women to play basketball back then, often lucky to just find a dirt court that had a goal set up at it.

In my day, girls' basketball existed in the younger school grades, high school and thousands of women were getting scholarships in college and playing the game, some appearing on national television.

Several professional women's basketball leagues had made a try of it but couldn't quite find the way to keep it going. Yet, by the mid 1990s the WNBA took to the court and hasn't looked back since.

I was part of a team, a legend and a way of life for women of other barnstorming teams that helped define where the game is today.

How cool is that?

Donna Geils (Orender)

Career 1975-81, 85
Queens College, 1978-81 Stars/Gems/Hustle (WBL), Maccabi Games USA Team

As told by Donna Geils Orender

The Real Lessons of Going for Gold

The game of basketball is my poetry, my dance and my song. I came to it later than some and I did not want to let it go, EVER. It's mystery and magic was still revealing itself to me when my collegiate career at Queens College was coming to a close.

Who knew that when I decided to go to Queens College, the crown jewel of the City University System of New York that we would be game changers, history makers and pioneers. Heck, I was just following the bouncing ball as it continued to mesmerize me and teach me the lessons of life that until then were never contemplated in my playbook. We were the first women's team to ever play in the Mecca of basketball Madison Square Garden. It just does not get bigger than the Garden. We were so dominant in New York State that we were not invited to play in any state tournaments and we were proud to host a national team from China, the first international visit from that country. We were ranked top 10 in the nation all four years I played, at a time when the women's game was certainly underappreciated by those who allocated dollars and resources for the game. The truth at the time, while we were aware our coach was fighting for us behind the scenes — we were there to play. We played very simply because we loved the game. No scholarships, fancy team rooms or even much meal money. We feasted on the pure exhilaration of a game that steeled our bodies, our minds and forged a team, a team that won and won often. I was fortunate that the end of my collegiate career, rumors as to the starting of a new professional league were flying.

If luck is the currency of the fortunate, that I was blessed with great timing. The WBL was the real deal — real teams, owners, uniforms and mascots. For a time we actually received real checks that delivered real currency when you brought them to the bank. Not even 23 years old and the game had served up two life-shaping and formative experiences that still define how I look at life and opportunity today.

The league was rough and tumble, but putting on my sneakers and tube socks, making sure the stripes matched my shorts, was a delight every morning. The league provided me an elite designation — professional athlete. It was membership in a very elite club, especially for women. I had scaled the heights and worked my butt off everyday to make sure that I would stay at the top of the mountain.

Three years in the league — statistical honors, an all-star team, three cities, many coaches and several owners — it was a whirlwind. I blinked, my last paycheck bounced and the league was over, folded, kaput. I felt sad but lucky. I was there from the first day to the last and I got to live a dream that I dared never dream, that of being a professional athlete.

The WBL was history in the making. I was thrilled to play the game I loved. The fact that people came to watch us and that I got paid, well that was all bonus. And perhaps we seeded the desire and potential opportunities for the young women who could now have the dream of careers that could extend past college and work for the next league that hopefully would last.

Being an athlete led to a "real" job in sports television. Pick up games with the guys was salve on the open wound of not being able to compete anymore. I missed it. It wasn't like we had a big locker room culture — more happened on our team bus — but hitting the gym floor for three hours a day. plus weight workouts, and agility training that I did on my own was like a drug and I was definitely in withdrawal. But the adult world was calling and I felt like it was time for me to jump in. It wasn't easy to be washed up unceremoniously retired by 23 years old.

And then, who could have predicted? Someone asked me if I had heard about the Maccabiah Games. I hadn't but came to learn that they are the Jewish Olympics, hosted every four years in Israel. Over 35 countries would be participating, with 7000 athletes, making them the third largest sporting competition in the world. I wanted to go. Are you kidding? The chance to be on a team, have USA emblazoned on my chest, to practice, to put on my socks and shoes and run the lanes freely and with abandon. I could not contain my excitement. The opportunity to play again, to have officials (yes, I even missed the black amd white up and down the sidelines) and to play in Israel. Talk about motivation.

So I began training. Pick-up games had renewed purpose and my training runs got longer. I was on a mission. It had been four years since college and I had landed a great job working for PGA Tour Productions, a brand new company seeking to emulate the model of NFL Films and NBA Entertainment. I had spent a few years in network television and the burgeoning cable television industry before being recruited for this pretty cool opportunity. The company was founded by a professional golfer, known for his tough talk and tough attitudes and perhaps a bit rough of around the edges.

So, perhaps tougher than being on the free throw line with two to win the game, was the conversation I had to have with my boss about taking three weeks off, should I have the good fortune of making the team. Actually, give me the free throws any day of the week — I knew this was going to be tough. At this point, I was in charge of programming and producing the newly launched show "Inside the PGA Tour." It was a great job and I loved it, but who says you can't have it all?

The first conversation did not go well, nor did the second, or any other. The verdict was simple — "You go, Donna, and you won't have a job when you return." That was like asking me to choose between food and water. I needed both to live. Ultimately, the decision was clear. If I did not try at the ripe old age of 27 to make this national team, I would always wonder. What if? No "what ifs" for me, what I was absolutely certain about was that I did not ever want to look back and have regrets. I decided that I would continue to give work my best while I continued to pursue the dream. What's a job when there were dreams to chase? One window may be closing, but perhaps a big beautiful door was in the process of opening.

Nine-mile runs, weight training, purpose and passion and nothing was going to stop me. I showed up to try-outs fit and looked around the gym at the "youngins." I recall a time in my career when I looked at girls who played basketball past the age of 16 as a little odd. I truly believed that 16 was the expiration date. Now here I was at 27, relishing in every moment, every drill, every scrimmage. Every coach's command had my full attention and I would leave everything I had on that court. Life moved quickly and I wanted to make sure I availed myself of all of its pleasures.

Try-outs went well and I was thrilled to join the kids as an official member of the USA Women's Open Basketball team for the Maccabiah Games. I can tell you, I still have that uniform in my drawer and the pride I felt being a part of that team and of the Maccabiah movement was palpable. So much so that I still serve on their executive committee, helping others to have the same opportunity that I have had.

We flew to Israel for training camp. Once again, I cherished every drill and every dribble. Sweat was as sweet as nectar and I scheduled my training runs in the hottest time of day so I could feel every degree of the Mediterranean sun. I found my game and my game found me. The two best teams were USA and Israel. We battled back and forth, with each of us winning one in a pair of qualifying games. The tiebreaker would be for the gold medal.

We played in small gyms around the country and I recall that one of the games was the first to be played on the West Bank, in a town called Ariel. The mayor came. I may have scored 30 that game and I received an invitation to stay and play in the country. I was flattered, but there was no time to think of that as we had a medal to win. We had come far and were focused.

The day of the game I was walking around the K'far, the resort where many of the teams stayed for the games. I suddenly heard a familiar voice yell for me. It was Coach Landa, a Hall of Fame coach who made me laugh, pushed me hard and to this day I love as a member of my own family. He was our USA assistant coach, part of a great duo led by another one of my favorite basketball mentors, Coach Bernie Fine. Coach Landa was my coach when I played for the WBL New Jersey Gems and he kept me and my backcourt partner Annie Meyers laughing.

"There she is, go ask her," I heard in his signature Philadelphia accent. "She will know what to do." I remember thinking, I have no idea what is going on here, but I did not come here to make any more decisions than whether I should make a chest or bounce pass to complete a fast break. It was then that I would learn that I had a lot more to think about than just the break. We had a serious break in the action and the game of life was looking to write new rules, utilizing basketball as its conduit.

The gold medal was going to be hanging around some team's neck in about four hours' time. We anticipated that we would face a hard-hitting, fast-paced, elbow-flying game. We were scheduled to play at a high school gym about 30 minutes away. We were guests, so we did not think much about this arrangement, nor the fact that the men, whose gold medal game would be contested that evening, would be playing in the big arena in Ramat Gan. The Israeli women were incensed. This was the final insult in a culture they felt did not provide them the commensurate respect they deserved. The gym assignment was the straw that broke the camel's back. The message was simple — unless we play in a gym worthy of our efforts and communicates that what we do is as important as the men, we will not play. This demand, I would like to remind you, happened 30 years prior to the USA Women's Soccer National Team demanding more equitable pay. The Israelis' message was simple to the USA delegation — do as you will, but we are not showing up.

I remember Coach Howie sort of yelling at me. He wasn't mad, just apoplectic. So was the rest of the USA delegation. The USA team gathered and slowly got on the bus that came to take us to the game site. Game officials joined us and family and friends would be following behind.

This was a big deal. Families had traveled from across America to see their daughters play in this esteemed event. They spent thousands of dollars for the privilege, planned for many years, and at long last here we were on the cusp of glory. A gold medal was ours for the taking. The precious metal that we all coveted was just a game away. There was a hope that a compromise would be offered and that all of this was just a bad dream. So as the bus left the K'far everyone kept asking, what are we going to do?

I was tucked into my seat on the aisle, a few rows up from the back, thinking and talking with my teammates. They were looking to me. We arrived at the gym and it was then when everything seemed to move in slow motion. I could see the game officials and the committee executive's mouths moving and their hands gesturing wildly as we remained on the bus. The message was delivered — 30 minutes. If you do not take the court in 30 minutes you will forfeit the game.

Tic-Toc.

We sat. What was a gold medal worth? A look out the window and we see, voices raised, and I feel my parents angst. For them, to see their daughter play one more game, a golden moment of accomplishment to behold on the podium, was a life highlight for them. My parents were joined by many other parents and fans who no doubt felt the same.

Tic-Toc.

We sat. At one time, we made a motion to go. We got back in our seats.

TIC-TOC.

The minutes were flying by. My heart was racing. What was the real value of this experience? We looked out of the bus windows and knew the gold medal was on the other side of those gym doors.

TIC-TOC.

At that very minute I think we all understood that we were competing for something so much more important than a medal. We were competing for *respect*. And this was not just our game, this was something much bigger than ourselves. To honor our fellow competitors, our sisters, and their desire and demand to be recognized as athletic equals was the game we wanted to win.

TIC-TOC!

The game was declared a forfeit and a very disappointed delegation packed up to return to the K'far.

No gold medals for us. I lost my job, traveled thousands of miles, worked 'til my muscles screamed in protest, and yet we felt like winners. Winners in the biggest game of all, the place it counts most,

US National Maccabiah team, 1985. Donna Geils (Orender) is front row center.

the game of life. The Israeli team found us before we departed and gave to each of us a beautiful stone wall hanging as a thank-you for our solidarity. It has hung on my wall for all of these years, a revered and cherished reminder of what is most important in life, the real lessons of going for gold.

So here I am, once again thinking of the game that I love. It is poetry, it is music and it is dance. It is a teacher of life's lessons and the more you open your heart to it, the more it will teach you.

Postscript

My boss recognized that I was dedicated to my job and that bringing me back was a good idea and so my career at the PGA Tour continued and lasted an additional 17 years. I eventually worked in the Commissioner's office as one of the four top senior executives in the organization.

The Maccabiah World Union did not schedule women's basketball for the next games. Eight years later both a woman's open and junior division were scheduled and continue to this day. Since that time I have volunteered to Co-Chair the USA Women's Open team for two separate games as well as the Boys Youth team on which my sons played.

Twenty-five years after this game took place I am sitting in the second row at Madison Square Garden, watching a New York Liberty game. Even all these years later and now as the president of the WNBA, I find myself fighting for the respect of women who love the game. A gentle tap on my shoulder caused me to look up at face that I tried to recall but just couldn't place. Once she began to speak, her accent revealed the familiar cadence of an Israeli, as she said to me, "you may not remember me, but I remember you. I was on that Israeli team that refused to play. We will always appreciate what you did for us!" Twenty-five years later, the truth be known, the truth reinforced, we did medal, with the mettle that mattered most — that of a human spirit that prevailed where standing up to be counted, counted most of all.

Rosters of Teams

The listings in this section are based on exhaustive research and networking and are not presented as an authoritative list of all players who were members of the teams. Neither the author nor the publisher are responsible for errors or omissions, but if you know of names that have been left out, please e-mail the author at WomensBasketball@aol.com so that the lists can be updated for future printings of this book.

Ozark Hill Billies

Bernard Cowden *(Coach)*
Lorene "Danny" Daniels
Darlene "Tex" Nabors Gould
Ruth Haines
Marvalee Jo Darrow Hickman
Nora Muncrief Isaacs
Eleanor Laich
Minnie Lee Moore
Helen Onson
Lucy Peters
Vinia Hobbs Poe
Monica Ryan
Joe Statovich
Louise White

Southern Belles

Phillis Brown
Lenna Carey Tucker
Sandra Duran
Mickey Gay
Kathy Gaither
Madeline Hoing
Dianne Kirkland Warren
Glenda Ledbetter Litaker
Carolyn Linzay
Sandy Mann
Diane Mitchell
Sue Petzold Dudek
Linda Shanks
Lucille "Lucy" Thomason Whetsel
Pat Overman
Connie Sanders
Nita Sherrod

All American Red Heads

Ina Mae Absire
Charlotte "Sweetie" Adams *(Player/Coach)*
Marcia Adams
Paula Albritton
Jolene Ammons *(Player/Coach)*
Jewel Hair Armijo
Justine Glover Arthur
Lorene Milligan Atwell
Mary Bennet Baker
Jessie Banks
Pauline Barbo
Emogene Barns
Peggy Padget Baugher
Mary Benton
Teresa Bergeron
Sandra Berry
Annette Binkley
Torcey Blasch
Tammy Bledsoe
Lila Blue
Julie Boles
Rhonda Waters Boatwright
Marie Reynolds Boggess
Beth Bohanon
Carolyn Grantham Booth
Sheryl Wood Borgman
Beth Borkman
Florence Boyles
Jackie Bray
Janet Grady Broadway *(Player/Co-Coach)*
Philip Brooks *(Driver)*
Mabel Brady Brown
Majorie Brown
Sandra Bishop Brown
Patty Bruce
Patty Eubank Bruce
Nota Lee McCain Brunson
Bonnie Buel
Pat Burgess
Kay O'Bryan Burk
Patty Burton
Linda Mitchell Cain
Judy Cameron
Joy Carol
Mary Carpenter
Marla Carroll
Emogene Shelton Carter
Lera Dunford Chadwick
Celeste Chartier
Shirley Beckman Cheatum
Mickey Hendricks Childress
Dolores "Dody" Petersen Clack
Cheryl Clark *(Player/Coach)*
Jo Ann Boone Clements
Wilda Kelley Clettenburg
Karen Milner Coggins
Wilbur Coggins *(Coach)*
Juanita Coleman
Annette Colvin
Hazel Vickers Cone
Susan "Spike" Callahan Cooper
Bernard Cowden *(Coach)*
Emily Cowden
Janet Cox
Hollis Cox *(Driver)*
Joyce Webster Crabtree
Ann Cragger
Kay Shinall Craig
Sandy Crist
Lorene "Danny" Daniels
Helen Daughdrill
Brenda Moon Davis
Sue Dawson
Margaret O'Neal Day
Gail Guthrie Dewberry
Catherine Jones Deweese
Dorsey Anderson Dinkla
Alice Washington Dockins
Jeannine Gogel Doe
Denise Maurais Doucette
Beverly Turley Douglas
Karen Riggs Dowty
Marcia Schmidt Drinkart
Angela Reed Dunigan
Shirley Durrow
Patricia Dyer
Joyce Eastman
Tammy Elkins
Bessie Shelton Elliot
Theda Vanwinkle Ely
Larry Emison *(Coach)*
Emma Bartmass Etue
Betty Everett
Shelby Tedder Faulkner
Kay Ferguson
Judy Eifling Fletcher
Carolyn Reeves Flowers
Joanne Foster
Lee Kaschmitter Freiburger
Myrtle Wallace Frost
Mickey Gay
La Rae Gibbs
Jana Giles
Bonnie Gilliand
Joy Ribitski Goff
Retha Carter Goodson
Sammy Lee Autrey Gordon
Darlene "Tex" Nabors Gould
Paula Gragg
Alice McHughes Gray
Richard Gray *(Coach)*
Velma Barnett Gray
Charlene Green
Glenn Green *(Coach)*
Janie Green
Barbara Wells Gwinn
Eloise Haines
Ruth Haines
Vicky Halbert
Margie Arrends Hannaman

Margaret McNeil Hansman
Jan Hardy
Ruth Harms
Kelli Horrell Harris
Alice Hatcher
Ruby Hayes
Kathy Jones Heck
Sharon Glenn Helterbrant
Delphia Allen Hemphire
Reva Henry
Mary Carlton Hester
Marvalee Jo Darrow Hickman
Barbara Baty Hicks
Jo Underwood Hightower
Carolyn Gooch Hix
Martha Hix
Kathy Holbrook
Red Holder
Jerry Holt *(Driver)*
Barb "Gabby" Hostert
Mary Hounsell
Aaronette Eifling Housely
Shirley "Trooper" Howard
Connie Howe
Nellie Marlow Hudgen
Leo Hutton *(Driver)*
Gretchen Pinz Hyink
Katie Watson Ingrahm
Nora Muncrief Issac
Doris Jones
Linda Jones
Pat Vaughn Johnson
Sylvia Jean Johnson
Tina Treat Johnson
Betty Keith
Herman Keith *(Driver)*
Zethel Mathews Keith
June Kelley
Linda Chandler Kidd
Alice Hammond Kilgore
April Jensen Kocken
Brenda "Brooksie" O'Bryan Koester
Sue Branham Kohler
Jackie Krutsinger
Trudy Babcock Kurtz
Eleanor Laich
Joy Lane
Gene Langerman
Jo Langerman
Cheryl Leffler
Denise Levy
Judith Coghlan Lewis
Wanda England Lewis
Sally Leyse
Glenda "Twinkles" Ledbetter Lilker
Elvera Lindgren
Carolyn Linzay
Lisa Livingston
Karen Logan
Gladys Lommler
Dean Lorrance *(Driver)*
Donna "Spanky" Losier
Barbara Eyde Lovette
Beverly Searcy Lyle
Mamie Holder Lynch
Ujeta Mack
Ann Taft Madden
Donna Granger Mahan
Nancy Malone
Sandy Mann
Gail Marks
Diane Martinson
Willa Faye "Red" Mason *(Player/Coach)*
Judith Matlock
Mabel Matlock
Sherri Mattson
Pam McAnally
Glenda "Okie" Hall McClain *(Player/Coach)*
Gene "Careless" Love McHughes
Lavella Polston McWilliams
Virginia Morris Merril
Phyllis Meyers
Eloise Purkey Mlaska
Betty Moore
Burnice Moore
Burnie Moore *(Coach)*
Jack Moore *(Coach)*
James Moore *(Driver)*
Lorene "Butch" Adams Moore
Mayonna Moore
Minnie Lee Moore
Orwell Moore *(Owner/Coach, 1948–1986)*
Velma Morrison
Brenda Ragan Nalepa
Cindy Laliberte Nelson
Marilyn Nelson
Georgia Washington Norris
Kathy Smith O'Brien
Jeanne Ohleman
Martha Olsen
C.M. "Ole" Olson *(Owner/Coach, 1936–1954)*
Doyle Olson
Helen Onson
Wilma Orr
Ruth Osborn
Benny Wayne Overman *(Coach)*
Pat Rimer Overman
Betty Bradshaw Owens
Jamie Pace
Kristi Pack
Debra Parashak
Mary Parsons
Patty Peterson
Joni Phillips
Kay Kirkpatrick Phillips
Charles Plummer *(Coach)*
Virginia Poe
Paula Haverstick Pollock
Virgina Posey
Mary Prater
Marya Leasure Prater
Penny Prater
Becky Harp Pritchett
Barbara Shrable Pyle
Pat Rakowitz
Kathy Tipton Ramsey
Frank Ray *(Driver)*
Gwen Reed *(Player/Coach)*
Hazel Reynolds
Johnnye Farley Riggs
Earlene Risenger
Pam Rowlett
Cindy Roybal
Mickey Ryan
Monica Ryan
Esther Taylor Sanderson
Francis Saunders
Sonia Schoolfield
Donna See
Linda Shanks
Jessie Shelton *(Driver)*
Beth Lively Shipman
Ruth Simmons *(Player/Co-Coach)*
Betty Jo Bollinger Simpson
Lois Glover Sitler
Lynnea Sjoquist
Lynnette Sjoquist
Pauline Smedley
Hazel Smith
Katherine Pitcock Smith
Kathy McCall Smith
Marcells Staggs
Helen "Fulton Flash" Stephens
Bill Stotts *(Driver)*
Jane Hounsel Stotts
Kathy Styles
Peggy Lawson Surface
Wilbur "Wiggles" Surface (Coach)
Betty Arrends Tamas
Marsha Tate
Shirley Bray Taylor
Lynn Holst Thomas
Becky Birtcher Thompson
Bertha Thompson
Loretta Thompson
Billie Thurber
Evelyn "Toby" McGee Turner
Wilson Turner *(Coach)*
Hazel Walker *(Player/Coach)*
Harlene Walls
Brenda Hubbard Watson
Patricia "Watusie" Daroche Weber
Mechelle Pollard Weyer
Louise White
Phyllis White
Sue "Rosie Red" Whitten
Eunice Wilkening
Carolyn Wooldrige Williams
Carolyn Williamson
Allegre "Stubby" Winters
Tommie Woods
Jackie Wranger
Lethco Wren *(Coach)*
Ella Cross Wright
Kim Wright
Betty Springer Wronka
Shari Marshall Wutherman
Maurine Moore Wychopen
Jackie Wrage Zitiau

Phoenix/Indianapolis Pink Panthers

Jolene Ammons
Gwen Bachman
Martha Carswell
Lois Glover
Mary Housell
Jackie Junkman
Karen Logan
Rex Smith
Connie Vance
Linda White

About the Author

John A. Molina

John Molina grew up playing in the tobacco and corn fields on the Connecticut River Valley in South Glastonbury, Connecticut. Upon graduation from high school he attended Sterling College in Vermont before heading to Idaho to become a 'Hotshot' forest firefighter in the Rocky Mountains.

Upon returning to Connecticut he went back to school and ended up working in computers becoming a systems analyst. During this time, he met and married the love of his life, Roxanne. John and Roxanne were busy raising their family when John became involved in the history of women's basketball. All-American and Olympian Carolyn (C.J.) Jones would become friends of the family and serve as additional inspiration to learn about the history of women's basketball.

John started off doing local exhibitions with artifacts he had collected over the years. He moved on to doing exhibitions at the NCAA Regional Finals and Final Four, as well as at colleges and other venues. He became Historian of the National Women's Basketball League for three years, and even had his own column in a short-lived women's basketball magazine.

He has been inducted into the Connecticut Women's Basketball Hall of Fame (2007), New England Basketball Hall of Fame (2013) and was on stage with the All American Red Heads when they were inducted into the Naismith Memorial Basketball Hall of Fame (2012).

John and Roxanne have three children—Sandra, C.J. and Rebecca-Lee. They reside in Rocky Hill, Connecticut and enjoy down time on the shores of Maine.

Photo Acknowledgments

Many of the photographs and images in this book are part of the private collections of the individuals listed below. The author and publisher would like to acknowledge and thank them for their permission to reproduce them as part of this historical record.

Marcia Adams
Jolene Ammons
Jessie Banks
Teresa Bergeron
Sandra Berry
Cyndi Meserve Bona
Sheryl Wood Borgman
Patty Bruce
Pat Burgess
Kay O'Bryan Burk
Ginny Hill Butz
Martha Carswell
Janet Cox
Brenda Moon Davis
Patti Decker
Joyce Eastman
Kathleen Ethington
Shelby Tedder Faulkner
Frances Garroutte
Barbara Wells Gwinn
Althea Gwyn
Cardte Hicks
Bernice Holladay Shafer
Aaronette Eiffling Housley
Bernnie Hudgens King
Harlean Hudson
Pat Deroche Hymel
Alan Isaacs
Molly Bolin Kazmer
Bob Knutson
Brenda O'Bryan Koester
Sue Branham Kohler
Glenda Ledbetter Litaker
Debbie Smith Loftice
Donna Losier
Sandra Mann
Gail Marks
Jeanie Marks
Diane Martinson
John Molina
Brenda Ragan Nalepa
Elvera Newman
Kathy Smith O'Brien
Donna Geils Orender
Mary Kay Pfeiffer
Becky Harp Pritchett
Gwen Reed
Ruth Simmons
Marsha Tate
Lynn Holst Thomas
Cindy Wilkes Thoren
Evelyn Turner
Dianne Kirkland Warren
Mechelle Pollard Weyer
Sue Whitten
Carolyn Wooldridge Williams

Index *(Roster of Teams not included in the index.)*